Mastering PyQt

Build Fast, Modern Applications with Python

Williams Asiedu

Mastering PyQt

Build Fast, Modern Applications with Python

Ouereila Publishing House
Email: ouereila@gmail.com
Forms: ouereila?

Ouereila Publishing House
Mastering PyQt
2025

ISBN: 979-8-3494-7408-8

Author: Williams Asiedu

MASTERING PYQt
Build Fast, Modern Applications with Python

Table of Contents

Preface

Mastering PyQt is more than just a book—it is an essential guide for passionate developers who want to create modern, high-quality desktop applications with beautiful user interfaces and great user experiences (UI/UX).

This book focuses on delivering the core concepts of Python programming and PyQt, helping readers develop the creative and technical skills needed to build powerful applications. PyQt is one of the most popular and widely used Python toolkits for building cross-platform desktop software, and this book provides everything you need to know to develop fully functional, professional-grade applications.

Who Is This Book For?

This book is organized in two broad sections:

- **An Overview of Python Programming**—designed to give readers without prior Python experience a solid foundation.
- **Building Applications with PyQt**—focusing on designing and developing complete desktop apps by integrating Python with PyQt.

Overall, *Mastering PyQt* is written for anyone—whether you're an experienced developer or just starting out—who wants to build desktop applications with Python.

The instructions are presented in clear, accessible English, with thorough explanations and practical examples that make learning both easy and engaging.

Structure of the Book

This book is divided into nine chapters. The first two chapters (*Starting Python* and *Overview of Python*) can be skipped by readers who are already comfortable with Python and its setup.

Chapter 1 – Starting Python
Covers setting up Python on different platforms (Windows, Linux, and macOS). It also explains how to choose the right editor and other essential tools needed to start coding in Python.

Chapter 2 – Overview of Python
Introduces the foundations of Python programming, offering clear, beginner-friendly explanations to help those new to the language get started confidently.

Chapter 3 – Graphical User Interface
Explores the concepts of frontend and backend in desktop applications. This chapter introduces the available GUI frameworks for Python, helping readers understand their roles and use cases.

Chapter 4 – PyQt/PySide
Dives into the PyQt and PySide frameworks: their history, architecture, modules, classes, properties and methods. It explains different syntax styles for using widgets and shows readers how to build their first PyQt application. This chapter also demonstrates how to integrate CSS and HTML for styling within PyQt.

Chapter 5 – Basic Widgets
Covers essential PyQt widgets used to create simple applications, including design and decoration elements. The chapter's objective project is building a simple calculator.

Chapter 6 – Inputs
Focuses on widgets for collecting user input, building on concepts from previous chapters. The chapter's objective project is creating a functional login page.

Chapter 7 – Pages and Menus
Teaches how to design a full-featured windowed application with multiple screens or pages and menus. The objective project is building a complete English-learning app.

Chapter 8 – Files and Media
Covers working with device files and handling audio and video playback widgets. The objective project is developing a full-featured music player.

Chapter 9 – Packaging Applications
Explains tools and techniques for creating standalone executable applications. This chapter also guides readers on how to find additional resources to deepen their understanding of the PyQt framework.

The book concludes with a **back matter section** offering further guidance, references, and useful resources for continued learning.

Learning Aids Used in This Book

This book uses carefully designed learning aids to help you fully grasp each topic and concept.

✔ Code Samples

Displayed in clearly marked code blocks, these samples show you exactly how to implement concepts in Python and PyQt. They're written to be easy to follow even if you're reading without a computer in front of you, reinforcing understanding through direct illustration.

✔ Notes

Highlight important instructions, concepts, or reminders you should keep in mind as you read.

✔ Deep

Offer in-depth explanations of key ideas to help you achieve a stronger and more thorough understanding of challenging topics.

✔ Tips

Share extra guidance, best practices, and helpful insights that can enhance your development process and deepen your knowledge of PyQt.

Objective of This Book

By the end of this book, any Python developer—whether experienced or completely new—will have the knowledge and practical skills to design, build, and deploy modern desktop applications for a variety of purposes.

I encourage every reader to go further by trying out challenging projects and continuing to practice. And remember: coding is even better with a good cup of coffee! ☕ 😊

Chapter 1

Starting Python

Chapter Objectives

- ◈ Understand the origin and history of Python
- ◈ Appreciate the importance and relevance of learning Python
- ◈ Install Python on your computer
- ◈ Set up a Python development environment
- ◈ Identify and use popular code editors
- ◈ Run Python scripts from different platforms
- ◈ Understand Python modules and libraries

Python

Python is a versatile and powerful programming language renowned for its readability, simplicity, and broad applicability across various domains. Developed by Guido Van Rossum in the late 1980s at the National Research Institute in the Netherlands, Python officially debuted in 1991. Since then, it has gained widespread adoption and popularity, becoming one of the most widely used programming languages globally.

Python's distinguishing features include being high-level, object-oriented, interactive, interpreted, and general-purpose. Its flexibility makes it suitable for a wide range of applications, including app development, data science, robotics, artificial intelligence, machine learning, web development, and game development.

One of Python's key strengths lies in its readability and simplicity. Python code is designed to resemble plain English, with keywords and syntax that are easy to understand and remember. This high-level scripting language allows developers to write concise and elegant code, facilitating rapid development and prototyping.

Moreover, Python boasts a vibrant and supportive community of developers and enthusiasts. This extensive community support ensures a wealth of resources, libraries, and frameworks readily available for developers to leverage in their projects, further enhancing Python's appeal and utility.

In essence, Python's combination of readability, versatility, and community support makes it an excellent choice for both beginners and experienced developers seeking to tackle a diverse range of programming challenges. Whether you're building web applications, analyzing data, or developing machine learning algorithms, Python offers the tools and resources necessary to bring your ideas to life effectively and efficiently.

Installing Python

Python is an open-source programming language, which means it is free to use and modify. It can be freely downloaded from the Python software Foundation's website at https://www.python.org

Windows

Installing Python on Windows is indeed straightforward and hassle-free. Here's a concise guide:

1. Download Python: Visit the Python Software Foundation website (https://www.python.org/) and download the Python installer suitable for your Windows version.

2. Run the Installer: Once the download is complete, navigate to the location of the downloaded executable file (.exe) and double-click on it to launch the Python installer.

3. Installation Wizard: The installation wizard will guide you through the setup process. You can customize the installation by selecting optional features or changing the installation directory if desired.

4. Configure Environment Variables: During the installation process, ensure that you check the box labeled "Add Python to PATH." This option automatically configures the system environment variables to include the Python executable, making it accessible from any command prompt or PowerShell window.

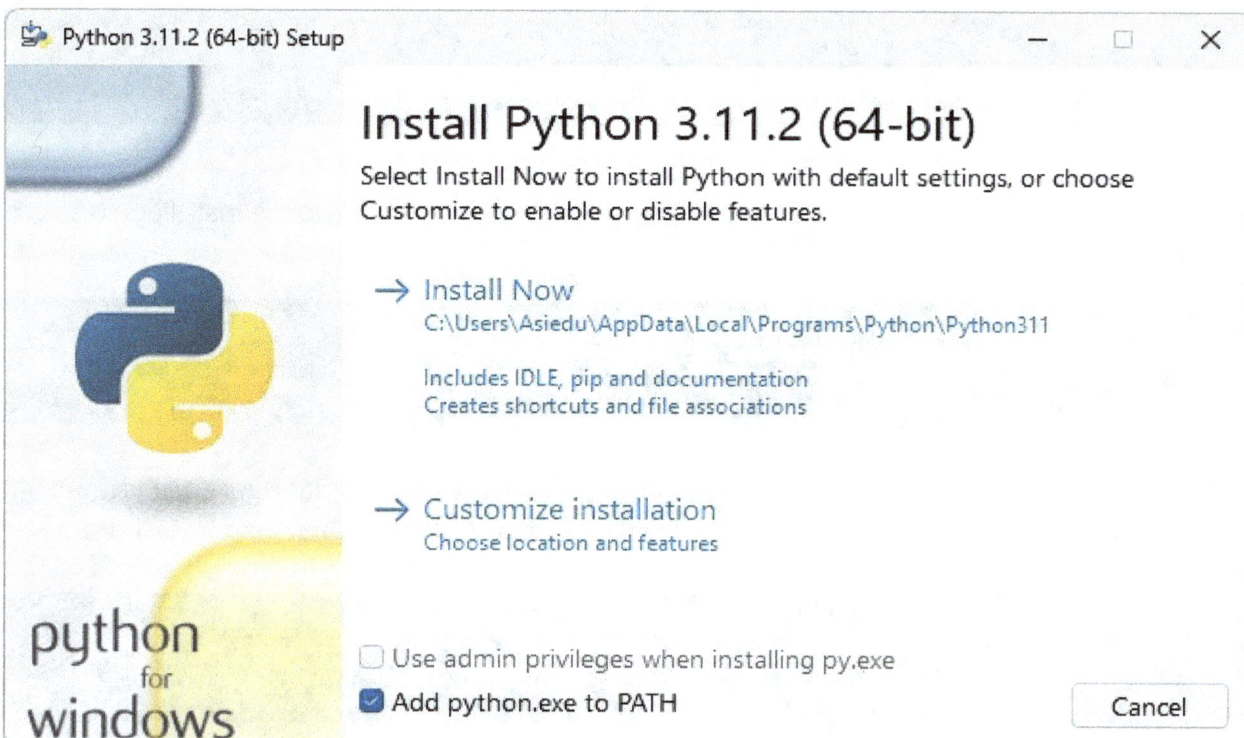

Figure 1.0 : Installation wizard

5. Complete Installation: Follow the prompts in the installation wizard to complete the installation process. Once the installation is finished, you can verify that Python is correctly installed by opening a command prompt and typing python --version. You should see the installed Python version displayed.

Linux

Indeed, Linux distributions often come with Python pre-installed. However, users may wish to install a different version or manage Python installations themselves. Here are the steps to install Python on Linux:

1. Update Package Lists: Open a terminal and update the package lists to ensure you have the latest information about available packages. Use the command:

```
$ sudo apt update
```

2. Install Python: Use the package manager to install Python. The package name might vary slightly depending on your distribution. For Python 3, you can use:

```
$ sudo apt install python3
```

3. Verify Installation: After the installation is complete, verify that Python is installed correctly by running:

```
$ python --version
```

4. Optional: Install **pip** (Python Package Manager): Pip is a package manager for Python that allows you to install and manage additional libraries and packages. You can install pip using the following command:

```
$ sudo apt install python3-pip
```

MacOS

1. Check Python Version (Optional): macOS usually comes with a pre-installed version of Python 2.x. You can check the version by opening the Terminal and running:

```
python --version
```

2. Install Homebrew (Optional): Homebrew is a package manager for macOS that simplifies the process of installing software. If you don't have Homebrew installed, you can do so by running the following command in Terminal:

```
/bin/bash -c "$(curl -fsSL
https://raw.githubusercontent.com/Homebrew/install/HEAD/install.sh)"
```

3. Update Homebrew (Optional): After installing Homebrew, it's a good idea to update it to ensure you have the latest version of available packages:

```
brew update
```

4. Install Python with Homebrew: Use Homebrew to install Python by running the following command in Terminal:

```
brew install python
```

5. Verify Installation: After the installation is complete, verify that Python is installed correctly by running:

```
python --version
```

6. Optional: Install pip (Python Package Manager): If pip is not installed automatically, you can install it using the following command:

```
sudo easy install pip
```

Editors

Editors, or Integrated Development Environments (IDEs), are applications that enable users to write, edit, debug, and run programming code. They typically feature user-friendly interfaces with integrated tools, compilers, and debuggers tailored for specific languages. Some editors support multiple languages, while others are designed for a particular language.

Popular editors for Python development include:

- PyCharm
- Visual Studio Code
- Sublime Text
- Notepad++

Additionally, Python comes with its own integrated environment called IDLE. IDLE provides an interactive environment for writing and running Python code, making it particularly useful for practicing coding skills.

Using IDLE

Using IDLE for Python coding is straightforward. Here's how to get started:

1. **Launch IDLE:**
   On Windows, open the Start menu and type "IDLE" to launch the IDLE editor.
   On Linux, open a terminal and type "idle" to launch IDLE.

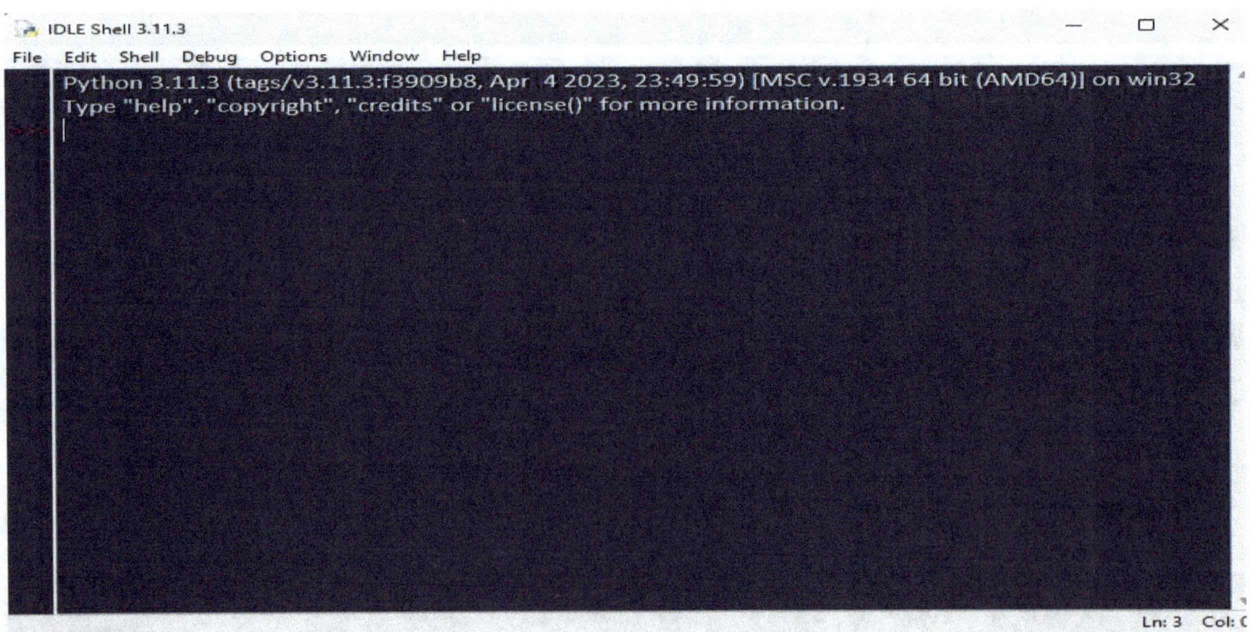

Figure 1.1 – Python IDLE

2. Create a New File:
Once IDLE is open, click on the "File" menu and select "New File," or simply press Ctrl + N. This will open a new window where you can start writing your Python code.

3. Write Your Code:
Start writing your Python code in the new file window. You can use all the features of the IDLE editor, such as syntax highlighting and auto-indentation, to make coding easier.

4. Run Your Code:
After writing your code, you can run it by clicking on the "Run" menu and selecting "Run Module," or by pressing F5.
IDLE will execute your code and display the output in the interactive shell window.

Additionally, Python provides other interactive environments like **IPython**, which offers more advanced features and graphical capabilities for Python coding.

You can also use the native **OS** shell or command interface for simple Python coding tasks. This approach works the same way across all operating systems, including Windows, Linux, and macOS. Simply open a terminal or command prompt, type *"python"* to enter the Python interactive shell, and start coding directly in the shell environment.

Using the Python Interactive Shell

1. Open the Command Line Interface (CLI):

- On Windows, type "cmd" into the Windows search bar and press Enter to open the Command Prompt.
- On Linux or macOS, open a terminal window.

2. Launch the Python Interactive Shell:

- In the Command Prompt or terminal window, type "python" and press Enter.
- This command starts the Python interpreter and opens the interactive shell, allowing you to enter Python code and receive immediate feedback.

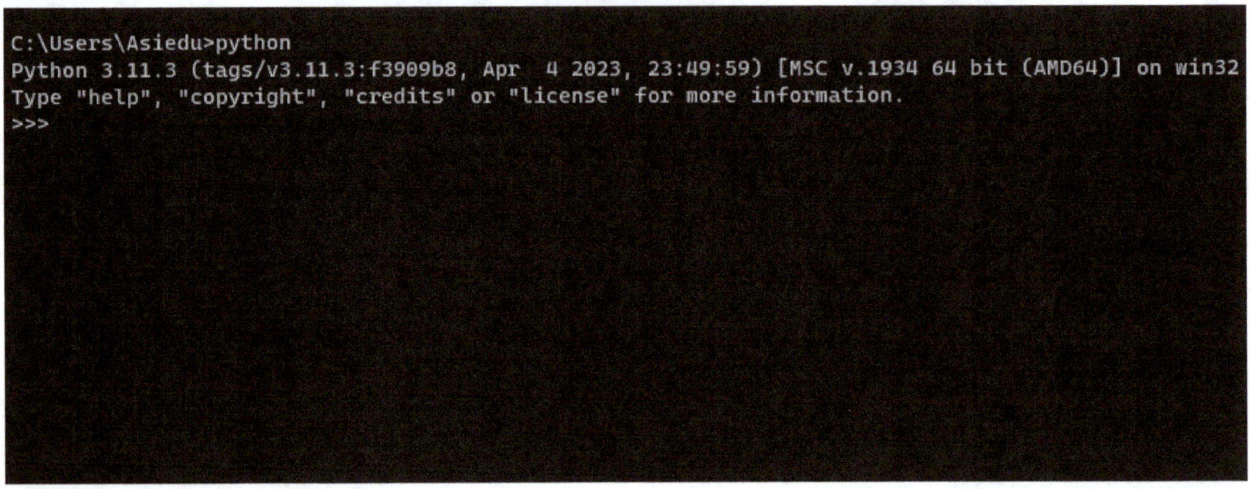

Figure: 1.2 - Python in CMD

That's it! You're now using the interactive Python shell, where you can experiment with Python code, test small snippets, and explore the language's features in real-time.

Running Python

Running Python code can be accomplished through various methods and integrated development environments (IDEs) like PyCharm, Visual Studio Code, and IDLE. Here's a specific example using Visual Studio Code:

The Visual Studio Code (VS Code)

VS Code is a versatile IDE developed by Microsoft, supporting numerous programming languages such as C, C++, Java, Python, C#, JavaScript, and HTML/CSS. It offers *IntelliSense* extensions to streamline programming tasks by providing suggestions for classes, functions, variables, and bug detection and correction. Additionally, VS Code is lightweight and features a user-friendly interface with buttons for running and *debugging* code.

Windows

1. Download VS Code:
   Visit the Visual Studio Code website or use the following link to download the VS Code executable file: *Visual Studio Code Download*.

2. Run the Installer:
   Once the download is complete, double-click on the downloaded executable file (usually named something like VSCodeSetup.exe) to run the installer.

3. Follow Installation Instructions:
   Follow the on-screen instructions provided by the installer to complete the installation process. You can choose installation options such as adding VS Code to the PATH and creating desktop shortcuts.

Linux

1. Download VS Code:

   On Linux, you can install Visual Studio Code using your distribution's package manager. For example, on Ubuntu, you can use the following commands in the terminal:

```
$ sudo apt update
$ sudo apt install code
```

MacOS

1. Download VS Code:
   Visit the Visual Studio Code website or use the following link to download the VS Code for macOS: *Visual Studio Code Download*.
2. Install VS Code:
   Once the download is complete, open the downloaded .dmg file.
   Drag the Visual Studio Code icon to the Applications folder to install VS Code on your macOS system.

After installing Visual Studio Code, you can launch it from the Start menu (Windows), applications menu (macOS), or by typing "code" in the terminal (Linux).

Running Python code in Visual Studio Code

1. Install Python Extension (if not already installed):
   - ✓ Open Visual Studio Code.
   - ✓ Go to the Extensions view by clicking on the square icon on the sidebar or pressing Ctrl + Shift + X.
   - ✓ Search for "Python" or *"Pylance"* in the Extensions view and install the Python extension provided by Microsoft.

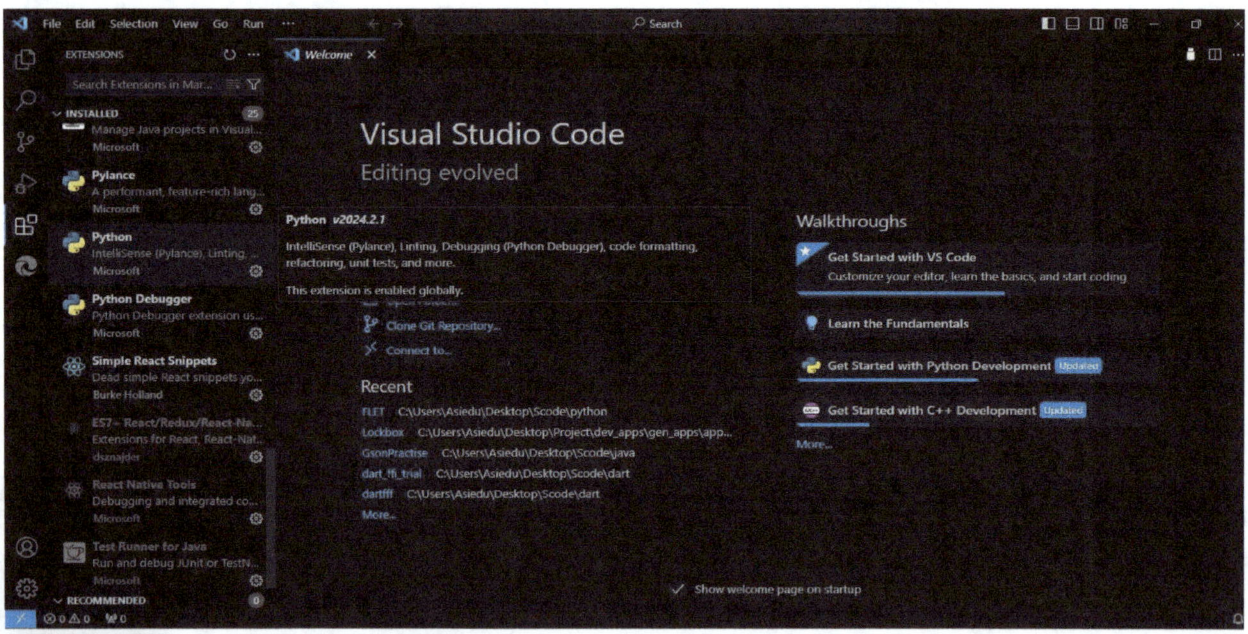

Figure: 1.3 - Visual Studio Code (extension)

2. Create or Open Python File:

   Create a new Python file or open an existing one in Visual Studio Code.
   - ✓ Click on the **"File"** menu at the top of the VS Code window.
   - ✓ Select **"New File"** to create a new file.
   - ✓ Name Your Python File:
     Type the preferred name of your Python file (e.g., "my_python.py").

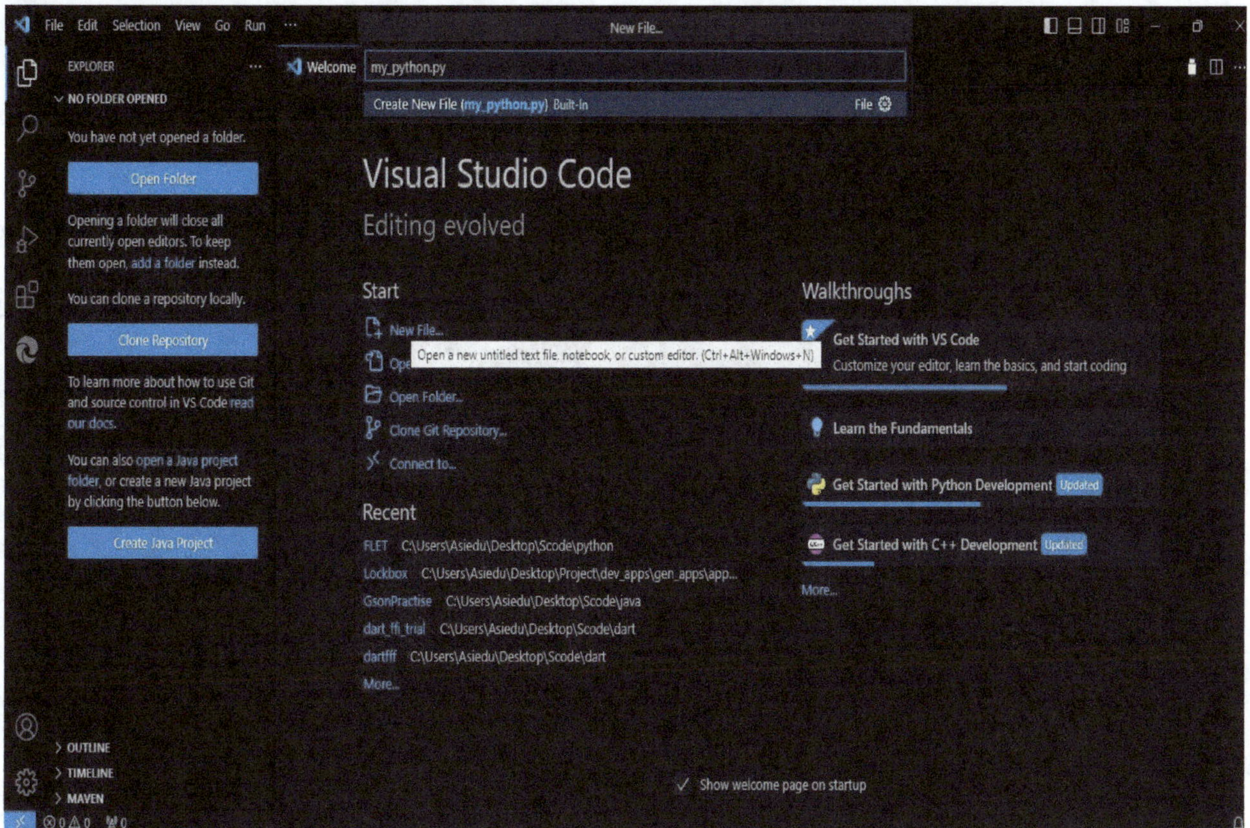

Figure: 1.4 - Visual studio code (start page)

3. Write Python Code:

   Write your Python code in the editor window. VS Code provides syntax highlighting and IntelliSense suggestions to assist you while coding.

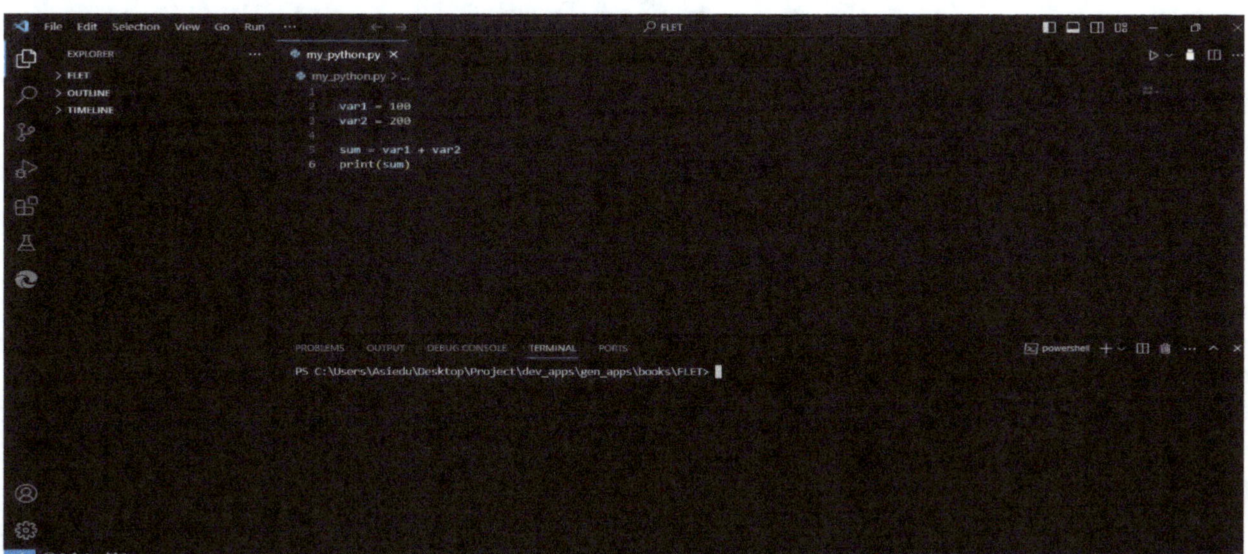

Figure: 1.5 - Visual studio code (using terminal)

4. Run Python Code:

   ✓ To run your Python code, you can use the Run button located in the toolbar at the top of the editor window. Alternatively, you can use the keyboard shortcut Ctrl + F5.

   VS Code will execute your Python code and display the output in the integrated terminal.

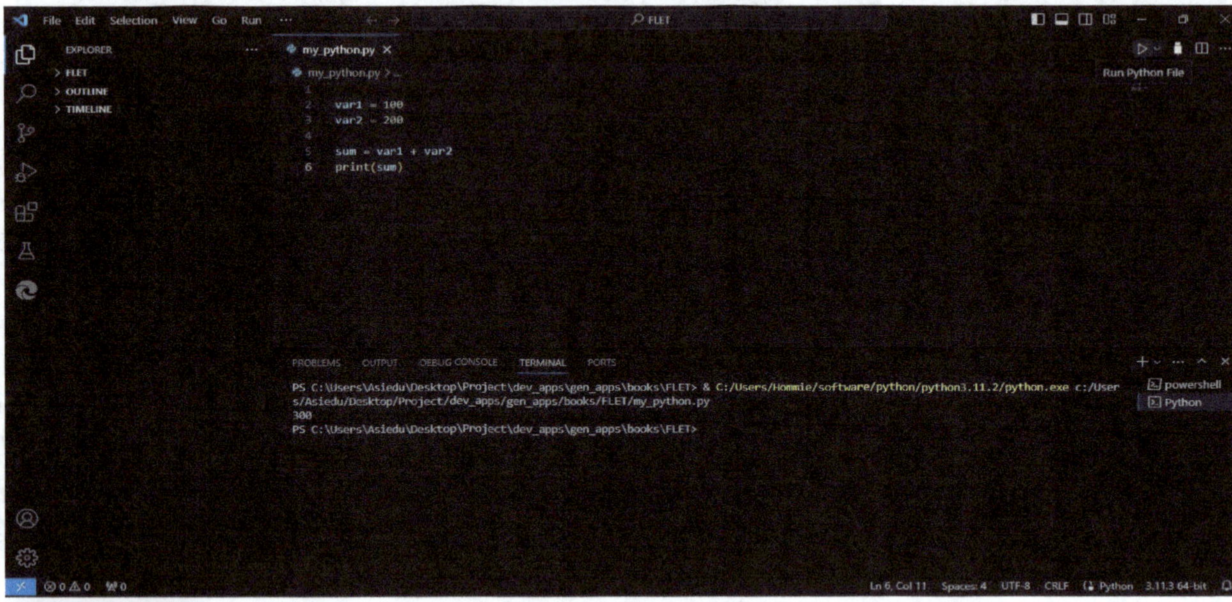

Figure: 1.6 - Visual studio code (running Python script)

Executing Python from the Command Line

Running Python code from the command line or shell using the python command is a simple and universal approach that works across all operating systems, including Windows, Linux, and macOS.

Here's how you can run Python code from the command line:

Open the Command Line or Terminal:

1. On Windows, open the Command Prompt by searching for *"cmd"* in the Start menu.
2. On Linux or macOS, open the Terminal application.

Navigate to the Directory Containing Your Python File (Optional):

3. Use the **cd** command to navigate to the directory containing your Python file if it's not already there.

Run the Python File:

4. Type **python** followed by the name of your Python file and press the **Enter** key. For example: python my_script.py

```
PS C:\Users\Asiedu\Desktop\Project\dev_apps> python my_python.py
```

View Output (If Any):

If your Python script produces any output, such as printed messages or results, it will be displayed in the terminal after running the script.

This method provides a straightforward way to execute Python code directly from the command line or shell, making it convenient for quick tests or running scripts without the need for an integrated development environment (IDE) or text editor.

Deep

Python files are commonly recognized by their extension. **.py** for regular Python scripts or file and **.pyw** for scripts that run without displaying the console window.

Modules or Libraries

Python modules are collections of code that provide additional functionality to Python programs. These modules are essentially Python files containing classes, functions and objects that can be imported and used in other Python scripts. They help simplify coding tasks by providing pre-defined solutions to common problems, thus saving developers time and effort.

While some modules are included in the Python standard library, many others are developed and maintained by the Python community. These external modules cover a wide range of domains and purposes, catering to diverse needs and preferences. For example, there are modules for web development, data analysis, machine learning, game development, and much more.

The beauty of Python modules lies in their versatility and flexibility. Developers can choose and install only the modules they need for their specific projects, allowing for a lightweight and efficient development process. For example, game developers may focus on installing modules essential for game development, while graphic designers may prefer using image processing libraries or modules to enhance their workflow.

Moreover, the open-source nature of Python encourages collaboration and contribution to module development, ensuring a rich ecosystem of tools and resources for Python programmers worldwide.

Installing Python Modules with Pip

Installing Python modules is straightforward using the pip command, which is included as part of the Python package. Here's how you can install a Python module using pip on the command line or shell of any operating system:

1. Open the Command Line or Terminal:
2. Use the pip Command:

```
pip install module_name
```

Press Enter to execute the command.
For example, to install the NumPy module, you would type:

```
pip install numpy
```

Once the installation is complete, you can start using the module in your Python code. Using the module in your Python code is as simple as using the import keyword followed by the name of the module. For example,

```python
>>> import numpy
>>>
```

This statement imports the specified module into your Python script, allowing you to use its *classes*, *functions*, and *variables* within your code.

Note

Import statement will be covered in more detail in later chapters.

Deep

Bugs, also known as errors, are issues in the code that prevent it from running correctly or producing the expected output. They can occur due to various reasons, such as logic error, semantic error, syntax error and runtime error.

Chapter 2

Overview of Python

Chapter Objectives

- Variable
- Reserved Words
- Operators
- String
- List
- Tuple
- Dictionary
- Set
- Decision Making Statements
- Loops
- Function
- Class and Object
- Handling Errors and Exceptions

Variable

Variable, also known as an identifier, is a term used to describe a letter or word that stores a value. Variables represent data stored in the computer's memory and can consist of any combination of letters, alphabets, or alphanumeric characters.

For example,

```
</> Python
>>> var = 100              #single value assignment
>>>
>>> var1, var2 = 2, 5      #multiple value assignment (var1 = 2, var2 = 5)
>>>
>>> x = y  = "computer"    #multiple value assignment (x = "computer", y = "computer")
```

In the above example:

- var is assigned to 100. Therefore, it holds a value of 100 in the computer memory.
- var1 and var2 are assigned to 2 and 5 respectively.
- x and y are assigned to the same value "computer".

Rules for naming Variables

- Variables are case sensitive.
  example: myvar is not equal to Myvar.

- Variables cannot begin with a number but can be followed by numbers.
  example: myvar25, my63var.

- Variables can begin with underscores.
  example: _myvar

Kinds of Variable

Variables exist in two forms: local and global. Both serve the same purpose of storing values in computer memory, but their functionality is determined by the scope in which they are used.

Local Variables

Local variables are declared **within** a function or block and can only be accessed by members within the same function. They are **not available** outside that block or function.

</> Python

```
global_var = 3

def math:                   #function
    local_var = 2           #local variable
    value = local_var + 5   #using variable
```

For example, the variable local_var is defined inside a function called math, no object outside the math function can access it.

Global Variables

Global variables are declared **outside** any function or block, making them **accessible** to all functions and objects within the program.

</> Python

```
global_var = 3                          #global variable
add = global_var + 10

def math:                               #function
    local_var = 2                       #local variable
    value = local_var + global_var      #using global variable
```

For instance, if a variable global_var is defined globally, it can be used both inside and outside functions. However, **global variables can only be accessed but not modified** from within a function unless explicitly specified using the global or nonlocal keyword.

</> Python

```python
city = "London"

def withoutGlobal():
    city = "New York"

def withGlobal():
    global city
    city = "New York"

withoutGlobal()             #Executing function
print(city)

withGlobal()
print(city)
```

```
#Ouput
London
New York
```

In a scenario where a variable city is modified inside a function withGlobal, the global keyword ensures that the change affects the original global variable, setting its new value to "New York".

Think about it ?

The **nonlocal** keyword works similarly to global, but it is primarily used within nested functions.

But wait... what exactly is a nested function?

Deep

To check if an object is a valid variable name or identifier, use the .isidentifier() method on the string.

```
>>> "100var".isidentifier()
False
>>> "_var".isidentifier()
True
>>>
```

Using None in Python

In most programming languages, especially **C++, Java, JavaScript, and Dart**, variables can be declared without assigning an initial value. These variables are often set to null or left empty, allowing them to be assigned a value later.

However, Python does not allow variables to be declared without assigning a value. Every declared variable must have an initial value. If a value is meant to be defined later, Python provides the special keyword **None**, which represents an empty or uninitialized variable that will be assigned a value in the future.

Example Use Case

</> Python

```python
country = None
city = "New York"

country = "USA"
print(country)
```

```
#Ouput
USA
```

None is commonly used as a placeholder for variables that will receive a value later in the program. It helps indicate that a variable is intentionally left empty rather than undefined.

Think about it ?

Are any of these valid variables?

- xyz
- 45var
- myVar
- _6var1
- #num
- n@um
- --first

Reserved Words

Python, like many programming languages, has a set of reserved *keywords* that serve specific purposes and functions within the language. These keywords are not available for use as variable names or for any other purpose in a Python program. Each reserved word carries a distinct and predefined functionality that is essential for the language's structure and operation.

print	chr	hex	max	super	finally
len	else	range	raise	next	type
set	if	bin	sum	map	or
int	True	try	as	with	global
dict	False	eval	bool	while	local
list	and	not	str	for	catch
object	import	oct	ord	zip	super
exec	del	dir	any	def	return
yield	hash	filter	format	enumerate	delattr
compile	bytearray	bytes	ascii	min	complex
id	local	help	in	open	lambda
input	None	is	nonlocal	assert	class
elif	break	continue	pass	from	case
match	async	await	pow		

Table 2.0 : Some keywords used in Python programming

Here are the uses of some keywords

input()

The input() function is used to receive data from the user through a prompt. By default, it takes input as a string, but the input data can be converted to any desired type and assigned to a variable.

</> Python

```
>>> num1 = int( input("first number: "))          #converting input to integer
...... first number: 2
>>> num2 = int( input("second number: "))
...... second number: 3
>>>
>>> total = num1 + num2
>>> total
....... 5
>>>
```

Note

The **int** used above belongs to the integer data type and is used to convert other types to integers. Integers and other data types will be covered in detail in the upcoming chapters.

eval()

The eval() function evaluates expressions in string format and applies mathematical operations to compute the result.

</> Python

```
>>> eval( "5+2*3-1/2" )
...... 10.5
>>> eval( "pow(2,4) -5 + max(10,5)" )
...... 21
```

Operators

Operators are special symbols that appear between two operands (values or variables) and instruct the computer to perform specific operations. These operations can involve mathematical calculations, comparisons, assignments, and logical evaluations.

The various kinds of Python operators include:

- Arithmetic Operators
- Relational Operators
- Assignment Operators
- Logical Operators
- Identity Operators
- Membership Operators
- Bitwise Operators

Arithmetic Operators

Arithmetic operators are used to perform various mathematical functions on numeric data types in programming. They enable you to perform fundamental mathematical operations like addition, subtraction, multiplication, division, and more.

Addition(+)

```
</> Python
>>> x = 5
>>> y = 3
>>> result = x + y
>>> print( result )
...... 8
>>>
```

Subtraction(-)

```python
>>> x = 10
>>> y = 6
>>> result = x - y
>>> print( result )
...... 4
>>>
```

Multiplication(*)

```python
>>> num1 = 4
>>> num2 = 2
>>> product = num1 * num2
>>> print( product )
...... 8
>>>
```

Division(/)

```python
>>> first = 6
>>> second = 2
>>> first / second
...... 3
>>>
```

Modulo(%)

```python
>>> x = 3
>>> y = 11
>>> y % x
...... 2
>>>
```

Floor division(//)

```
</> Python
>>> x = 9
>>> y = 2
>>> x // y
...... 4
>>>
```

Exponential (**)

```
</> Python
>>> _exp = 2
>>> _num = 4
>>> _num **  _exp
...... 16
>>>
```

Relational Operators

Relational operators, also known as comparison operators, are essential components of conditional statements in Python. They are used to compare two values or operands and determine the relationship between them. Relational operators return a Boolean value, either **'True'** or **'False'**, based on the result of the comparison.

Relational operators are crucial for making decisions in programs. They help answer questions like "Is this value equal to that one?" or "Is this value greater than that one?"

Equal to (==)

```
</> Python
>>> "wheat" == "whaet"   #equal to
...... False
>>> x, y = 100, 100
>>> x == y
.....  True
```

Not equal to (!=)

</> Python

```
>>> "Computer" != "computer"
...... True
>>> x = y = 4
>>> x != y
...... False
```

Less than or equal to (<=)

</> Python

```
>>> 10 <= 20
...... True
>>> m = n = 5
>>> m <= n
...... True
```

Greater than or equal to (>=)

</> Python

```
>>> 10 >= 20
...... False
>>> x, y = 4 , 2
>>> x >= y
...... True
```

Think about it ?

- How is **>** different from **>=**?
- What about **<** and **<=**?

Data Types

Data encompasses raw values that can manifest in various forms, such as numbers, letters, special characters or a blend thereof. Data types serve to classify data based on their attributes and functionalities.

In Python, data types represent instances or objects of specific classes, each characterized by unique traits and behaviors. The Python programming language encompasses approximately eight fundamental data types. The various types of data types in Python include:

- Numbers (Integer and Float)
- String
- List
- Dictionary
- Tuple
- Set
- Boolean
- Bytes

Deep

To check the data type of an object, use the type() function.

```
>>> var = 3
>>> type(var)
...... class <'int'>
>>> mystr = "Computer"
>>> type(mystr)
...... class <'str'>
```

Numbers

Number data types include all real numbers, such as positive and negative integers, decimals, and other numerical values.

Integer

The integer class encompasses all numbers, including negative numbers, without decimal points. Examples include, 2, 13, -5, 100, 2000 ......

Deep

The int() function is employed to convert from one type to the integer type

```
>>> num = "5"       #string to integer
>>> int(num)
...... 5
>>> var = 12.58     #float to integer
>>> int(var)
...... 12
```

Float

On the other hand, floats represent the class of all numbers with decimal points. Examples include, -6.25, 8.5245, -5.3, 100.6 ......

Deep

To convert from one type to the float type, the float() function is utilized.

```
>>> dec = "8.258"     #string to float
>>> float(dec)
...... 8.258
>>> var = 35          #integer to float
>>> float(var)
...... 35.0
```

The math Module

The **math** module provides a wide range of mathematical functions and constants for performing numerical computations. It includes methods for working with equations, geometry, trigonometry, logarithms, and more. These functions are essential for handling mathematical concepts in Python.

Deep

You can explore more methods of math with the dir() function.

```
>>> import math
>>> dir(math)
...... [............]
```

Commonly Used Functions in the math Module

Function	Description
math.sqrt(x)	Returns the square root of x.
math.pow(x, y)	Returns x raised to the power of y (equivalent to x ** y).
math.exp(x)	Returns e raised to the power of x.
math.log(x)	Returns the natural logarithm (base e) of x.
math.log10(x)	Returns the logarithm of x to base 10.
math.log2(x)	Returns the logarithm of x to base 2.
math.factorial(x)	Returns the factorial of x (x!).
math.gcd(x, y)	Returns the greatest common divisor (GCD) of x and y.
math.lcm(x, y)	Returns the least common multiple (LCM) of x and y.
math.fabs(x)	Returns the absolute value of x.
math.ceil(x)	Rounds x up to the nearest integer.
math.floor(x)	Rounds x down to the nearest integer.
math.trunc(x)	Returns the truncated integer part of x.
math.modf(x)	Splits x into its fractional and integer parts as a tuple.
math.copysign(x, y)	Returns x with the sign of y.
math.fsum(iterable)	Returns the precise sum of an iterable of numbers.
math.isfinite(x)	Checks if x is a finite number.
math.isinf(x)	Checks if x is infinite (+∞ or -∞).
math.isnan(x)	Checks if x is NaN (Not a Number).

Table 2.1 : The math functions

pow(x, y)

```
</> Python
import math
>>> pow( 2, 4)
...... 16
>>> math.pow(3, 2)
...... 9.0
```

sqrt(x)

```
</> Python
import math
>>> math.sqrt( 25 )
...... 5.0
```

log10(x)

```
</> Python
import math
>>> math.log10( 10 )
...... 1.0
```

ceil(x)

```
</> Python
import math
>>> math.ceil( 3.845 )
...... 4
```

floor(x)

```
</> Python
import math
>>> math.floor( 5.389 )
...... 6
```

factorial(x)

```
</> Python
import math
>>> math.factorial( 6 )
...... 720
```

String

A string is a sequence of characters, including alphabets, numbers, or special characters, enclosed within quotes. String can be in a single or double quote.

For example,

</> Python

```
>>> var1 = 'single'
>>> var2 = "double"
>>> var3 = '''triple'''
>>> var4 = """triple"""
```

Deep

The str() method is used to convert other data types to a string.

```
>>> var = 3.45
>>> string_var = str(var)
>>> print(string_var)
..... '3.45'
>>>
```

String indexing

Indexing refers to the position of each character in a string. The index of a string starts from zero and goes up to the length of the string minus one (0 to length-1). The first character or element of a string typically occupies index 0, the next character takes index 1, and so on.

For example, using “computer”

0	1	2	3	4	5	6	7
c	o	m	p	u	t	e	r
-8	-7	-6	-5	-4	-3	-2	-1

```python
>>> var = "computer"
>>> var[0]
...... 'c'
>>> var[1]
...... 'o'
>>> var[-6]
...... 'm'
>>>
```

Concatenating string

Concatenating strings involves adding two or more separate strings to form one complete string using the plus (+) operator.

For example,

```python
>>> var1 = "com"
>>> var2 = "puter"
>>> var3 = var1 + var2
>>> print(var3)
...... 'computer'
>>>
```

Slicing a string

String slicing allows you to extract substrings from a string. The syntax for string slicing is **string**[start : end], where *start* indicates where the slicing should begin and *end* indicates where it should end. Both start and end parameters can be omitted, in which case Python will set them to default values (0 for start and the last index of the string for end).

Formulas for String Slicing

string[start: end] → Returns a substring starting from the specified start index up to (but not including) the end index.

string[start:] → Returns a substring starting from the specified start index to the end of the string.

string[: end] → Returns a substring starting from the beginning (index 0) up to (but not including) the specified end index.

string[:] → Returns the entire string from index 0 to the last character.

For example,

</> Python

```
>>> var = "Hello World"
>>> var[0:5]                #start = 0, end=5
...... 'Hello'
>>> var[6:]                 #start = 6, end= length of string
...... 'World'
>>> var[:3]                 #start = 0, end=3
...... 'Hel'
>>> var[1:5]                #start = 1, end=5
...... 'ello'
>>>
```

String Methods

Deep

To view the various methods available for a string, use the dir() function on a string object.

```
>>> mystring = "Hello World"
>>> dir(mystring)
...... [............]
```

Case Conversion Methods

Method	Description
upper()	Converts all characters in the string to uppercase.
lower()	Converts all characters in the string to lowercase.
capitalize()	Converts the first character of the string to uppercase and the rest to lowercase.
title()	Converts the first character of each word in the string to uppercase.
swapcase()	Swaps uppercase characters to lowercase and vice versa.
casefold()	Converts the string to lowercase, more aggressive than lower(), used for case-insensitive comparisons.

</> Python

```
>>> var = "The brown fox"
>>>
>>> var.upper()
...... 'THE BROWN FOX'
>>>
>>> var.lower()
...... 'the brown fox'
>>>
>>> var.capitalize()
...... 'The brown fox'
>>>
>>> var.title()
...... 'The Brown Fox'
>>>
>>> var.swapcase()
...... 'tHE BROWN FOX'
>>>
>>> var.casefold()
...... 'the brown fox'
>>>
```

Searching and Finding Methods

find(substring, start, end)	Returns the index of the first occurrence of substring in the string. Returns -1 if not found.
rfind(substring, start, end)	Similar to find(), but searches from the right.
index(substring, start, end)	Similar to find(), but raises an error if the substring is not found.
rindex(substring, start, end)	Similar to rfind(), but raises an error if the substring is not found.
count(substring, start, end)	Counts the occurrences of substring in the string.

</> Python

```
>>> var = "Programming"
>>>
>>> len( var )                  #returns the length of the string
...... 11
>>>
>>> var[0]                      #returns a character by the index
......  'P'
>>>
>>> var.find( "o" ,1, 6)
...... 2
>>> var.find( "g" )             #returns the first occurrence of  g
...... 3
>>>
>>> var.rfind( "g" )            #returns the last occurrence of g
...... 10
>>>
>>> var.index( "r" , 1, 6 )     #start from index 1  ( r ) , end at index 5 (a)
...... 1
>>>
>>> var.rindex( "r" , 1, 6 )    #start from index 1  ( r ) , end at index 5 (a)
...... 4
>>>
>>> var.count( "m")
...... 2
>>>
```

String Modification and Replacement Methods

replace(old, new, count)	Replaces occurrences of old with new. The optional count limits the number of replacements.
removeprefix(char)	Removes the specified leading character or substring from a string.
removesuffix(char)	Removes the specified trailing character or substring from a string.

```
</> Python
>>> newstring = "The big brown cat"
>>>
>>> newstring.replace("cat", "fox")
...... 'The big brown fox'
>>>
>>> substring = "Crack Codes and Coffee ".replace("C", "K", 2)
>>> print(substring)
...... 'Krack Kodes and Coffee'
```

```
</> Python
>>> var = "*programming"
>>>
>>> var.removeprefix("*")
...... 'programming'
>>>
>>> var.removesuffix("ming")
...... '*program'
```

String Checking Methods (True or False)

startswith(prefix, start, end)	Returns True if the string starts with prefix.
endswith(suffix, start, end)	Returns True if the string ends with suffix.
isalpha()	Returns True if the string contains only alphabetic characters (A-Z, a-z).
isdigit()	Returns True if the string contains only digits (0-9).
isalnum()	Returns True if the string contains only alphanumeric characters (letters and numbers).
isspace()	Returns True if the string contains only whitespace characters.
islower()	Returns True if all characters in the string are lowercase.
isupper()	Returns True if all characters in the string are uppercase.
istitle()	Returns True if the string follows title case (each word starts with an uppercase letter).
isnumeric()	Returns True if the string contains only numeric characters, including Unicode numerals.
isdecimal()	Returns True if the string contains only decimal characters.
isidentifier()	Returns True if the string is a valid Python identifier (variable name).
isascii()	Returns True if the string contains only ASCII characters (0-127).

</> Python

```
>>> "computer".startswith("com")
..... True
>>> "computer".endswith("k")
..... False

>>> "coding".isalpha()
..... True
>>> "code250".isalpha()
..... False

>>> "code250".isdigit()
..... False
>>> "250".isnumeric()
..... True
```

```
>>> "code250".isalnum()
..... True

>>> "code250@_#".isalnum()
..... False

>>> "code250@_#".isascii()
..... True

>>> second_char = "I love programming"[1]
>>> second_char.isspace()
..... True

>>> "Programming".isupper()
..... False
>>> "PROGRAMMING".isupper()
..... True

>>> "Programming".islower()
..... False
>>> "programming".islower()
..... True

>>> "Python Programming".istitle()
..... True
>>> "Python programming".istitle()
..... False

>>> "_var".isidentifier()
..... True
>>> "23var".isidentifier()
..... False
```

String Formatting

In Python, inserting variables into a string to make the output dynamic is called **string formatting**. Instead of directly placing a variable inside a string (which would be treated as plain text), Python provides multiple ways to format strings properly.

❌ Wrong formatting

</> Python

```python
var = 100
print(" Total is var")
```

```
#Output
Total is var
```

Here, var is treated as part of the string instead of a variable.

Python provides three main ways to format strings properly:

1. Using f-strings (f"" notation) – Recommended

Introduced in Python 3.6, **f-strings** allow embedding variables directly into a string using curly brackets { }.

Syntax:

```
f"{variable or expression}"
```

Example

</> Python

```python
var = 100
print(f" Total is { var }")
```

```
#Output
Total is 100
```

2. Using .format() method

Before f-strings, the .format() method was commonly used. It replaces {} placeholders with values passed inside .format().

Syntax:

```
"{}".format(variable)
"{}{}".format(variable1, variable2)
"{1} {0}".format(variable1, variable2) # Positional indexing
```

Example

```python
var = 25
results = "Alice is {} years".format( var )
print( results )
```

```
#Output
'Alice is 25 years'
```

Escape Characters in Python

In programming, escape characters are special sequences used to format strings by providing short commands that instruct the compiler on how to display text. These commands help in creating new lines, adding tab spaces, inserting special symbols, and more.

Escape characters always begin with a backslash (\), followed by a specific character that represents an action. Below is a list of commonly used escape characters in Python:

Escape Character	Description
\n	Inserts a new line (line break)
\t	Adds a horizontal tab space
\\	Inserts a backslash (\)
\'	Inserts a single quote (') inside a string enclosed in single quotes
\"	Inserts a double quote (") inside a string enclosed in double quotes
\r	Carriage return – moves the cursor to the beginning of the line
\b	Backspace – removes the previous character
\f	Form feed – moves to the next page (used in printing)
\v	Vertical tab – adds a vertical tab space
\000	Represents an octal value (e.g., \101 represents 'A')
\xhh	Represents a hexadecimal value (e.g., \x41 represents 'A')

Table 2.2 : The escape characters

Example, using newline (\n)

</> Python

```
print( "Hello everyone! \nDo you like Python?" )
```

```
#Output
Hello everyone!
Do you like Python?
```

List

A list is a collection of items of the same type or different types, enclosed in square brackets [ ]. Lists perform functions similar to arrays in C, C++, and Java. They can contain other lists, making them a preferred choice for storing large data of different types.

For example,

```python
>>> even = [2, 4, 6, 8, 10]                                        #list of numbers
>>> items = ["mouse", "keyboard", "microphone"]                    #list of string
>>> mix = [ 5, "mouse", 4.25, ('age', 30), {'name' : "John"}, [2, 4] ]   #list of different types
>>>
```

Note

The first element of a list occupies index **0**, the next at index **1** and so on.
For example, cities = ["London", "New York", "Ontario", "Chicago"]

item	London	New York	Ontario	Chicago
index	0	1	2	3

Accessing Items in a List

Elements of a list can be retrieved by specifying their index within square brackets ([]).
For example,

```python
>>> cities = ["London", "New York", "Ontario", "Chicago"]
>>> cities[0]
...... 'London'
>>> cities[2]
...... 'Ontario'
>>>
```

Deep

The list() function is used for converting other data types to list.

```
>>> list("programming")
...... ['p', 'r', 'o', 'g', 'r', 'a', 'm', 'm', 'i', 'n', 'g']
>>>
```

Slicing a list

Lists can be divided to obtain sub-lists using slicing notation list[start : end]. The *start* parameter is optional and specifies where the division should begin. If start is not set, Python begins the division from the first element (index 0). Similarly, the *end* parameter is optional. If not specified, Python sets it to the last index of the list.

Formulas for Slicing a List

list[start: end] → Returns a sub list starting from the specified start index up to (but not including) the end index.

list[start:] → Returns a sub list starting from the specified start index to the end of the list.

list[: end] → Returns a sub list starting from the beginning (index 0) up to (but not including) the specified end index.

list[:] → Returns the entire list from index 0 to the last character.

For example,

</> Python

```
>>> cities = ["London", "New York", "Ontario", "Chicago"]
>>> cities[1:3]
...... ['New York', 'Ontario']

>>> cities[1:]
...... ['New York', 'Ontario', 'Chicago']

>>> cities[:2]
...... ['London', 'New York']
>>>
```

Tuple

Tuples are collections of elements of different data types enclosed in parentheses ( ) and separated by commas. The elements of tuples are immutable, meaning they cannot be changed once created, but they can still be accessed.

For example,

</> Python

```
>>> tup1 = (3, 4, 2)                                                    #tuple of numbers
>>> tup2 = ("Python", "Java", "C++")                                    #tuple of strings
>>> tup3 = (5, 3.25, ('id', 30), "Texas", {'name' : "Alice"}, [6, 2] )  #tuple of different types
>>>
```

Deep

The tuple() function is used to convert other data types to tuple.

```
>>> var = "code"                    #string to tuple
>>> tuple(var)
.....  ('c', 'o', 'd', 'e')

>>> var = ["USA", "Spain", "Italy"]     #list to tuple
>>> tuple(var)
.....  ('USA', 'Spain', 'Italy')

>>> var = {2, 4, 6, 8}              #set to tuple
>>> tuple(var)
...... (8, 2, 4, 6)
```

Accessing Elements from a Tuple

Tuples, like other iterables such as **strings** and **lists**, allow elements to be accessed using **indexing**. Each element in a tuple is assigned an **index**, starting from **0** for the first element, **1** for the second, and so on. For example,

```
</> Python
>>> planets = ("mercury", "venus", "earth", "mars")
>>> planets[0]
..... 'mercury'

>>> planets[2]
...... 'earth'

>>> profile = ( ("Alice", 25), ("John", 30), ("Bob", 10) )

>>> profile[0]
...... ('Alice', 25)

>>> profile[1][0]
..... 'John'

>>> profile[2][1]
...... 10
```

Tuple Methods

Method	Description
index(item, start, end)	Returns the index of the first occurrence of the specified value. Raises a ValueError if the value is not found.
count(item)	Returns the number of times a specified value appears in the tuple.

index(item, start, end)

```
</> Python
>>> tup = ("apple", "berry", "banana")
>>> tup.index("apple")
..... 0

>>> tup.index("banana")
..... 2
```

Dictionary

A dictionary is a data structure that consists of a collection of **key-value** pair items, separated by commas, and enclosed within curly braces { }. Dictionaries can contain items of various data types. In a key-value pair, one item (the key) is associated with another item (the value), and they are linked by a colon (key : value).

For example,

```
Dictionary_name = { key : value }
```

</> **Python**

```
>>> dict1 = {'name' : "Alice", 'age' : 20, 'country' : "USA"}
>>> dict2 = {'numbers' : [2, 4],  'languages' : ("Python", "Java") }
>>> dict3 = { 1 : 100,  2 : 200,  3 : 300}
>>>
```

Note

Dictionary keys can be either numbers or strings, whereas values can be any object, including strings, numbers, dictionaries, tuples, sets, and bytes. Dictionary keys are immutable.

Deep

The dict() function is used to convert other data types (tuple) to dictionary.

```
>>> var = ( ("name", "John"), ("ID", 250), ("city", "London") )       #Tuple
>>> dict(var)
...... {'name': 'John', 'ID': 250, 'city': 'London'}
>>>
```

Dictionary Methods

Method	Description
get(key, default)	Returns the value of the key. If the key is not found, returns the specified default value.
items()	Returns a view of all dictionary key-value pairs as tuples.
keys()	Returns a view of all dictionary keys.
values()	Returns a view of all dictionary values.
pop(key, default)	Removes and returns the value for the specified key. If the key is not found, returns the default value.
popitem()	Removes and returns the last inserted key-value pair as a tuple.
update(iterable)	Updates the dictionary with key-value pairs from another dictionary or iterable of key-value pairs.
setdefault(key, default)	Returns the value of the key if present; otherwise, inserts the key with the specified default value.
fromkeys(seq, value)	Creates a new dictionary from a sequence of keys, all having the specified value.
copy()	Returns a shallow copy of the dictionary.
clear()	Removes all key-value pairs from the dictionary.

Table 2.3 : Dictionary methods and properties

In a dictionary, values can be accessed using their corresponding keys in two ways:

① Using Square Brackets (dictionary[key])

This method retrieves the value associated with the specified key. However, if the key does not exist in the dictionary, it raises a KeyError.

</> Python

```
>>> program = {1: "Python", 2: "Java",  3: "C++"}
>>> program[1]
...... 'Python'

>>> program[3]
...... 'C++'

>>> profile = {"name": "Alice",  "age": 25}
>>> profile["name"]
..... 'Alice'

>>> profile["age"]
...... 25
```

② Using the get(key) Method

The get() method returns the value associated with the specified key. Unlike square brackets, if the key is not found, it returns None (or a default value if specified), preventing potential errors.

get(key)

```
</> Python
>>> profile = {"name": "Alice",  "age": 25}

>>> profile.get("name")
...... 'Alice'

>>> profile.get("age")
...... 25
```

Updating Dictionary Items

Dictionary values can be updated in two ways:

① Using the square bracket notation (dictionary_name[key] = value)

This method updates the value of an existing key or adds a new key-value pair if the key does not exist.

dictionary_name[key]

```
</> Python
>>> profile = {"name": "Alice",  "age": 25}

>>> profile["name"] = "Bob"
>>> print(profile)
...... {'name': 'Bob', 'age': 25}

>>> profile["country"] = "Italy"
>>> print(profile)
...... {'name': 'Bob', 'age': 25, 'country': 'Italy'}
```

② Using the update() method

This method allows multiple updates at once by passing a dictionary of key-value pairs.

update(iterable)

```python
>>> profile = {"name": "Alice",  "age": 25}

>>> profile.update({"name": "Bob",  "city": "London"})
>>> print(profile)
...... {'name': 'Bob', 'age': 25, 'city': 'London'}
```

setdefault(key, default)

```python
>>> person = {"name": "Bob"}

>>> person.setdefault("name", "Alice")
......  'Bob'
>>> print(person)
...... {'name': 'Bob'}

>>> person.setdefault("college", "Harvard")
......  'Harvard'
>>> print(person)
.....  {'name': 'Bob', 'college': 'Harvard'}
```

copy() and clear()

```python
>>> profile = {"name": "Alice",  "age": 25}

>>> new_dict = profile.copy()
>>> print(new_dict)
...... {'name': 'Alice', 'age': 25}

>>> profile.clear()
>>> print(profile)
...... { }
```

Set

A set is an unordered collection of unique elements. Sets enclose their members within curly braces { }. Sets can hold members of strings, integers, floats, and tuples, but not dictionaries, lists, or other sets. Sets are commonly used to perform mathematical operations such as intersection, union, or symmetric difference.

For example,

</> **Python**

```
>>> set1 = {1, 3, 5, 7}

>>> set2 = {"a", "b", "c", "d"}

>>> set3 = {2, 4, 6, "orange", "apple" }
```

Deep

The set() function is used to convert other data types to set.

```
>>> list_var = [2, 3, 5]        #list to set
>>> set(list_var)
...... {2, 3, 5}

>>> string_var = "Hello"   #string to set
>>> set(string_var)
..... {'l', 'H', 'o', 'e'}

>>> tuple_var = (2, 5, 8)    #string to set
>>> set(tuple_var)
...... {8, 2, 5}

>>> dictionary_var = {1:'Python', 2:'Java', 3:'C#'}   #dictionary to set
>>> set(dictionary_var)
...... {1, 2, 3}
```

Set Methods

Method	Description
add(item)	Adds an element or item to the set. If the element already exists, it does nothing.
copy()	Returns a shallow copy of the set.
clear()	Removes all elements from the set, making it empty.
difference(*sets)	Returns a new set with elements that are in the original set but not in the given set(s).
difference_update(*sets)	Removes elements from the original set that are present in the given set(s). Modifies the original set.
discard(item)	Removes the specified item from the set if it exists. Does nothing if the element is not found.
remove(item)	Removes the specified item from the set. Raises a KeyError if the element is not found.
pop()	Removes and returns a random element from the set. Raises a KeyError if the set is empty.
intersection(*sets)	Returns a new set containing elements common to the original set and all given set(s).
intersection_update(*sets)	Modifies the original set to keep only elements also found in all given set(s).
isdisjoint(set)	Returns True if the set has no elements in common with other set, otherwise returns False.
issubset(set)	Returns True if all elements of the set are in other set, otherwise returns False.
issuperset(set)	Returns True if the set contains all elements of other set, otherwise returns False.
union(*set)	Returns a new set containing all unique elements from the original set and given set(s).
update(*sets)	Adds elements from given set(s) to the original set. Modifies the original set.
symmetric_difference(set)	Returns a new set with elements that are in either the set or other set, but not both.
symmetric_difference_update(set)	Modifies the original set to include only elements unique to either set.

Table 2.4 : Methods and properties of Set

add()

</> Python

```
>>> even = {2, 4, 6}
>>> even.add(8)
>>> print(even)
```

```
..... {8, 2, 4, 6}
>>>
```

update(*set)

```
</> Python
>>> set1 = {2, 4}
>>> set2 = {1, 3}
>>> set1.update(set2)
>>> print(set1)
..... {1, 2, 3, 4}

>>> rainbow = {"blue","purple", "white"}
>>> primary, secondary = {"red", "green"}, {"yellow","orange"}
>>> rainbow.update(primary, secondary)
>>> rainbow
...... {'red', 'blue', 'white', 'orange', 'purple', 'green', 'yellow'}
```

copy()

```
</> Python
>>> even = {2, 4, 6}
>>> copied = even.copy()
>>> print(copied)
...... {2, 4, 6}
>>>
```

discard(item)

```
</> Python
>>> even = {1, 4, 8}
>>> even.discard( 4 )
>>> print(even)
...... {8, 1}
>>>
```

Decision Making Statements

Decision making is crucial in programming, especially when you want your program to execute only when a certain condition is true or false. These statements, known as conditional statements, are based on a Boolean value (True or False). There are three different kinds of conditional statements:

① if Statement:

This is a simple conditional statement that executes a program or instructions if a condition is true or false

</> Python

```python
if condition:
  #code
```

For example,

A program to print "Hello World!" when an input number is greater than or equal to 10.

</> Python

```python
var = int(input("type any number: "))  #convert input to integer

if var >= 10:
  print("Hello World!")
```

```
#Output
type any number: 20
Hello World!
```

② if – else Statement:

The if-else conditional statement provides two options for program execution. If the given condition is true, the program executes the statements in the if block; otherwise, if the condition is false, the statements within the else block execute.

</> Python

```
if condition:
  #code
else :
  #code
```

For example:

A program to print *"Great Python"*, if a variable is greater than 5, otherwise print *"Awesome Python"*.

</> Python

```
var = int(input("type any number: "))  #convert input to integer

if  var > 5:
    print("Great Python!")
else:
    print("Awesome Python!")
```

```
#Output
type any number: 8
Great Python!
```

Example 2,

A program that asks the user to input their age. If the age is below 18, it prints *'You are underage, sorry you cannot vote'*. Otherwise, it prints *'You can vote'*.

```python
age = int(input("How old are you?: "))

if  age < 18:
    print("You are underage,\nSorry, you cannot vote")
else:
    print("You can vote")
```

```
#Output
How old are you?: 16
You are underage,
Sorry, you cannot vote
```

③ if – elif – else Statement:

This conditional statement is necessary for multiple decision making

```python
if condition1:
  #code
elif condition2:
  #code
elif condition3:
   #code
.......
.......
else :
   #code
```

For example:

A program to print *"great Python!"*, if a variable is equal to 5. If it is greater than 5, print *"awesome Python"*; otherwise print *'good Python'*.

</> Python

```
var = 3
if   var == 5:
     print("Great Python")
elif var < 5:
     print("Awesome Python")
else :
     print("Good Python")
```

#Output
Awesome Python

Loops

A loop is a control structure that enables the repetitive execution of a statement or a group of statements. Loops are built around **conditions**, **steps**, and **statements**. They continue executing as long as the condition remains true. There are two main types of loop structures in Python: for loops and while loops.

Needed for Loops:

Automate repetitive tasks
Loops are ideal for automating tasks that need to be repeated multiple times, saving time and effort.

Handle large amounts of data
Loops are efficient for processing items in a list, dictionary, or any other data structure.

Improving code readability
Reduces redundancy by eliminating the need for repeated statements.

Iterate over sequences
You can use loops to go through sequences like strings, lists, or ranges without manually indexing each item.

Perform calculations or updates
Loops can be used to continuously calculate or update variables until a specific condition is met.

Reduce human error
By automating repetitive tasks, loops minimize the chances of mistakes.

The for loop

The for loop is a control structure that allows the repetitive execution of statements in a top-to-bottom approach. It is used to iterate over elements of sequential data types such as lists, strings, or tuples.

Syntax:

```
for item in iterable:
    #code
```

Note

Iterable is an object capable of returning its members one at a time. It can be traversed or looped over using **for** loops. Examples include list, tuple, string, dictionary and set.

For example,

</> **Python**

```python
var = "code"

for i in var:
    print(i)
```

```
#Output
c
o
d
e
```

Example2,

A program that calculates the sum of a list of numbers by iterating through the list and adding each item.

</> Python

```python
num = [ 1, 2, 3, 4]
total = 0

for i in num:
    total = total + i
    print(total)
```

```
#Output
1
3
6
10
```

Note

- Indentation is crucial in **for** and **while** loops.
- Every **for** or **while** statement must end with a colon (:).

Range

Loop structures execute code based on user-given instructions, specifying where to begin, end, and the steps. These instructions can be easily implemented using the ***range()*** function.

The range(start, end, step) function is used to specify the range of values and steps a control structure must follow to execute the program. The *start* parameter is optional and denotes where to begin the loop. It is set to **0** by default. The *end* parameter must always be specified and denotes the integer to end the loop. The *step* is also an optional parameter that specifies the interval of execution. It is set to **1** by default.

For example,

range(end)

```python
for  i in range( 4 ):     #end = 4
      print( i )
.....
```

```
#Output
0
1
2
3
```

range(start, end)

```python
for  i in range( 2, 6 ):     #start = 2 , end = 4
      print( i )
.....
```

```
#Output
2
3
4
5
```

range(start, end, step)

</> Python

```
for i in range( 0, 10, 2 ):      #start = 0 , end = 10, step = 2
      print( i )
.....
```

```
#Output
0
2
4
6
8
```

The while loop

The while loop is another control structure used to iterate or repeatedly execute a set of statements based on a true condition. The loop terminates when the condition is no longer true.

Syntax

```
while condition:
     #code
```

For example,

</> Python

```
i = 0                #initial value set to 0
while i < 4:         #repeat iteration until i >= 4  (condition becomes false or no longer true)
....    i = i + 1    #increment i by one in each iteration
....    print( i )
```

```
#Output
1
2
3
4
```

Deep

To create an infinite loop, set the condition to always be True and terminate with Ctrl + C.
Infinite loop:

```
while True:
    print("Hello World!")
.....

#output
Hello World!
Hello World!
Hello World!
....
....
```

Think about it ?

Did the loop run forever using the True condition? How true is that? Infinite loops can gradually consume system resources, degrading performance. You can interrupt the iteration using Ctrl + C.

The break statement

The break statement is a Python keyword used mostly in loop structures to halt or terminate execution prematurely once a given condition is true.

For example,

</> Python

```python
for i in range( 1, 5 ):
    if i == 3:          #terminate loop once i = 3
        break
    print( i )
.....
```

```
#Output
1
2
```

Example 2,
A program that continuously accepts numbers and computes their sum. The program should terminate when the input is "=" and then display the final result.

</> Python

```python
total = 0

while True:
    num = input("type number: ")

    if num == "=":
        print(f"total = {total}")
        break
    else:
        total = total + float(num)
```

```
#Output
type number: 2
type number: 5
type number: =
total = 7
```

The continue statement

The continue statement is also a Python keyword implemented in loops to skip a step or iteration when a particular condition is true.

For example,

```python
for i in range( 1, 5 ):
    if i == 3:          #skip step 3
        continue
    print( i )
.....
```

```
#Output
1
2
4
```

Example 2,
A program that prints all odd numbers from 1 to 10. If a number is even, the program should skip it.

```python
i = 0

while i < 10:
    i = i +1
    if i % 2 == 0:
        continue
    print(f"{i} is odd number")
```

```
#Output
1 is odd number
3 is odd number
5 is odd number
7 is odd number
9 is odd number
```

Function

A function is a block of organized and related statements used to perform a specific task. It can contain variables, loops, decision-making statements, other functions, statements, and objects that can be used repeatedly in different parts of a program. Functions are also referred to as methods, procedures, subprograms, routines, or subroutines.

Importance of Functions:

- Enhanced Readability and Comprehensibility:

Functions improve the readability and comprehensibility of a program by breaking it down into smaller, logical units. Each function performs a specific task, making the code easier to understand.

- Efficiency through Minimization of Repetitions:

Functions help minimize repetitions in code by encapsulating repetitive tasks into reusable blocks. This reduces the amount of code duplication and makes the program more efficient to maintain.

- Breaking Complex Programs into Smaller Segments:

Functions allow complex programs to be broken down into smaller and more manageable segments. Each function focuses on a specific aspect of the program's functionality, making it easier to develop and debug.

- Improved Time Efficiency:

By organizing code into functions, developers can optimize performance and improve time efficiency. Functions enable code reuse, which reduces development time and effort, leading to faster and more efficient programming.

Types of Functions:

There are two types of functions in the Python programming language: Built-in Functions and User-defined Functions.

Built-in Functions:

Built-in functions are provided by the Python language and are readily available to be used in programs. They serve various purposes and are commonly used for tasks such as mathematical operations, data conversion, string manipulation, and more.

Examples include: sum(), eval(), hex(), bin(), oct(), chr(), ord(), dir(), del(), max(), min() and len()

Example of using built-in functions

</> Python

```
>>> var = [2, 4, 6]
>>> total = sum( var )
>>> print( total )
...... 12
>>>
```

User-defined Functions:

User-defined functions are functions created by the user according to Python syntax. These functions allow developers to encapsulate specific tasks or operations into reusable blocks of code, enhancing code modularity and reusability.

Syntax

```
def function_name(param):
    #statement

    return  #statement
```

The def Keyword:

The def keyword is used to define a function in Python. It is the keyword used to create a function.

Function Name:

The function name is the identifier given to the function. It can start with either a capital or lowercase letter and can include underscores, but it cannot start with a number.

Parameters:

Parameters, also known as arguments, are optional and used to pass data or values to the function. They are specified within the parentheses following the function name.

Colon:

A colon (:) marks the end of the function header, indicating the start of the function block or body.

Statement(s):

Every function block or body contains at least one statement, which defines the actual logic or purpose of the function. These statements are executed when the function is called.

The return Statement:

The return keyword is optional and is used if the function is defined to return or produce a value. If the function is designed to return no value, there is no need to use the return statement.

Example 1 : A function to print "Hello World!"

</> Python

```python
def hello( ):
    print( "Hello World!" )
```

Example 2 : A function to accept two numbers and return their sum

</> Python

```python
def total( x, y ):
    result = x + y

    return result
```

Calling Functions

Calling a function simply means executing the function. Function calls can be made through the Python prompt, within another function, or within a program.

① **Executing a function call directly in the interpreter.**

```python
>>> def greetings():
.......     print( "Hi\nGoodmorning" )
.......
>>> greetings()      #calling the greetings function
...... Hi
       Goodmorning
>>>
```

② Executing a function within a program.

```python
def myFun():
    var = 200
    return var

value = myFun( )                 #calling the myFun function
print( value )
```

```
#Output
200
```

③ Invoking a function from within another function.

```python
def myFunc():
    num = 10
```

```
    return num

def price():
    myfun = myFunc()          #calling the myFunc  function within price()
    return  myfun + 5

value =  price()              #calling the price function
print( value )
```

```
#Output
15
```

Argument Functions

Functions in Python can be designed to perform tasks automatically using variables and other objects without requiring user interaction. These types of functions do not take any parameters and are called **argumentless functions**.

On the other hand, some functions require input data to operate, either from the user or another function. These inputs, known as **parameters** or **arguments**, can include numbers, strings, lists, dictionaries, or even other functions. The function processes these parameters during execution.

Unlike some other programming languages, Python does not require specifying the data type of parameters. Instead, Python determines the type dynamically based on the value assigned to them.

Syntax

```
def myFun(x, y):
    pass
```

Example,

</> **Python**

```
def average( x, y, z):
    total = x + y + z
    avg = total/3

    return avg


result =  average( 6, 8, 10)    #x=6,  y= 8, z= 10
print( result )
```

```
#Output
8.0
```

Optional Arguments

Some functions are designed to accept parameters, but they can still function without them. These parameters are called **optional arguments** because they are not required for the function to execute successfully.

If a parameter is not optional, it must always be provided when calling the function; otherwise, an error will occur. To make a parameter optional, you assign it a **default value**. If the argument is not supplied, the function will use the default value instead.

Syntax

```
def myFun( x= 0, z=None):
    pass
```

In this example, x has a default value of 0, and z is set to None, making them optional parameters. If no value is passed for x or z, their default values will be used.

Note

When defining a function with both required and optional parameters, the required parameters must always come first, followed by the optional parameters.
This ensures that Python correctly assigns values to the parameters when the function is called.

```
def myFun(x, y=5):        ☑ Correct
    print( x, y)
```

```
def myFun(x=0,  y):       ✗ Wrong
    print( x, y)
```

If optional parameters are placed before required ones, Python will not know how to correctly assign values, leading to a syntax error.

Executing Argument Functions

When calling or executing functions with arguments, values can be passed in two ways:

1. **Positional Arguments** – Values are supplied in the same order as the function parameters.
2. **Keyword Arguments** – Parameters are explicitly assigned values using their names, allowing flexibility in the order.

</> Python

```
def products( x, y):
    results = x * y
    return results


value1 = products( 10, 2 )          #positional argument (x=10,  y= 2)
value2 = products( y= 2,  x= 10 )   #keyword arguments
```

```
print( value1 )
print( value2 )
```

```
#Output
20
20
```

Unlimited Arguments

In programming, there are situations where a function needs to accept a large or **unknown number of arguments.** Defining each argument separately is not practical, especially when the number of inputs varies.

To handle this efficiently, Python allows using *** (asterisk) notation** before a parameter. This collects all passed arguments into a **tuple**, enabling the function to accept multiple values without explicitly defining them.

Key Points:

- The * notation allows a function to accept an unlimited number of arguments.
- The collected arguments are stored as a **tuple**, which can be accessed using indexing.
- Arguments must be passed separated by commas inside the function call.

Syntax

```
def myFun( *args):

    pass
```

Example,
A program to sum all passed arguments

</> Python

```
def total( *args ):
    result = 0
    for item in args:                    #iterating through the args (contains the arguments)
        result = result + item

    return result


value = total( 2, 5, 10, 3, 4 )        #calling the total function with multiple arguments
print( value )
```

```
#Output
24
```

Understanding the pass Keyword

The pass keyword, as used in the function block above, is not limited to functions alone—it can also be used in other code structures such as loops and conditional statements.

It serves as a **placeholder** when a function, loop, or block of code is defined but does not yet contain any statements. This is useful when writing code that will be implemented later, preventing syntax errors that would occur if the block were left empty.

A function or block cannot be left empty without using pass, as Python requires at least one statement inside it.

</> Python

```
def total( ):
    pass

def greetings():
    return "Hello, Friend!"
```

Lambda Function

Python functions are normally defined with the **def** keyword, but there is another way to create functions without using the def keyword and a function name. This can be achieved using Python Lambda functions.

Syntax

```
>>> variable = lambda arguments : expression
```

- **Variable:** This is the variable that will store the lambda function.
- **Argument:** These are the input values provided to the lambda function.
- **Expression:** This is the logic that defines the function.

Example 1 : Lambda function to add two numbers.

```python
>>> add = lambda x , y : x + y
>>> add( 2, 5)
...... 7
>>>
```

Example 2 : Lambda function to return the square of a number.

```python
>>> square = lambda x  : x ** 2
>>> square( 4 )
...... 16
>>>
```

Example 3 : Lambda function to check if a number is even.

```python
>>> even = lambda x  : x % 2 == 0
>>> even( 6 )
...... True
>>>
```

Using map() and filter() with Lambda Functions

Lambda functions can be used to create new iterables by transforming or filtering elements from an existing iterable. This is achieved using the **map()** and **filter()** functions.

map() Function

The map() function applies a given function to each element of an iterable and returns a new iterable with the modified values.

Syntax

```
new_iterable = type(map(lambda argument: expression, iterable))
```

Example 1,

```python
numbers = [1, 2, 3, 4]
squared = list(map(lambda x: x**2, numbers))
print(squared)
```

```
#Output
[1, 4, 9, 16]
```

Examples 2,

```python
import math

numbers = [3, 4, 5, 6]
factorial = set(map(lambda x: math.factorial(x), numbers))
print(factorial)
```

```
#Output
{6, 24, 120, 720}
```

filter() Function

The filter() function is used to select elements from an iterable based on a given condition. It returns a new iterable containing only elements that satisfy the condition.

Syntax

```
new_iterable = type(filter(lambda argument: condition, iterable))
```

Example 1

</> Python

```python
numbers = [1, 2, 3, 4, 5, 6]
evens = list(filter(lambda x: x%2 == 0, numbers))
print(evens)
```

```
#Output
[2, 4, 6]
```

Example 2

</> Python

```python
numbers = [2, 3, 4, 5, 6, 7, 8, 9]
multiple_three = tuple(filter(lambda x: x%3==0, numbers))
print(multiple_three)
```

```
#Output
(3, 6, 9)
```

Multiprocessing

Multiprocessing refers to the execution of multiple functions or processes simultaneously. In programming, functions are typically executed sequentially in a linear manner, following a first-come, first-served basis. This means that the function called first is executed before any subsequent functions. Execution progresses from the top of the program to the bottom, and any function waiting to execute must remain idle until the currently running function completes. This happens because execution occurs within the system's single thread by default.

Drawbacks of Sequential Execution:

- It is inefficient for tasks that require real-time processing or produce crucial results needed for subsequent operations.
- It slows down performance, especially when dealing with CPU-intensive tasks.
- It prevents full utilization of multi-core processors, as only a single core is used at a time.
- Functions that take longer to execute can block the execution of other functions, causing delays.

</> Python

```python
import time

def first():
    time.sleep(5)              #delay execution for 5 seconds
    print("First Function")

def second():
    print("Second Function")

first()     #calling the first() function
second()    #calling the second() function
```

```
#Output
First Function
Second Function
```

In the example above, **second()** runs only after **first()** has finished executing. This demonstrates a performance issue, as subsequent functions must wait for the previous ones to complete, leading to potential delays and inefficiencies.

To overcome these limitations, functions or processes can be executed concurrently on different threads, allowing multiple tasks to run simultaneously. This is made possible using threading for lightweight concurrent execution and **multiprocessing** for parallel execution across multiple CPU cores.

Threading

Threading allows multiple functions or processes to execute simultaneously without waiting for the completion of another process before starting. This improves performance by enabling parallel execution. In Python, the **threading** module provides various methods for managing and working with threads.

Threading Methods

Function	Description
Thread()	Creates a thread
active_count()	Returns the currently executing thread object.
current_thread()	Returns a list of all active Thread objects.
enumerate()	Returns a list of all active Thread objects.
excepthook()	Used to handle uncaught exceptions in threads.
get_ident()	Returns the thread identifier (a unique integer for each thread).
get_native_id()	Returns the native (OS-level) thread identifier.
getprofile()	Retrieves the profiling function for the current thread.
gettrace()	Returns the trace function for the current thread.
local()	Creates thread-local data storage. Each thread maintains its own separate copy.
main_thread()	Returns the main thread object.
setprofile()	Used to set a profiling function for threads.
settrace()	Sets a trace function for debugging threads.
stack_size()	Returns the stack size used when creating new threads.

Table 2.5 : Methods of the Python thread

Thread(target, name, args, kwargs, daemon, group)

- target → Specifies the function that the thread will execute when started. If None, no function runs, and the thread does nothing.
- name → A string representing the thread's name. If None, a default name like "Thread-1", "Thread-2", etc., is assigned.
- args → A tuple containing arguments to pass to the target function. If the function requires multiple arguments, they must be passed as a tuple.
- kwargs → A dictionary containing keyword arguments (key=value pairs) for the target function.
- daemon → Determines whether the thread is a **daemon thread** (runs in the background and stops when the main program exits). If None, it inherits the main thread's daemon status.
- group → Reserved for future implementation. Always set to None.

</> Python

```python
import time
import threading


def first():
    time.sleep(5)
    print("First Function")

def second():
    print("Second Function")

def third(x, y):
    print(x + y)


#creating threads

thread1 = threading.Thread( target = first)
thread2 = threading.Thread( target = second, name = "second_thread" )
thread3 = threading.Thread( target = third, args = (10, 20), daemon= True )
```

Thread Object Methods

start()	Starts the execution of the thread.
daemon	A boolean attribute that determines whether a thread is a daemon thread. Daemon threads run in the background and automatically terminate when the main program exits.
name()	Retrieves or sets the thread's name.
indent()	Returns the thread's unique identifier (assigned by Python).
is_alive()	Returns True if the thread is still running, False otherwise.
join()	Waits for the thread to finish execution before continuing.
native_id()	Returns the OS-assigned native thread ID.
run()	Defines the code that runs when the thread starts. Typically, you override this method when creating a custom thread class.

Table 2.6 : Methods of thread object

Example 1

</> Python

```python
import time
import threading

def worker1():
    time.sleep(5)
    print("First Function")

def worker2(x, y):
    value = x + y
    print(f"Sum: { value }" )


#creating threads

thread1 = threading.Thread( target = worker1)
thread2 = threading.Thread( target = worker2, args = (10, 20) )

#running the threads
thread1.start()
thread2.start()
```

```
#Output
Sum: 30
First Function
```

Example 2

</> Python

```python
import threading
import time

def worker():
    time.sleep(2)
    print("Thread is running")


#creating thread
thread = threading.Thread( target = worker)

thread.daemon = True
thread.start()


#wait until thread finish executing
thread.join()

name = thread.name
status = thread.is_alive()


print(f"Name: {name}")
print(f"Status: {status}")
```

```
#Output
Thread is running
Name: Thread-1 (worker)
Status: False
```

active_count()

```python
import threading
import time

def worker():
    time.sleep(2)
    print("Thread is running")


threading.Thread( target = worker).start()
print(threading.active_count())
```

```
#Output
2
Thread is running
```

current_thread()

```python
threading.Thread( target = worker).start()
print(threading.current_thread())
```

```
#Output
<_MainThread(MainThread, started 17988)>
Thread is running
```

stack_size()

```python
threading.Thread( target = worker).start()
print(threading.stack_size())
```

```
#Output
0
Thread is running
```

Class and Object

Python is a **multi-paradigm language**, but it is primarily **object-oriented** (OOP), meaning **everything in Python is an object**. Objects in Python can include fundamental data types such as integers, floats, strings, lists, dictionaries, functions, and even modules.

Classes and Objects

A **class** is a blueprint or template for creating objects. It is a user-defined data type, similar to built-in types like list, dict, str, float, and int.
An **object** is a specific instance of a class. When a class is defined, no memory is allocated until an object is created. Objects store data and behavior defined by their class.

Attributes and Methods

Classes contain two main components:

1. **Attributes (Instance Variables)** – These are variables that hold data specific to each object.
2. **Methods** – These are functions defined inside a class that operate on the object's attributes and define its behavior.

Example:

</> Python

```
class MyClass:                    #class name
    num = 10                      #class attribute (variable)
    name = "Bob"

    def greetings():              #class method (function)
        value = "Hello World!"
        return value
```

Key Points

- **Classes** define the structure and behavior of objects.
- **Objects** are created from classes and hold specific data and functionality.
- **Methods** (functions inside classes) define the behavior of objects.
- **Instance variables** store object-specific data.

Deep

Similar to functions, class names can contain both letters and numbers. However, they must begin with a letter if they include both. Class names can start with either an uppercase or lowercase letter, but by convention, Python follows PascalCase (e.g., MyClass, StudentRecord).

Creating Object

Objects are created by assigning a class to a variable. The variable then becomes an instance (or object) of the class. This means the object inherits the class's attributes and methods, allowing it to access and manipulate them independently.

Syntax

```
class MyClass:
    num = 10

    def greetings():
        return "Helloo"
```

```
myobject = MyClass       #instantiating the class
```

Accessing Methods and Attributes of a Class

Methods and attributes of a class can be accessed using the instance or object of the class.

Syntax

```
var  = myobject.num
hello = myobject.greetings()
```

Example 1

</> **Python**

```python
class StudentRecords:

    school = "Harvard"
    school_ID = 5879

    def student(input):
        data = {'name':"George Wood", 'age': 25, 'index':3056, 'course':"Computer Science"}

        value = data.get(input)
        return value


#creating object of the class StudentRecords
obj = StudentRecords

#Accessing attributes
sch = obj.school

#Accessing method
name = obj.student("name")
age = obj.student("age")
course = obj.student("course")

print(f"School: {sch}")
print(f"Name: {name}")
print(f"Age: {age}")
print(f"Course: {course}")
```

```
#Output
School: Harvard
Name: George Wood
Age: 25
Course: Computer Science
```

Example 2

</> **Python**

```
import math

class Calculation:

    greetings = "Hello\nThis is a calculation class. Just crack the numbers!...."

    def sum( *input ):
        value = 0
        for i in input:
            value = value + i
        return value

    def factorial( input ):
        value = math.factorial( input )
        return value


#creating object of the class Calculation

cal = Calculation
greet = cal.greetings
total = cal.sum(10, 20, 5)
factor = cal.factorial( 6 )

print(f"Greetings: {greet}")
print(f"Total: {total}")
print(f"Factorial: {factor}")
```

```
#Output
Greetings: Hello
This is a calculation class. Just crack the numbers!.....
Total: 35
Factorial: 720
```

The __init__ Method

In Python, the __init__() method serves as a **constructor**, used to initialize objects, variables, and methods within a class. When an instance of a class is created, the __init__() method is automatically executed.

This approach is similar to other programming languages like C, C++, Dart, and Java, which use a main() function to initiate execution. However, unlike main(), __init__() is specific to object instantiation.

Accessing Class Attributes in Methods

By default, methods cannot directly access attributes declared at the class level. To ensure that attributes are accessible across methods and instances, they must be assigned using the self keyword inside __init__().

Understanding self

- The self keyword represents the instance of the class, allowing access to attributes and methods within the class.
- Attributes prefixed with self become instance attributes, meaning they can be accessed and modified by any method within the class.
- Attributes without self are considered **class attributes** (shared across all instances) or private attributes if prefixed with double underscores (__).

Public and Private Attributes

- **Public attributes:** Declared using self.attribute_name, making them accessible within and outside the class.
- **Private attributes:** Defined with double underscores (__attribute_name), restricting access from outside the class.

Public and Private Methods

- **Public methods:** Defined with self as the first parameter (e.g., def my_method(self):).
- **Private methods:** Prefixed with double underscores (e.g., def __my_method(self):), making them inaccessible outside the class

Example

Python

```python
class Geometry:

    def __init__(self):
        self.pi = 3.14

    def area_circle(self , radius ):
        area =  pow(radius, 2) * self.pi
        return area

    def area_square( self , size ):
        area = size *size
        return area

    def area_rectangle( self , width, height ):
        area = width * height
        return area


geo = Geometry()
pi = geo.pi
circle = geo.area_circle( 7 )
square = geo.area_square( 12 )
rec = geo.area_rectangle( 4, 6 )


print(f"pi = {pi}")
print(f"Area of a circle : {circle}")
print(f"Area of a square: {square}")
print(f"Area of a rectangle: {rec}")
```

```
#Output
pi = 3.14
Area of a circle : 153.86
Area of a square: 144
Area of a rectangle: 24
```

Deep

In Python, instantiating a class with or without the __init__() constructor behaves differently.

1. Without __init__()
When a class does not have an __init__() method, an instance can be created simply by referencing the class name:

```
class MyClass:
    pass

#Instantiating
object = MyClass
```

2. With __init__()
When a class has an __init__() constructor, it must be instantiated with parentheses:

```
class MyClass:
    def __init__(self):
        print("instance")

#Instantiating
object = MyClass()
```

Argument Class

In Python, arguments can be passed to a class in the same way they are passed to functions. These arguments are processed by the __init__() constructor, allowing the class to initialize instance attributes that can be used by methods and objects.

The __init__() method takes self as its first parameter, followed by any additional arguments:

```
def __init__(self, arg1, arg2, ....):
    self.arg1 = arg1
    self.arg2 = arg2
```

The arguments are assigned to instance attributes using self, making them accessible within the class.

These arguments must be provided when instantiating the class:

```
obj = MyClass(value1, value2)
```

Example

</> Python

```python
class Statistic:

    def __init__(self, scores):
        self.scores = scores
        self.average = self.average()

        print("average: { self.average }")

    def average(self ):
        total = sum(self.scores)
        length = len(self.scores)

        print("total: { total }")
        avg = total/length
        return avg


data = [65, 30, 84, 72]
stat = Statistic( data )
```

```
#Output
total: 251
average: 62.75
```

Running a Class

In Python, a class can be used in different ways within a program. Generally, classes are instantiated by creating objects, but in some cases, they can be executed without explicitly creating an object.

① Instantiating a Class

Normally, to use a class, you create an instance (object) of it:

```
</> Python
class Greet:
    print("Hello,\nGood day Buddy")

# Creating an object and calling a method
obj = Greet
```

```
#Output
Hello,
Good day Buddy
```

② Running a Class Without Instantiation

In Python, a class can contain class-level methods that can be called without creating an object.

```
</> Python
class Greet:
    print("Hello,\nGood day Buddy")

# Calling the method without an instance
Greet
```

```
#Output
Hello,
Good day Buddy
```

③ Using if __name__ == "__main__":

This approach ensures that the class runs only when the script is executed directly, and not when imported as a module.

</> Python

```
class Greet:
    print("Hello,\nGood day Buddy")

if __name__ == "__main__":
    obj = Greet
```

```
#Output
Hello,
Good day Buddy
```

Handling Errors and Exceptions

Programming inherently involves errors or *bugs*. Writing code requires applying human logic while adhering to the programming language's structure, syntax, and semantic rules. However, mistakes in logic, incorrect syntax, or unforeseen runtime conditions can lead to errors or exceptions.

Errors in a program are commonly referred to as *bugs*. Regardless of a programmer's experience, encountering bugs is inevitable, making error handling an essential part of software development. Errors can cause programs to behave unexpectedly, produce incorrect results, or fail to run entirely.

Python is an interpreted language, meaning it executes code line by line. When an error occurs, execution stops immediately, preventing further code from running. To ensure smooth execution and prevent abrupt program crashes, error handling is crucial.

Reasons for Handling Errors in Programming

- **To prevent program crashes:** Proper error handling ensures that a single error does not cause the entire program to terminate unexpectedly.
- **To allow a program to continue running despite encountering an error:** Handling exceptions gracefully allows a program to recover from errors and continue execution.
- **To display user-friendly error messages:** Instead of showing cryptic system-generated messages, developers can provide clear error messages to guide users on what went wrong.
- **To use errors as conditions for executing alternative tasks:** Some exceptions may indicate an expected situation that can be handled by executing a fallback solution.
- **To log errors for debugging and future reference:** Logging errors helps developers identify issues and improve the software over time.
- **To enhance security:** Some unhandled errors can expose sensitive information or allow attackers to exploit vulnerabilities in the software.
- **To improve software reliability and maintainability:** Well-structured error handling ensures that software remains stable and easy to maintain in the long run.

Errors in Python Programming

In Python, errors can arise due to several factors. They may be caused by logic mistakes, syntax violations, structural misconfigurations, incorrect data handling, incompatible data types, or missing dependencies.

Python errors are broadly categorized into two main types:

1. **Syntax Errors**
2. **Runtime Errors**

Syntax Errors

Every programming language follows a strict set of structural rules for using **variables, objects, functions, keywords, operators, punctuation, and mnemonics**. When these elements are not used correctly, or the required syntax is not followed, Python raises a *syntax error*. Syntax errors occur during the parsing stage and prevent the program from running.

Common Causes of Syntax Errors:

Incorrect indentation – Python enforces indentation to structure code blocks properly.

</> Python

```python
def myFunc():
print("Hello World!")    #incorrect indentation
```

```
#Output
IndentationError: expected an indented block after function definition on line 2
```

Missing colons (:) – Required for defining functions, loops, and conditionals.

</> Python

```python
def myFunc()                #missing colons
    print("Hello World!")
```

```
#Output
SyntaxError: expected ':'
```

Empty code blocks without the pass keyword – Python does not allow empty function or loop bodies.

```
</> Python
def myFunc():                  #empty block

def hello():
    print("Hello World!")
```

```
#Output
IndentationError: expected an indented block after function definition on line 3
```

Misspelled keywords or function names – Example: writing prnt() instead of print().

```
</> Python

prnt("Hello World!")   #wrong spelling of print
```

```
#Output
NameError: name 'prnt' is not defined. Did you mean: 'print'?
```

Mismatched parentheses, brackets, or braces – Example: print("Hello World" (missing closing parenthesis).

```
</> Python

print("Hello World!"   #no closing parentheses
```

```
#Output
SyntaxError: '(' was never closed?
```

Incorrect use of assignment (=) instead of comparison (==) – Example: if x = 5: instead of if x == 5:.

```
</> Python
var = 5
if var = 5:            #incorrect  use of assignment (==)
```

```
print("Hello World!"
```

```
#Output
SyntaxError: invalid syntax. Maybe you meant '==' or ':=' instead of '='?
```

Unclosed string literals – Example:

```
</> Python
var = "Python     #unclosed string
```

```
#Output
SyntaxError: unterminated string literal (detected at line 2)
```

Using reserved words as variable names – Example: def = 10 (since def is a keyword).

```
</> Python
def = 10          #def is a keyword
```

```
#Output
SyntaxError: invalid syntax
```

Runtime Exception

Runtime errors occur during the execution of a program rather than during compilation or syntax checking. These errors are not caused by violations of the language's syntax or structure but rather by **logical mistakes, incorrect operations, invalid data handling, or unexpected conditions.** Unlike syntax errors, which prevent the program from running, runtime errors appear while the program is running and may cause it to crash or behave unexpectedly.

Common Causes of Runtime Errors:

Runtime exception	Description
ZeroDivisionError	Occurs when a number is divided by zero
KeyError	Attempting to access a dictionary key that does not exist.
NameError	Trying to use a variable that has not been declared.
IndexError	Attempting to access a list, tuple, or string index that does not exist.
TypeError	Performing operation on incompatible types. For example, trying to add a string and an integer.
IndentationError	Wrong indentation in program
FloatingPointError	Operations on floating point fail
ImportError	Imported module is not found
AssertionError	Assertion statements fail
FileNotFoundError	Trying to open a non-existent file
AttributeError	An invalid attribute reference or assignment is attempted
RecursionError	When recursion exceeds the system limit.
UnicodeError	An encoding or decoding operation fails
EOFError	The input() function reaches the end-of-file condition

Table 2.7 : Some runtime exceptions in Python

Handling Errors and Exceptions

Errors and exceptions can be addressed in a program during debugging, allowing developers to correct them before deployment. However, some errors may only occur under specific conditions, such as user input errors, file access issues, or network failures. These types of errors are unpredictable and can arise during the production stage of an application. To prevent a program from crashing and to ensure it continues running smoothly, **error handling** is necessary.

Python provides **two main ways** to handle errors and exceptions:

1. **try-except Block** – Used to catch and handle specific errors, preventing the program from crashing when an exception occurs.
2. **try-finally** or **try-except-finally Block** – Ensures that certain cleanup operations (e.g., closing files or releasing resources) are executed, regardless of whether an exception occurs.

try-except

In this approach, the code that is likely to raise an exception is placed inside the try block. If an exception occurs, the except block is executed to handle the error. However, if no exception occurs, the statements inside the except block will not run.

Syntax

```
try:
    #statement or code

except ErrorType:
    #statement or code
```

Note

The **ErrorType** is optional and can be any of the runtime errors listed above. It allows the execution of specific statements when multiple statements are likely to raise different types of errors. However, the program will still handle errors properly even without specifying an ErrorType.

Example 1, the following code demonstrates handling a ZeroDivisionError:

#Handled exception

```python
try:
    result = 200 / 0

except ZeroDivisionError:
    print("Error: Number was divided by zero")
```

```
#Output
Error: Number was divided by zero
```

#Unhandled exception

```python
result = 200 / 0
```

```
#Output
    result = 200 / 0
            ~~~~^~~
ZeroDivisionError: division by zero
```

try-finally

The try-finally approach is useful in situations where certain statements or functions must execute regardless of whether an error occurs.

- The code that might raise an error is placed inside the try block.
- The except block is optional and can be used to handle specific exceptions.
- The finally block always executes, whether an error occurs or not. The finally block is mainly used for **cleanup operations**, such as closing files, releasing resources, or disconnecting from databases.

Syntax

```python
try:
    #statement or code

finally:
    #statement or code
```

```python
try:
    #statement or code

except ErrorType:
    #statement or code
```

```
finally:
    #statement or code
```

Example the following code demonstrates handling NameError

```python
try:
    result = var + 20            #variable is not defined
finally:
    print("Execution completed")
```

```
#Output
Execution completed
result = var + 20
         ^^^
NameError: name 'var' is not defined. Did you mean: 'vars'?
```

Chapter 3

Graphical User Interface (GUI)

Chapter Objectives

- ◈ Understand how a GUI works
- ◈ Explain frontend and backend interactions
- ◈ Identify kinds of GUI frameworks available in Python

Graphical User Interface (GUI)

Now that you've built a strong foundation in Python—with a good grasp of variables, operators, data types, functions, loops, and object-oriented programming—you're ready to take the next big step: building real applications with a visual interface.

So far, you've worked with code in the console, but real-world apps are often more than just lines of text. They have buttons you can click, forms you can fill, windows you can move around—these are all part of the **Graphical User Interface**, or **GUI**.

In this section, we'll dive deep into GUI development using **PyQt**, a powerful library that lets you build desktop applications with Python. Whether it's a simple calculator or a full-featured productivity tool, PyQt gives you the tools to design clean, interactive, and professional-looking apps.

What is a GUI?

A GUI is the visual part of your application—the buttons, text fields, sliders, checkboxes, menus, and everything else users can interact with. It's what people see and use. Behind the scenes, your Python code—the logic, processing, and decision-making—acts as the backend, making everything work.

For example, when a user clicks a button in your app, that button triggers an event. Your backend code then listens for that event and responds accordingly—maybe by showing a message, calculating something, or saving data.

Why Build a GUI?

Here's why GUI development is such an important skill:

- **Simplifies user interaction** – Instead of typing commands, users can just click and go.
- **Makes apps accessible** – People who don't know how to code can still use your programs.
- **Improves user experience** – A well-designed GUI makes your app intuitive and enjoyable to use.

- **Professional and presentable** – Your apps look polished and ready for real-world use.
- **Platform-friendly** – GUI apps can often run across Windows, macOS, and Linux.
- **Event-driven structure** – Lets your app respond in real-time to what users do.

As you go through this chapter, you'll learn how to create windows, add widgets like buttons and text boxes, and handle user actions—all with PyQt. By the end, you'll be able to turn your Python scripts into full-fledged desktop applications.

How a GUI Works

A **Graphical User Interface (GUI)** is made up of all the visual elements you interact with in an application—text fields, buttons, icons, frames, color schemes, sliders, checkboxes, and more. These visual components are known as **widgets**, and each one is created using a combination of a programming language (in this case, Python) and a GUI framework like **PyQt**.

All these widgets together form the **frontend** of your application. The frontend is what users see and interact with. But behind the scenes, these visual elements are connected to the **backend**—the core logic of the application written in Python. This includes your functions, loops, classes, and objects that define how the app behaves.

The Interaction Between Frontend and Backend

When a user interacts with a widget—whether by clicking a button, pressing a key, selecting a radio option, toggling a switch, dragging an item, scrolling, resizing a window, or typing in a text field—these actions trigger specific **events**. These events are connected to backend functions that handle what should happen in response. For example, clicking a "Submit" button might trigger a function that processes user input and displays a result.

This interaction forms an **event-driven loop**, where user actions continuously trigger responses from the backend, creating a seamless and interactive experience. This cycle keeps running as long as the application is open.

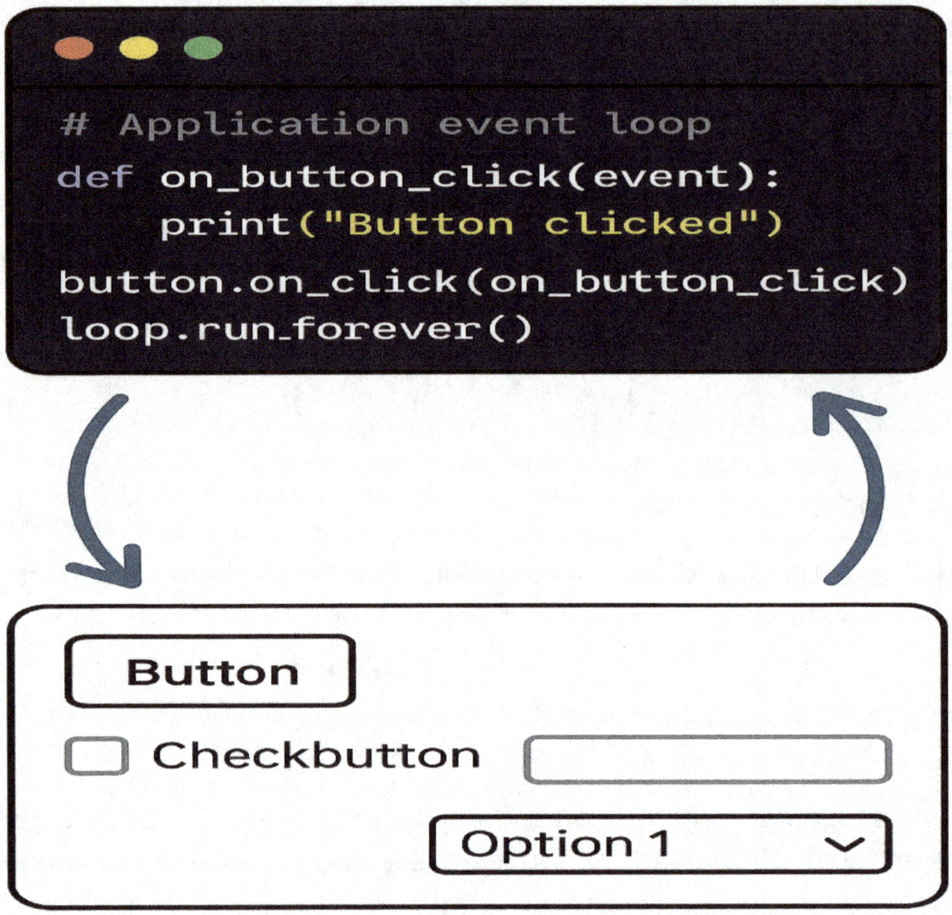

Figure 3.0 : An application event loop

What Powers a GUI Behind the Scenes

For a GUI application to run smoothly and respond efficiently, several key programming concepts must be implemented correctly:

- **Functions** – to encapsulate and reuse logic

- **Loops** – for repeating actions and handling dynamic behavior
- **Classes and Objects** – to structure your code using object-oriented principles
- **File Handling** – to read from and write to files as needed
- **Threading/Multithreading** – to keep the app responsive while performing background tasks
- **Exception Handling** – to catch and manage errors without crashing the app
- **Signal and Slot Mechanism** – to manage communication between widgets in PyQt
- **State Management** – to track and control the status of UI elements and app data
- **Resource Management** – to efficiently manage memory, files, and system resources

Together, these components ensure that your application not only looks good but also functions reliably and efficiently.

Kinds of GUI Frameworks in Python

GUI frameworks or toolkits are the tools that enable developers to build graphical user interfaces. These frameworks are not part of the core Python language—they are external libraries, often developed in Python or integrated with it through bindings. In most cases, GUI frameworks are designed to work with a specific programming language, meaning Python cannot directly use frameworks built for Java or JavaScript.

Different programming languages often have multiple GUI frameworks, each with its own architecture, syntax, and logic. Similarly, Python has a wide range of GUI libraries to choose from, allowing developers to build everything from simple desktop applications to cross-platform mobile and web apps.

Cross-Platform vs Platform-Specific Frameworks

Modern GUI frameworks are increasingly designed to be **cross-platform**, meaning they can run on multiple operating systems such as Windows, Linux, macOS, Android, and iOS. However, some frameworks are tailored to a single platform, focusing on maximizing performance or native look and feel.

Below is a list of some popular Python GUI frameworks:

Framework	Platform Support	Use Case
PyQt	Windows, Linux, macOS	Full-featured desktop apps
PySide	Windows, Linux, macOS	LGPL alternative to PyQt
Flet	Windows, Linux, macOS, Android, iOS, Web	Cross-platform GUI with Flutter-like syntax
Kivy	Windows, Linux, macOS, Android, iOS	Mobile-first, multitouch apps
KivyMD	Windows, Linux, macOS, Android, iOS	Material Design components for Kivy
TKinter	Windows, Linux, macOS	Lightweight GUIs, included with standard Python
Dear PyGui	Windows, Linux, macOS	GPU-accelerated GUIs, game-like UIs
WxPython	Windows, Linux, macOS	Native look-and-feel across platforms
PyGObject	Linux (GNOME), limited support on Windows/macOS	GNOME-based desktop apps
PySimpleGUI	Windows, Linux, macOS	Simplified wrapper over other frameworks (Tkinter, PyQt, etc.)

Table 3.0 : Some Python GUI Frameworks

Note

Version numbers may change over time—always check the official documentation or GitHub page for the most up-to-date release.

Choosing the Right Framework

Choosing the right GUI framework depends on your project requirements:

- For **professional desktop apps**, PyQt or PySide is recommended.
- For **mobile-friendly or touch-based apps**, Kivy or KivyMD is a good choice.
- For **fast prototyping**, PySimpleGUI or Tkinter may be ideal.
- If you want a **modern web+mobile style UI**, Flet offers a Flutter-inspired approach.

Chapter 4

PyQt / PySide

Chapter Objectives

- Learn about PyQt/PySide
- Explore features of PyQt
- Review apps made with PyQt
- Understand installation steps
- Study classes and modules in PyQt
- Examine classes in QtWidgets
- Examine classes in QtCore
- Examine classes in QtGui
- Understand widget properties
- Create your first PyQt app
- Categorize PyQt widgets
- Use common widget properties and methods

PyQt

PyQt (and its official alternative, PySide) are Python bindings for the Qt toolkit, a powerful cross-platform application framework developed by The Qt Company (originally by Trolltech, then acquired by Nokia, and later spun off into a standalone company). The Qt toolkit itself is written in C++ and is widely used for building native desktop applications across platforms such as Windows, Linux, and macOS.

While Qt is mainly used with C++, **PyQt** and **PySide** make it possible to use the same rich set of tools and widgets directly in Python. This opens the door for Python developers to build fully functional, professional-grade GUI applications without writing C++ code.

Although PyQt and PySide serve the same purpose and have very similar APIs, the key difference lies in their licensing:

📌 **PyQt** is available under GPL and commercial licenses.

📌 **PySide (also known as Qt for Python)** is licensed under LGPL, making it more permissive for commercial use without open sourcing your code.

Features of PyQt

PyQt offers a broad range of features that make it a powerful choice for GUI development:

✏️ **Comprehensive Widget Set**
Buttons, labels, sliders, text fields, tables, and many advanced widgets.

✏️ **Signal and Slot Mechanism**
Clean event handling and interaction between widgets.

✏️ **Cross-Platform Compatibility**
Write once, run anywhere (Windows, macOS, Linux).

✏️ **Integrated with Web Technologies**
Supports embedding HTML, JavaScript, and CSS via QWebEngineView.

✏️ **Support for 2D/3D Graphics**
Includes QPainter, QGraphicsView, and OpenGL integration.

Multithreading Support
Easily run background tasks without freezing the UI.

Database Integration
Supports SQLite, PostgreSQL, MySQL, and more via QSqlDatabase.

Advanced Layout Management
For dynamic and resizable UIs.

Rich Text and Markdown Support
Display styled text using QTextEdit, QLabel, etc.

Internationalization
Built-in support for multiple languages (translations, locales).

Plugin System
Extend apps using custom or third-party modules.

Extensive Documentation and Tutorials
Well-maintained official and community resources.

Why Use PyQt or PySide?

There are many reasons to choose PyQt or PySide for building Python GUI applications:

- **No External Dependencies** – Only requires Python and the PyQt/PySide library.
- **Tight Python Integration** – Smooth and intuitive use of Python's object-oriented capabilities.
- **Simple and Intuitive Syntax** – Faster development and easier learning curve.
- **Clean Architecture** – Modular and organized structure promotes maintainability.
- **Rich Set of Widgets and Tools** – Everything you need to build modern UIs.

- **Cross-Platform Development** – Write once, deploy across multiple operating systems.
- **Active Community and Support** – Help is available through forums, GitHub, Stack Overflow, etc.
- **Frequent and Stable Releases** – Keeps up with Python and Qt updates.
- **Good IDE and Designer Tools** – Tools like Qt Designer let you drag and drop UI elements.
- **OpenGL and Multimedia Support** – For graphics, animation, and media-rich apps.
- **Used in Industry** – Trusted by major companies and projects around the world.

Popular Apps Made with PyQt

PyQt is one of the most powerful and widely adopted GUI frameworks among both Python and C++ developers. Its popularity stems from its ease of use, fast development process, and lack of external dependencies. With cross-platform support and a rich set of widgets, PyQt has been used in a wide range of industries, including:

- Education
- Multimedia & Entertainment
- Utilities
- Data Science & Analytics
- Cybersecurity
- Software Development
- Networking Tools

Here are some **well-known applications** developed using PyQt:

Application	Description	Developer
Free Download Manager	Download manager for various file types	FDM Team
Bittorrent	Lightweight BitTorrent client	Christophe Dumez / Open Source
Anki	Flashcard app for spaced repetition learning	Damien Elmes
Spyder IDE	Scientific Python Development Environment	Spyder Dev Team
eric IDE	Full-featured Python and Ruby IDE	Detlev Offenbach
Calibre	eBook manager and reader	Kovid Goyal
OpenShot	Video editor with drag-and-drop UI	OpenShot Studios, LLC
Fman	Dual-pane file manager	Michael Herrmann
Veusz	Scientific plotting and graphing tool	Jeremy Sanders
Leo Editor	Outliner and literate programming editor	Edward K. Ream

Table 4.0 : Some applications, developed with PyQt

Installation

To start using PyQt or PySide, you only need to install the respective library via pip. There are no external dependencies required beyond Python itself.

As of the time of writing this book, the current versions are PyQt6 and PySide6.

Install PyQt:

```
pip install PyQt6
```

(Optional) If you prefer PySide:

```
pip install PySide6
```

Packaging and Prerequisite Installation

After successfully developing a full-fledged GUI application, the final step is **packaging**—converting your Python source code into a standalone application that can be run on any system without requiring the user to install Python or your source code files.

This process is essential for distributing, deploying, or commercializing your software. It includes bundling the Python code, required dependencies, application icons, metadata, and platform-specific resources into a single executable or installer file.

Platform Packaging Formats

Platform	Output Format	File Extension
Windows	Executable	.exe
macOS	Application	.app or .dmg
Linux	Executable/Binary	.deb, .bin, .AppImage
Cross-platform Python	Wheel	.whl

Table: 4.1 – Platform extensions

Once your code has been packaged into a proper application, it can be distributed like other software programs—installed, run, and even monetized or offered for free.

Popular Python Packaging Tools

Here are some of the most widely used tools for packaging Python GUI applications:

Tool	Mode of Use	Installation Command	Platform Support
PyInstaller	Command-line	pip install pyinstaller	Windows, macOS, Linux
auto-py-to-exe	GUI for PyInstaller	pip install auto-py-to-exe	Windows (GUI only), others via CLI
cx_Freeze	Command-line	pip install cx_Freeze	Windows, macOS, Linux
py2exe	Windows-specific	pip install py2exe	Windows only
py2app	macOS-specific	pip install py2app	macOS only
Briefcase	Cross-platform (CLI)	pip install briefcase	Windows, macOS, Linux, Android, iOS

Nuitka	Compiles to C-level binary	pip install nuitka	Windows, Linux, macOS
fbs (Fast Build System)	PyQt-specific	pip install fbs	Windows, macOS, Linux
shiv	Zipapp packager	pip install shiv	Cross-platform

Table: 4.2 – Packaging tools

Note

This book will explore packaging applications using several of these tools toward the end of this chapter, giving you hands-on experience with creating distributable apps.

PyQt Classes and Modules

PyQt (and its alternative, PySide) is organized into a variety of **modules** (or packages), each providing a collection of **classes** that handle specific aspects of GUI development. These classes are often grouped under three core modules:

Core Modules

Module	Description
PyQt6.QtWidgets / PySide6.QtWidgets	Contains all the standard GUI elements (widgets) like buttons, labels, text boxes, checkboxes, combo boxes, layouts, dialogs, and windows. This is the primary module for building the GUI.
PyQt6.QtGui / PySide6.QtGui	Handles 2D graphics, images, fonts, drag-and-drop, icons, painting, cursors, and other graphical elements.
PyQt6.QtCore / PySide6.QtCore	Contains core, non-GUI classes used for application logic—such as event handling, signals and slots, threading, file handling, timers, settings, and data models.

Table: 4.3 – The three core modules

Structure of the PyQt

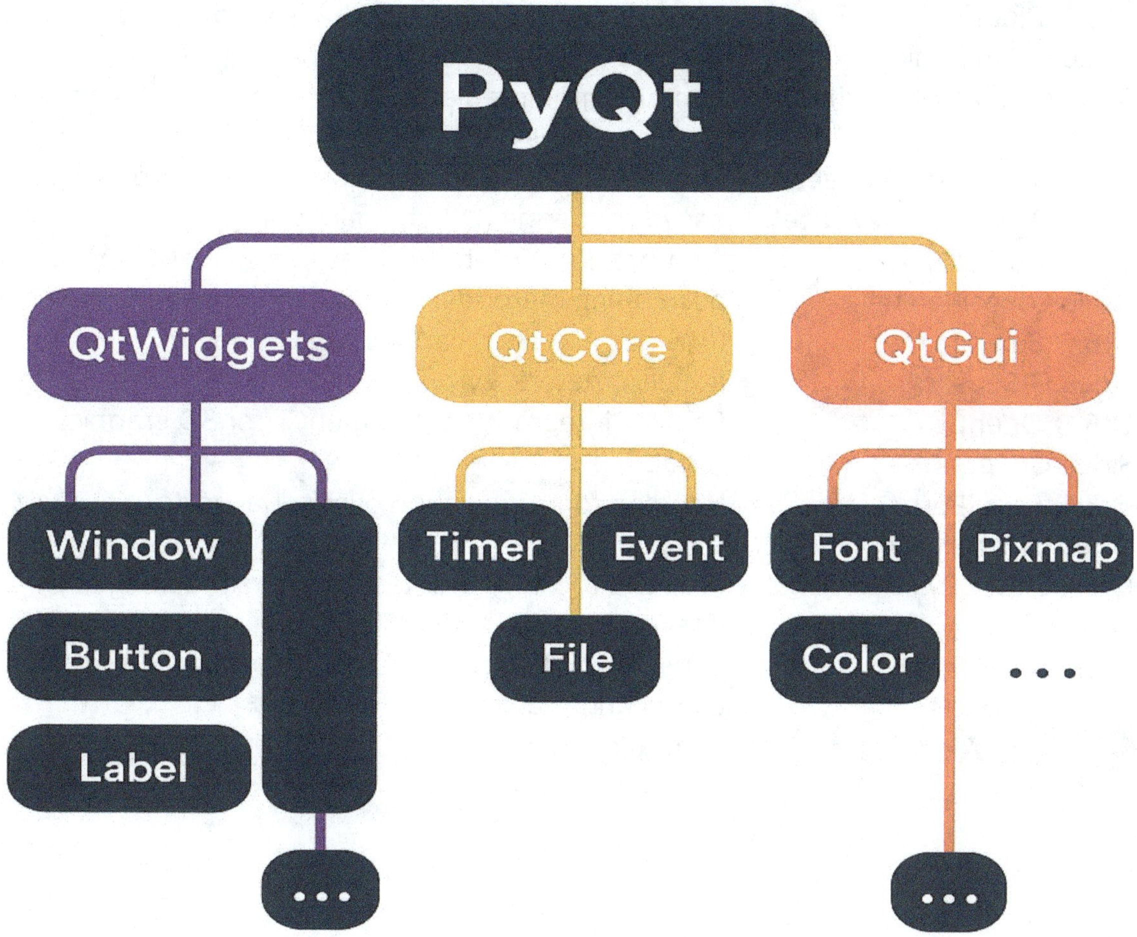

Figure 4.0 : A structure of the PyQt framework

Additional Modules

Module	Description
PyQt6.QtMultimedia / PySide6.QtMultimedia	Provides classes to handle audio and video playback, capture, recording, and processing.

PyQt6.QtNetwork / PySide6.QtNetwork	Enables network operations such as TCP/UDP socket communication, HTTP requests, and network access management.
PyQt6.QtBluetooth / PySide6.QtBluetooth	Offers support for Bluetooth device discovery, connection, and communication.
PyQt6.QtMultimediaWidgets / PySide6.QtMultimediaWidgets	Contains multimedia-specific widgets like QVideoWidget for embedding media playback in GUIs.
PyQt6.QtWebEngineWidgets / PySide6.QtWebEngineWidgets	Embeds full-featured web content using Chromium-based rendering (QWebEngineView).
PyQt6.QtPositioning / PySide6.QtPositioning	Supports location-based features using GPS and other positioning methods.
PyQt6.QtSensors / PySide6.QtSensors	Provides access to various device sensors like accelerometers, gyroscopes, etc.
PyQt6.QtOpenGL / PySide6.QtOpenGL	Enables integration with OpenGL for 3D graphics rendering.
PyQt6.QtSerialPort / PySide6.QtSerialPort	Handles communication over serial ports (e.g., COM, USB).
PyQt6.QtTest / PySide6.QtTest	Provides tools for unit testing and simulating user interactions.
PyQt6.QtCharts / PySide6.QtCharts	Offers widgets and classes to display a wide variety of charts and graphs.

Table: 4.4 – Additional PyQt modules

Deep

You can mix and match classes from multiple modules to build hybrid apps (e.g., using QtWidgets for layout, QtMultimedia for sound, and QtCharts for data visualization).

QtWidgets

QAbstractButton	QCommandLinkButton	QFocusFrame	QAbstractGraphicsShapeItem
QScrollArea	QCommonStyle	QFontComboBox	QAbstractItemDelegate
QScrollBar	QCompleter	QFontDialog	QStyleOptionToolBox
QAbstractItemView	QDataWidgetMapper	QFormLayout	QStyleOptionToolButton
QAbstractScrollArea	QDateEdit	QFrame	QStyleOptionViewItem
QAbstractSlider	QDateTimeEdit	QGesture	QStylePainter
QAbstractSpinBox	QDial	QGestureEvent	QStyledItemDelegate
QApplication	QDialog	QGestureRecognizer	QSwipeGesture
QBoxLayout	QDialogButtonBox	QGraphicsAnchor	QSystemTrayIcon
QButtonGroup	QDockWidget	QGraphicsAnchorLayout	QTabBar
QCalendarWidget	QDoubleSpinBox	QGraphicsBlurEffect	QTabWidget
QCheckBox	QErrorMessage	QGraphicsEffect	QTableView
QColorDialog	QFileDialog	QGraphicsEllipseItem	QTableWidget
QColumnView	QFileIconProvider	QGraphicsGridLayout	QTableWidgetItem
QComboBox	QWidget	QGraphicsItem	QTableWidgetSelectionRange
QTextBrowser	QWidgetAction	QPlainTextEdit	QLabel
QTextEdit	QWidgetItem	QProgressBar	QLayout
QTimeEdit	QWizard	QProgressDialog	QLayoutItem
QToolBar	QWizardPage	QProxyStyle	QLineEdit
QHBoxLayout	QMenu	QPushButton	QListView
QHeaderView	QMenuBar	QRadioButton	QListWidget
QInputDialog	QMessageBox	QRubberBand	QSplashScreen
QMainWindow	QTapGesture	QTreeWidgetItemIterator	QSplitter
QMdiArea	QToolBox	QUndoView	QSplitterHandle
QMdiSubWindow	QToolButton	QVBoxLayout	QStackedLayout
QPanGesture	QToolTip	QSlider	QStackedWidget
QPinchGesture	QTreeView	QSpacerItem	QStatusBar
QScrollBar	QTreeWidget	QSpinBox	QGraphicsWidget
QScroller	QListWidgetItem	QStyle	QGridLayout

QtCore

QAnimationGroup	QCoreApplication	QPoint	QDynamicPropertyChangeEvent
QBasicTimer	QCryptographicHash	QPointF	QLibrary
QBitArray	QDataStream	QProcess	QLibraryInfo
QBluetoothPermission	QDate	QProcessEnvironment	QMessageAuthenticationCode
QBuffer	QDateTime	QPropertyAnimation	QMessageLogContext
QByteArray	QDeadlineTimer	QRandomGenerator	QMessageLogger
QByteArrayMatcher	QDir	QReadLocker	QTextStream
QCalendar	QDirIterator	QReadWriteLock	QTextStreamManipulator
QCalendarPermission	QSaveFile	QRect	QTransposeProxyModel
QCameraPermission	QEasingCurve	QRectF	QTypeRevision

QCborError	QElapsedTimer	QThread	QXmlStreamAttribute
QLine	QEvent	QThreadPool	QXmlStreamAttributes
QLineF	QEventLoop	QTime	QXmlStreamEntityDeclaration
QLocale	QEventLoopLocker	QTimeLine	QXmlStreamEntityResolver
QLocationPermission	QFile	QTimeZone	QModelRoleDataSpan
QLockFile	QFileDevice	QTimer	QMutex
QLoggingCategory	QSize	QUrl	QMutexLocker
QMargins	QSizeF	QUrlQuery	QNativeIpcKey
QMarginsF	QSocketNotifier	QAbstractTableModel	QAbstractAnimation
QTemporaryDir	QSortFilterProxyModel	QCborKnownTags	QAbstractEventDispatcher
QTemporaryFile	QStandardPaths	QCborSimpleType	QAbstractItemModel
QTimerEvent	QStorageInfo	QCborStreamReader	QAbstractListModel
QTranslator	QStringConverter	QCborStreamWriter	QFileInfo
QItemSelection	QStringConverterBase	QChar	QFileSelector

QtGui

QtGui Modules	QFocusEvent	QDropEvent	QAbstractFileIconProvider
QWindow	QFont	QEnterEvent	QAbstractTextDocumentLayout
QTextFormat	QFontDatabase	QEventPoint	QPainterPath
QAction	QFontInfo	QExposeEvent	QPainterPathStroker
QActionEvent	QFontMetrics	QFileOpenEvent	QPalette
QActionGroup	QFontMetricsF	QFileSystemModel	QPdfOutputIntent
QBitmap	QGlyphRun	QKeyEvent	QPdfWriter
QBrush	QGradient	QShortcutEvent	QPen
QChildWindowEvent	QGuiApplication	QTextFrame	QPicture
QClipboard	QHelpEvent	QMatrix2x2	QPixelFormat
QCloseEvent	QHideEvent	QMatrix2x3	QPixmap
QColor	QHoverEvent	QMouseEvent	QPixmapCache
QColorConstants	QIcon	QMoveEvent	QTabletEvent
QColorSpace	QIconDragEvent	QMovie	QTextBlock
QColorTransform	QIconEngine	QPageSize	QTextBlockFormat
QCursor	QImage	QPagedPaintDevice	QTextBlockGroup
QDesktopServices	QImageIOHandler	QPaintDevice	QTextBlockUserData
QDoubleValidator	QImageReader	QPaintDeviceWindow	QTextCharFormat
QDrag	QImageWriter	QPaintEngine	QTextCursor
QKeyEvent	QInputDevice	QPaintEngineState	QTextDocument
QKeySequence	QInputEvent	QPaintEvent	QTextDocumentFragment
QLinearGradient	qPixelFormatAlpha	QPainter	QTextDocumentWriter
QPolygon	qPixelFormatCmyk	QTextItem	QTextOption
QPolygonF	QShortcut	QTextLayout	QTextTable
QQuaternion	qPixelFormatHsl	QTextLength	QTextTableCell
QRadialGradient	QPointerEvent	QTextLine	QTextTableCellFormat

QRasterWindow	QScreen	QTextList	QTextTableFormat
QRawFont	QScrollEvent	QTextListFormat	QTouchEvent
QRegion	QPageLayout	QTextObject	QTransform
QShowEvent	QPageRanges	QNativeGestureEvent	QUndoCommand

Deep

You can explore an exhaustive list of available classes and methods in any PyQt/PySide module using Python's built-in dir() function: For example,

```
>>> import PyQt6.QtWidgets
>>> widgets = dir(PyQt6.QtWidgets )
>>> print(widgets)
......
```

Importing and Using Widgets in PyQt / PySide

In PyQt and PySide, GUI components such as buttons, labels, layouts, and icons are part of various modules. These components—called **widgets**—must be imported into your program before they can be used.
You can import widgets in two main ways:

① Import Individual Widgets

</> Python

```python
from PyQt6.QtWidgets import QApplication, QPushButton, QWidget

from PyQt6.QtGui import QIcon
```

📌 This method imports only the widgets you need.

② Import All Widgets from a Module

</> Python

```
from PyQt6.QtWidgets import *

from PyQt6.QtCore import *
```

📌 This method is not recommended for large-scale projects because it pollutes the namespace and may cause conflicts.

💡 Tips

PySide Syntax

If you're using PySide6 instead of PyQt6, the import syntax is exactly the same, just change the module name:

```
>>> from PySide6.QtGui import QIcon        # Individual import
>>> from PySide6.QtCore import *           # Import all from a module
```

Understanding Widget Syntax

Most widgets in PyQt/PySide are initialized using the format:

```
QWidget(parent=None, **kwargs)
```

Parameters:

- parent: This specifies the parent widget that contains or hosts the current widget (also called the child widget). If not specified, the widget stands alone.
- **kwargs: These are optional named parameters used to customize the widget (e.g., size, alignment, text, tooltip, etc.).

Widget Properties

Each widget comes with properties that control its appearance and behavior. These can be common (shared by many widgets) or unique to a specific widget.

Setting Properties

To set a property for any widget, you first need to create an instance (object) of that widget. You can then access its methods to set various properties.

Example : Setting the text property of QPushButton

</> Python

```python
from PyQt6.QtWidgets import QPushButton

button = QPushButton()          # Creates the QPushButton instance
button.setText("Cancel")        # Sets the button text
```

Here, **setText()** is the method that modifies the widget's visible label.

Tips

Using setProperty() to Configure Widget Attributes

In PyQt, widget properties can be dynamically set using the setProperty() method. This provides a flexible way to assign values to widget attributes, especially useful when working with dynamic UIs, styling, or automation tools like Qt Designer.

Syntax

widget.setProperty("propertyName", value)

For example,

```
button = QPushButton()
button.setProperty("text", "Click me")
```

📌 In this example, the "text" property is assigned to the button, just as if you had used button.setText("Click me").

Getting Properties

Getting or retrieving a widget's property is often important when:

- You want to access the current value of a widget (e.g. user-entered text).
- You want to pass it to another widget or use it in logic.

Example : Getting the text of a QPushButton

</> Python

```python
from PyQt6.QtWidgets import QPushButton

button = QPushButton(text="Cancel")     # Creates a button with initial text
text = button.text()                    # Get the current button text
print(text)                             # Output: Cancel
```

Output

Cancel

Note

The widget must be stored in a variable (button) so it can be accessed later from other parts of the app.

Creating Your First PyQt Application

Example 1 : Basic Window Using QMainWindow

</> Python

```python
import sys
from PyQt6.QtWidgets import QMainWindow, QApplication

app = QApplication(sys.argv)        # Step 1: Create the application instance
window = QMainWindow()              # Step 2: Create the main window
window.setFixedSize(400, 300)       # Step 3: Set fixed dimensions
window.show()                       # Step 4: Show the window on screen
sys.exit(app.exec())                # Step 5: Run the application loop
```

Analysis

1. **import sys** – Enables command-line arguments and ensures proper app exit.
2. **QApplication** and **QMainWindow** are both widgets from QtWidgets.

3. **QApplication(sys.argv)** – Initializes the application environment and parses any command-line args.
4. **QMainWindow()** – Creates the main UI window that can host menus, toolbars, and other widgets.
5. **setFixedSize()** – Prevents resizing by setting a fixed window size.
6. **show()** – Displays the window on the screen.
7. **sys.exit(app.exec())** – Ensures the app closes gracefully when the user clicks the close button.

Example 2 : Same Logic Encapsulated in a Class

</> Python

```python
import sys
from PyQt6.QtWidgets import QMainWindow, QApplication

class MyApp:

  def __init__(self):
      app = QApplication(sys.argv)

      self.win = QMainWindow()          # Create window instance
      self.win.setFixedSize(400, 300)   # Set window size

      self.win.show()                   # Show the window
      sys.exit(app.exec())              # Start the event loop

if __name__ == "__main__":
  MyApp()
```

Analysis

1. **The app is run in a class** – This enables encapsulation of the app logic and UI.
2. **def __init__(self):** – Defines the constructor method that initializes the class when an object is created.
3. **self keyword** – Allows access to class-level variables and methods throughout the class. Variables prefixed with *self.* can be used in other functions within the class.
4. **if __name__ == "__main__":** – This ensures that the code block runs **only** when the script is executed directly, not when it's imported as a module in another script. It's Python's way of saying: "Run this part only if this is the starting file."
5. **MyApp()** – Creates an instance of the MyApp class, which triggers the constructor (__init__) and launches the app.

Note

The second app structure (class-based) is ideal for larger applications. You can define custom functions (methods) inside the class and each of them should include self as the first argument to access or manipulate class attributes.

Classes and Objects were discussed in earlier chapters. Readers are encouraged to review that section to fully understand how this works.

Example 3 : Using a QWidget-Based Class as the Main Window

</> Python

```
import sys
from PyQt6.QtWidgets import QMainWindow, QApplication

class MyApp(QMainWindow):
    def __init__(self):
        super().__init__()
        self.resize(600, 400)
        self.setWindowTitle("My App")
        self.setStyleSheet("background:#0e121a")

app = QApplication(sys.argv)
window = MyApp()
window.show()
sys.exit(app.exec())
```

Analysis

- **class MyApp(QMainWindow)**: This defines a new class MyApp that inherits from QMainWindow, making it a main window widget. By subclassing QMainWindow, you gain access to its built-in window management features like menus, toolbars, and status bars.
- **def __init__(self):** This is the initializer (constructor) method for the MyApp class. It is automatically called when an instance of the class is created.
- **super().__init__()**: This calls the constructor of the parent class (QMainWindow) to ensure the base class is properly initialized. This is a required step when subclassing Qt widgets.
- **self.resize(600, 400)**: This sets the initial size of the main window to 600 pixels wide and 400 pixels high. The self keyword refers to the current instance of MyApp, which is also an instance of QMainWindow.
- **self.setWindowTitle("My App")**: This sets the title of the window that appears in the title bar.
- **app = QApplication(sys.argv):** Creates the Qt application object. sys.argv is passed to allow Qt to handle command-line arguments if needed.
- **window = MyApp()**: Instantiates the MyApp class, which in turn creates and initializes a QMainWindow.
- **window.show()**: Makes the main window visible on the screen.
- **sys.exit(app.exec())**: Starts the Qt event loop. The program will continue running until the main window is closed. sys.exit ensures that the application exits cleanly, returning the exit status from the event loop.

Tips

At this point, we have explored three different approaches to creating a PyQt application. Each method offers its own advantages depending on the complexity and structure of the application. Developers are encouraged to adopt the approach that best aligns with their needs, coding style, and project requirements. Simplicity, readability, and maintainability should guide the choice of structure.

Categorization of PyQt Widgets by Functional Area

Below is a categorized list of common widgets and tools from ***QtWidgets***, ***QtGui***, and ***QtCore:***

Windows and Containers

Widget	Description
QMainWindow	Main application window
QWidget	Base class for all UI components
QDialog	Modal or non-modal dialog window
QGroupBox	Group container with a frame and label
QStackedWidget	Stack of widgets with only one visible
QTabWidget	Tabbed interface
QScrollArea	Enables scrollable views
QFrame	Used to create frames or panels

Table: 4.5 – Windows and containers widget group

Buttons

Widget	Description
QPushButton	Regular clickable button
QToolButton	Button for toolbars
QRadioButton	Radio (option) button
QCheckBox	Checkbox
QCommandLinkButton	Command-style button with description

Table: 4.6 – Button widget group

Text input and Editors

Widget	Description
QLineEdit	Single-line text box
QTextEdit	Rich-text editor
QPlainTextEdit	Plain text editor
QSpinBox / QDoubleSpinBox	Numeric input boxes
QComboBox	Dropdown list
QDateEdit, QTimeEdit, QDateTimeEdit	Date and time editors

Table: 4.7 – Text input and editor widget group

Layout Managers

Widget	Description
QVBoxLayout	Vertical layout
QHBoxLayout	Horizontal layout
QGridLayout	Grid-style layout
QFormLayout	Label-field layout
QSpacerItem	Adds space between widgets

Table: 4.8 – Layout managers widget group

Icons, Images and Media

Widget	Description
QIcon	Loads and displays icons
QPixmap	Handles images
QImage	Image manipulation
QMediaPlayer	Multimedia playback
QVideoWidget	Multimedia playback

Table: 4.9 – Icons, images and media widget group

Core Functionalities

Widget	Description
QTimer	Timing events
QDate, QTime, QDateTime	Date/time objects
QThread	Multithreading
QFile, QTextStream	File I/O
QObject	Base class for signals/slots

Table: 4.1.0 – Core functionalities widget group

Network, Bluetooth and Others

Widget	Description
QTcpSocket, QNetworkAccessManager	Network programming
QBluetoothDeviceDiscoveryAgent	Bluetooth discovery
QWebEngineView	Browsing the web

Table: 4.1.1 – Network and bluetooth widget group

Styling with HTML and CSS

PyQt allows developers to enhance the visual appeal and usability of their applications by integrating HTML and CSS-like styling. This makes it easy to create intuitive, flexible, and modern user interfaces.

HTML Support in Widgets

Some PyQt widgets, such as QLabel, support rendering rich text using a subset of HTML. This is particularly useful for displaying styled text, headings, links, and other inline formatting.

Example – Using HTML with QLabel:

</> Python

```python
label = QLabel(text="<h1>Heya! Look at my PyQt project</h1>")
```

CSS-like Styling with setStyleSheet()

PyQt widgets can be styled using a CSS-like syntax through the setStyleSheet() method. This property is available on most widgets and allows for powerful customization of appearance, including colors, borders, padding, and hover effects.

Example – Using CSS with QPushButton:

</> Python

```python
button = QPushButton("Click Me")

button.setStyleSheet("background-color: red; border-radius: 5px;")
```

Note

Note that style sheets should be written as string literals, enclosed in triple quotes ('''), single quotes ('), or double quotes ("), and passed to the setStyleSheet() method.

Commonly Supported CSS Properties in PyQt

PyQt supports a wide range of CSS properties (though not the full web CSS standard). Some commonly used ones include:

Properties	Function
color	Text color
background-color	Background
font, font-size, font-family, font-weight	Fonts
border, border-radius	Borders
padding, margin	Space around and within widget
min-width, max-width, min-height, max-height	Size control
qproperty-	Custom Qt properties

Table: 4.1.2 – Recognized CSS properties

Tips

General CSS Usage

```
*{
  background-color: #f0f0f0;
  color: black;
  font-size: 14px;
  font-family: "Arial";
  border: 1px solid gray;
  padding: 12px 24px;
  border-radius: 4px;
}
```

Common Properties

In **PyQt**, every widget (like QLabel, QPushButton, QMainWindow, etc.) has two types of properties:

- Common Properties:
  These are **shared by almost all widgets**. They manage basic aspects like size, visibility, fonts, tooltips, and window behaviors.
- Unique or Key Properties:
  These are **specific to a particular widget** and define its specialized behavior. (For example, a QLabel has setText() and setPixmap() methods, which are unique.)

Common properties ensure that different kinds of widgets still behave consistently in areas like geometry, event handling, visibility, and style.

Below are examples of some important common properties found across almost all PyQt widgets:

Group	Property or Method	Description
Visibility Control	show()	Displays the widget.
	hide()	Hides the widget.
	setVisible(bool)	Sets whether the widget is visible.
	isVisible()	Checks if the widget is currently visible.
	setHidden(bool)	Alternative way to hide the widget.
	showFullScreen()	Shows widget in full-screen mode.
	showMaximized()	Maximizes the widget window.
	showMinimized()	Minimizes the widget to taskbar.
Size and Geometry Control	resize(width, height)	Resizes the widget.
	adjustSize()	Auto-resizes to fit contents.
	setGeometry(x, y, width, height)	Sets both position and size.

	move(x, y)	Moves widget to a position.
	width() / height()	Returns the width/height of the widget.
	sizeHint()	Returns recommended size.
	maximumHeight(), maximumWidth()	Sets/retrieves maximum allowed height/width.
	minimumHeight(), minimumWidth()	Sets/retrieves minimum allowed height/width.
Style and Appearance	setStyleSheet("CSS")	Applies CSS styling.
	setFont(QFont)	Sets the font.
	setToolTip(str)	Adds tooltip text.
	setWindowIcon(QIcon)	Sets the window's icon.
	setWindowOpacity(float)	Sets transparency.
	setWindowTitle(str)	Sets the window's title text.
	backgroundRole() / foregroundRole()	Defines visual roles for theming.
Focus and Interaction	setFocus()	Gives keyboard focus to widget.
	setFocusPolicy(Qt.FocusPolicy)	Defines when widget can take focus.
	grabKeyboard() / releaseKeyboard()	Captures/releases keyboard input.
	grabMouse() / releaseMouse()	Captures/releases mouse input.
Event Handling	event(event)	Base event handler.
	eventFilter(obj, event)	Filters/intercepts events before handling.
	keyPressEvent(event)	Handles key press events.
	mousePressEvent(event)	Handles mouse press events.
	mouseReleaseEvent(event)	Handles mouse release events.
	timerEvent(event)	Handles timer-based events.

	showEvent(event)	Triggered when widget is shown.
	hideEvent(event)	Triggered when widget is hidden.
Window Management	setWindowFlags(Qt.WindowFlags)	Sets special window behaviors (frameless, stay on top, etc.).
	windowFilePath()	Retrieves the window's file path (if set).
	setWindowModality(Qt.WindowModality)	Makes window modal (blocks input to other windows).
	windowFlags()	Returns current window flags.
	activateWindow()	Brings window to front and gives it focus.
State and Persistence	saveGeometry() / restoreGeometry()	Saves/restores window size and position.
	saveState() / restoreState()	Saves/restores toolbars and dock widgets.
Action and Menu Management	addAction(action) / addActions(actions)	Adds one or multiple actions (buttons, menus).
	removeAction(action)	Removes an action.
	setMenuBar(QMenuBar)	Sets a menu bar (top bar with File/Edit/etc.).
	setMenuWidget(QWidget)	Sets a widget instead of a menu bar.
General Widget Info	isEnabled() / setEnabled(bool)	Enables or disables widget.
	isHidden() / isVisibleTo(widget)	Visibility relative to parent widget.
	isWindow() / isWindowType()	Checks if it's a standalone window.
	underMouse()	Checks if mouse is over widget.

Table: 4.1.3 – Shared methods and properties

Chapter 5

PyQt Widgets -SetA (Basic widgets)

Chapter Objectives

- ◈ Understand QMainWindow
- ◈ Use QIcon
- ◈ Work with QPushButton
- ◈ Apply QHBoxLayout
- ◈ Apply QVBoxLayout
- ◈ Use QGridLayout
- ◈ Implement QStackedLayout
- ◈ Use QFormLayout
- ◈ Explore QLayout
- ◈ Explore QBoxLayout
- ◈ Work with QLabel
- ◈ Use QFrame
- ◈ Draw with QPainter
- ◈ Customize with QPen
- ◈ Fill with QBrush
- ◈ Apply gradients

Project A – Building a Calculator

In this project, we will create a basic desktop calculator using PyQt. The goal is to apply the core concepts you've learned by combining multiple PyQt widgets into a cohesive, interactive application.

As we design the calculator, you'll become more familiar with commonly used widgets and their properties. This project will also highlight how layout management, signal-slot connections, and styling come together to form a complete user interface.

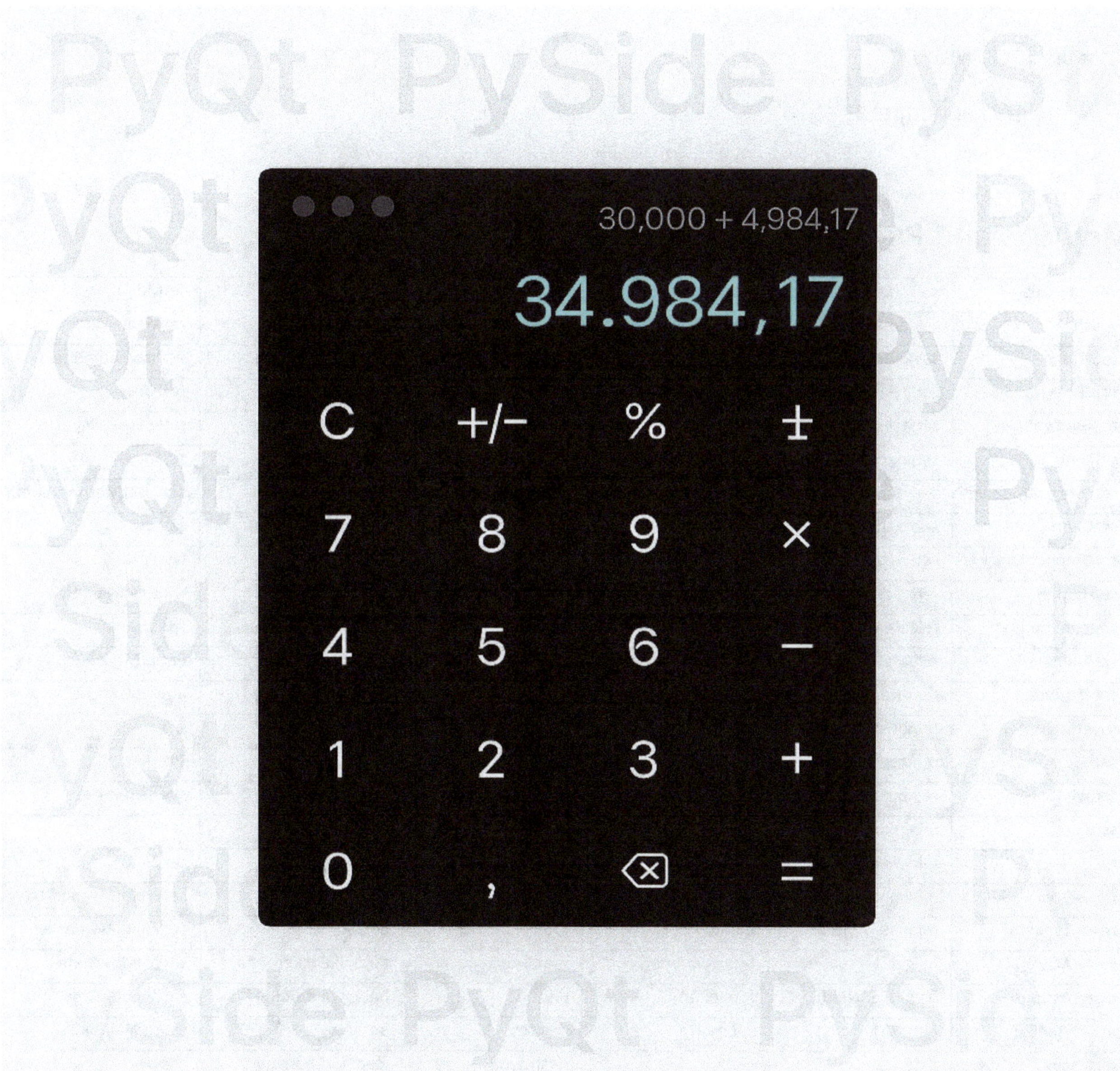

QMainWindow

QMainWindow serves as the core container widget in PyQt, forming the base upon which all other interface elements are built. It acts as the **main window** or **central board** that hosts and organizes the child widgets, tools, and components of your application.

As a part of the QtWidgets module QMainWindow provides a robust and flexible structure, supporting additional UI elements such as:

- Toolbars
- Menu bars
- Status bars
- Dock widgets
- Central widgets

Methods and Properties

windowTitle	setVisible	setWindowFlags	receivers	showEvent	setMenuBar
width	setToolButtonStyle	setWindowIcon	windowOpacity	showFullScreen	setMenuWidget
toolTip	setToolTip	setWindowIconText	windowIcon	showMaximized	setMaximumSize
toolTipDuration	setStyle	setProperty	thread	showMinimized	setFocus
toolButtonStyle	setStyleSheet	setScreen	timerEvent	keyboardGrabber	setFocusPolicy
setFont	setEnabled	setMaximumHeight	toolBarArea	isEnabled	setFocusProxy
setForegroundRole	setFixedHeight	setMaximumWidth	setBaseSize	isEnabledTo	setInputMethodHints
setGeometry	setFixedSize	setMinimumHeight	setCorner	isFullScreen	setLayout
setGraphicsEffect	setFixedWidth	setMinimumSize	setCursor	isHidden	window
setHidden	releaseKeyboard	setMinimumWidth	setDisabled	isLeftToRight	windowFilePath
setIconSize	releaseMouse	mouseGrabber	isVisible	isMaximized	windowFlags
setAnimated	releaseShortcut	mouseMoveEvent	isVisibleTo	isMinimized	underMouse
setAttribute	removeAction	mousePressEvent	isWidgetType	isModal	ungrabGesture
saveGeometry	removeDockWidget	mouseReleaseEvent	isWindow	actions	size
saveState	removeEventFilter	move	isWindowModified	activateWindow	sizeHint
screen	removeToolBar	maximumHeight	isWindowType	addAction	sizeIncrement
scroll	minimumHeight	maximumSize	keyPressEvent	addActions	setWindowFlag
resize	minimumSize	maximumWidth	keyReleaseEvent	addDockWidget	setWindowModality
resizeDocks	minimumSizeHint	menuBar	keyboardGrabber	addToolBar	setWindowModified
resizeEvent	minimumWidth	menuWidget	grabKeyboard	adjustSize	setWindowOpacity
insertAction	height	frameGeometry	grabMouse	autoFillBackground	setWindowState
insertActions	heightForWidth	frameSize	depth	backgroundRole	setWindowTitle
insertToolBar	heightMM	geometry	destroy	baseSize	sharedPainter
hasFocus	hide	grab	destroyed	iconSizeChanged	show

event	hideEvent	grabGesture	childAt	inherits	stackUnder
eventFilter	close	font	childEvent	initPainter	startTimer
find	closeEvent	fontInfo	children	statusBar	style
disconnect	colorCount	fontMetrics	isAnimated	setStatusBar	styleSheet

Tips

You can explore the full list of methods and properties available for ***QMainWindow*** using Python's built-in dir() function:

```
>>> import sys
>>> from PyQt6.QtWidgets import QMainWindow, QApplication

>>> app = QApplication(sys.argv)
>>> window = QMainWindow()
>>> print(dir(window))
.....
```

Python

```python
import sys
from PyQt6.QtWidgets import *

class MyApp(QMainWindow):
  def __init__(self):
      super().__init__()

      self.setWindowTitle("My Calculator")
      self.resize(300,800)
      self.move(100,50)
      self.setStyleSheet("background:#0e121a")

      self.mainWidget = QWidget()
      self.setCentralWidget(self.mainWidget)

app = QApplication(sys.argv)
window = MyApp()
window.show()
sys.exit(app.exec())
```

Explanation

- **setWindowTitle("My Calculator")**: Sets the title displayed in the window's title bar.
- **resize(300, 800)**: Sets the initial width and height of the main window.
- **move(100, 50)**: Positions the top-left corner of the window at coordinates (100, 50) on the screen.
- **setStyleSheet("**background: #0e121a**")**: Applies a dark background color using CSS-like syntax.
- **setCentralWidget(self.mainWidget)**: In a QMainWindow, this sets the central area widget. All other widgets and layouts are typically nested inside this central widget.

Sizing and Positioning

PyQt provides several methods to control the size and position of widgets. Here's a breakdown of the most commonly used ones:

resize(width, height)

Sets the widget's width and height. The widget remains resizable unless explicitly restricted.

setFixedSize(width, height)

Sets a fixed, unchangeable size for the widget. Users cannot resize the window manually.

</> Python

```python
window = QMainWindow()
window.setFixedSize( 500, 200)
```

move(x, y)

Moves the widget to a specific position. If used on a top-level widget (like a main window), the coordinates refer to screen space.

setGeometry(x, y, width, height)

Combines position and size into a single method. Equivalent to calling move(x, y) and resize(width, height) together.

</> Python

```python
window = QMainWindow()
window.setGeometry( 100, 70, 500, 200)
```

geometry()

Returns a ***QRect*** object containing both the widget's position and size: (x, y, width, height).

frameGeometry()

Similar to *geometry()*, but includes the window frame (if present). Useful for getting the true screen footprint of a top-level window.

width() and height()

Return the current width and height of the widget as integers.

size()

Returns a QSize object representing the widget's current width and height.

</> Python

```python
window.setGeometry( 100, 70, 500, 200)
winSize =  window.size( )
print(winSize)
```

```
Output
PyQt6.QtCore.QSize(500, 200)
```

x() and y()

Return the x and y coordinates of the widget's top-left corner relative to its parent.

</> Python

```python
window.setGeometry( 100, 70, 500, 200)
x =  window.x()
y =  window.y()

print(x)
print(y)
```

```
Output
100
70
```

pos()

Returns a *QPoint* object representing the widget's position (x, y) relative to its parent.

</> Python

```
window.setGeometry( 100, 70, 500, 200)
position = window.pos()
print(position)
```

Output
```
PyQt6.QtCore.QPoint(100, 70)
```

setMinimumSize(width, height) / setMaximumSize(width, height)

Define the minimum and maximum dimensions the widget is allowed to have.

minimumSize() / maximumSize()

Return the minimum and maximum size constraints currently set on the widget.

rect()

Returns a *QRect* representing the internal area of the widget, excluding window decorations.

contentsRect()

Returns the rectangle available for child widgets, accounting for padding or margins inside the widget.

Other QMainWindow Properties

setWindowOpacity(float)

Sets the transparency level of the window. Accepts a float between **0.0** (completely transparent) and **1.0** (fully opaque).

</> Python

```
window = QMainWindow()
window.setWindowOpacity( 0.5)
```

windowOpacity( )

Returns the current opacity level of the window as a float.

setToolTip(text)

Displays a tooltip message when the mouse hovers over the window or widget.

</> Python

```
window = QMainWindow()
window.setToolTip( "This is a calculator application" )
```

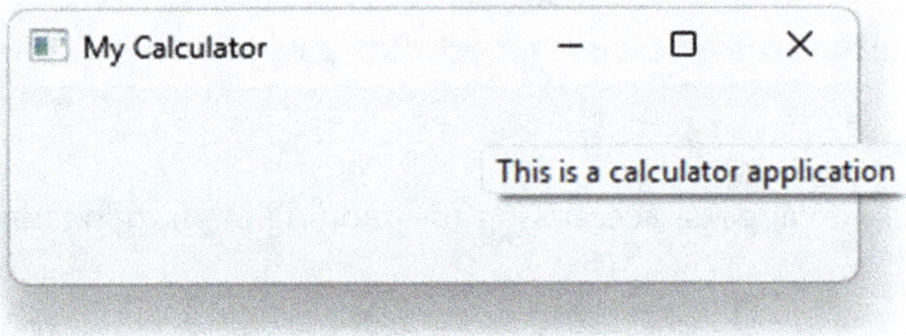

toolTip( )

Retrieves the tooltip text currently set for the widget.

setWindowIcon(QIcon)

Sets the window's icon using a *QIcon* object.

</> Python

```python
window = QMainWindow()
window.setWindowIcon( QIcon("images/rocket.png"))
```

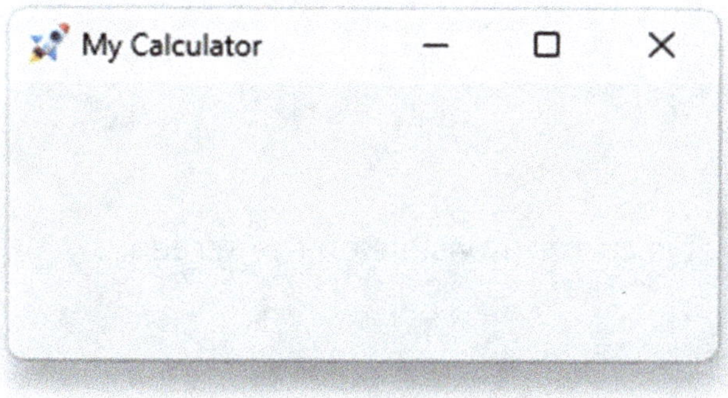

Tips

QIcon(path/to/image)

This can also be used with other widgets like ***QPushButton, QLabel*** etc., to display icons.

close()

Closes the window. Often used in response to events such as button clicks.

hide() and show()

- hide() – Hides the window from the screen.
- show() – Displays the window (or re-displays it if hidden).

These methods are useful for temporarily removing or restoring the window from view.

</> Python

```
window = QMainWindow()
window.hide()
window.show()
```

isVisible( )

Returns a Boolean indicating whether the widget is currently visible on the screen.

setWindowFlag(Qt.WindowType)

Controls the appearance and behavior of the window frame. This can be used to remove the title bar, disable resizing, hide minimize/maximize buttons, and more.

Common Qt.WindowType Flags:

- Qt.WindowType.Window – Standard top-level window
- Qt.WindowType.Dialog – Dialog-style window
- Qt.WindowType.FramelessWindowHint – No window frame or title bar
- Qt.WindowType.WindowStaysOnTopHint – Keeps the window on top of all others
- Qt.WindowType.Tool – A small utility window, typically used for tool panels

</> Python

```
window = QMainWindow()
window.setWindowFlag( Qt.WindowType.FramelessWindowHint)
```

Qt.WindowType.FramelessWindowHint

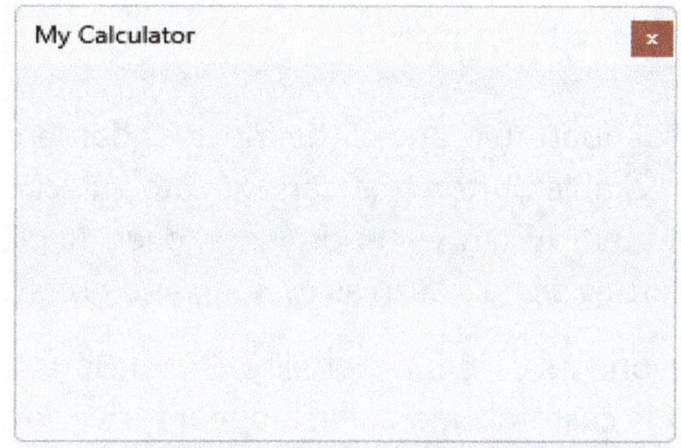

Qt.WindowType.Tool

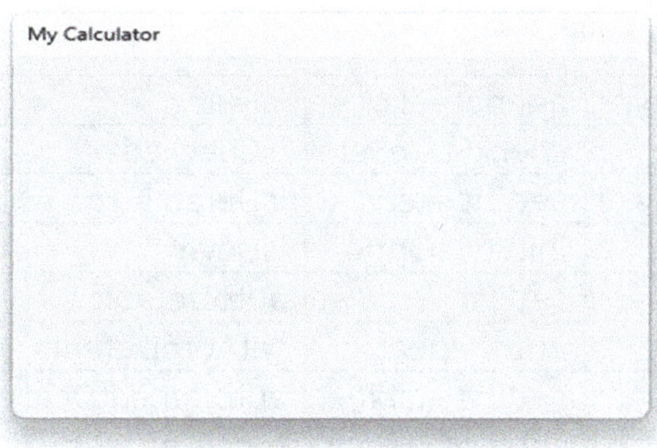

Qt.WindowType.CoverWindow

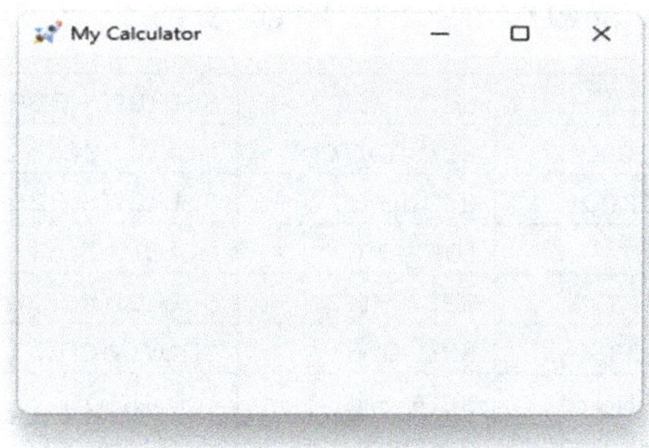

Qt.WindowType.NoDropShadowWindowHint

Other Qt.WindowType Flags:

Desktop	Sheet	WindowTitleHint
CoverWindow	Splashscreen	WindowCloseButtonHint
Drawer	SubWindow	WindowDoesNotAcceptFocus
ForeignWindow	ToolTip	CustomizeWindowHint
Popup	WindoType_Mask	MSWindowsOwnDC
Widget	WindowSystemMenuHint	MacWindowToolBarButtonHint

Table: 5.0 – Some Window types

QPushButton

QPushButton is one of the most fundamental and widely used widgets in PyQt. It represents a clickable button that can execute an action, trigger events, or control other widgets when pressed. As an event-driven widget, it plays a key role in signal-slot communication by emitting signals such as *clicked()* and *pressed()*.

Beyond its core functionality, QPushButton offers a variety of properties and methods that allow customization of its appearance and behavior. These include options for setting icons, toggling states, handling shortcuts, and integrating menus.

Key Methods and Properties

text	shortcut	setAutoRepeatInterval	animateClick	isFlat
pressed	setShortcut	nextCheckState	checkStateSet	isChecked
clicked	group	setAutoRepeatDelay	setChecked	isDefault
icon	toggled	autoExclusive	initStyleOption	isDown
setIcon	setText	setAutoExclusive	setFlat	autoDefault
released	setDown	showMenu	autoRepeat	setAutoDefault
menu	setMenu	hitButton	setCheckable	autoRepeatDelay
click	setDefault	setFlat	setAutoRepeat	toggle

Note

All the common widget properties and methods—such as setEnabled(), setVisible(), setStyleSheet(), setToolTip(), setGeometry(), and others—explained under previous widget sections are also fully applicable to QPushButton.

Tips

To explore all available properties, methods, and attributes of a QPushButton object—including inherited ones—you can use Python's built-in dir() function.
Example:
>>> print(dir(QPushButton()))

setText(text **) and text()**

The *setText()* defines the text label displayed on the button and *text()* returns the text.

</> Python

```
import sys
from PyQt6.QtWidgets import *

class MyApp(QMainWindow):
    def __init__(self):
        super().__init__()

        self.setWindowTitle("My Calculator")
        self.setProperty("setGeometry", (100, 100, 400, 300))
        self.setStyleSheet("background:#0e121a")

        self.button = QPushButton( self )
        self.button.setGeometry(100, 50, 100, 50)
        self.button.setText("Submit")


app = QApplication(sys.argv)
window = MyApp()
window.show()
sys.exit(app.exec())
```

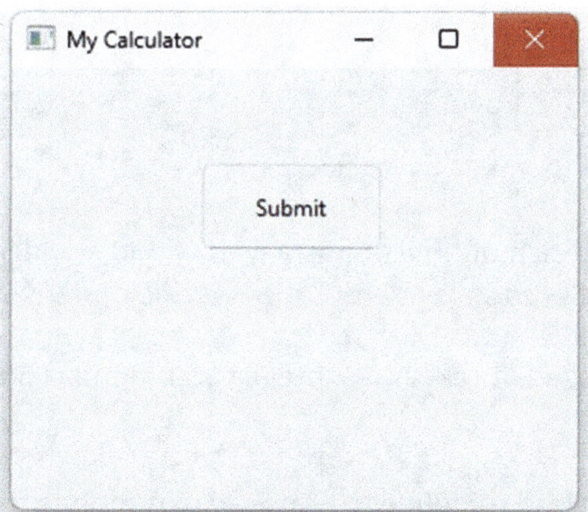

setIcon(QIcon(path)) and icon()

Allows an icon to be displayed on the button alongside or instead of text. The *icon()* returns the button's icon.

</> Python

```
buttonA = QPushButton( widget )
buttonA.setIcon(QIcon("images/home.png"))
buttonA.setIconSize(QSize(50, 50))

buttonB = QPushButton( widget )
buttonB.setText("Upload")
buttonB.setIcon(QIcon("images/upload.png"))
buttonB.setIconSize(QSize(50, 50))
```

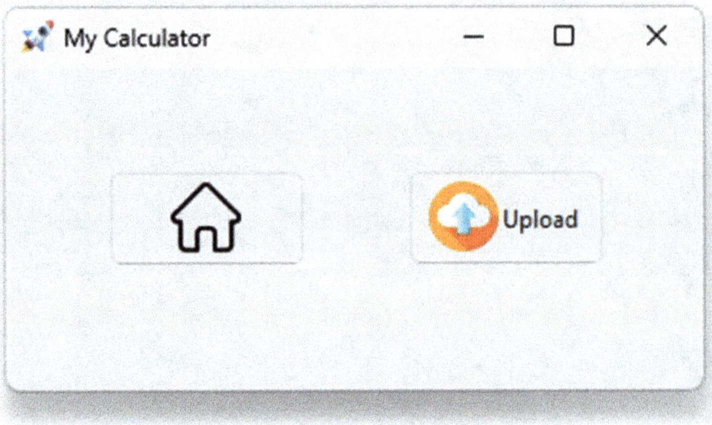

Tips

Controlling Icon Size with setIconSize()
The setIconSize() method is used to define the size of an icon displayed within a widget, such as a QPushButton. This ensures that the icon is rendered at a specific dimension, regardless of the original image size.
To specify the dimensions, the **QSize** class is used. It takes two integer arguments: width and height.

- **QSize(width, height)**
  Represents a two-dimensional size object. Used to define the desired dimensions for the icon.

setFlat(bool **)** and **isFlat()**

Removes the 3D frame, making the button appear flat and more visually minimalistic.

```
buttonA = QPushButton( self )
buttonA.setGeometry(50, 100, 100, 50)
buttonA.setText("Click")
buttonA.setFlat(True)

buttonB = QPushButton( self )
buttonB.setGeometry(200, 100, 100, 50)
buttonB.setText("Click")
buttonB.setStyleSheet("background:blue; color:white; border-radius:25px")
buttonB.setFlat(True)
```

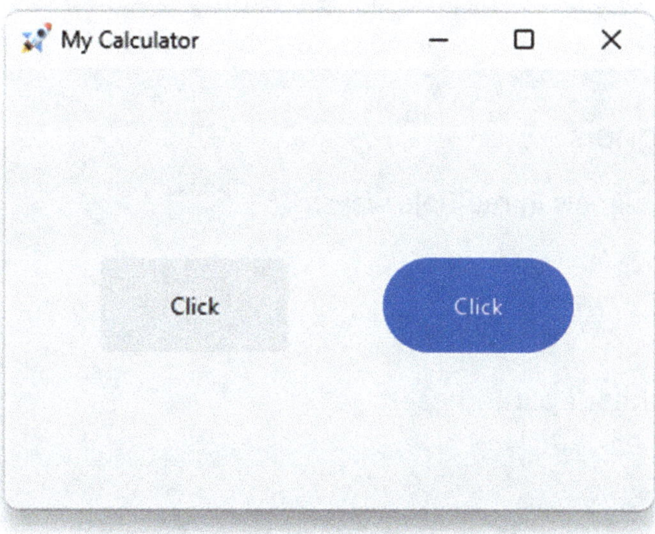

setDefault(bool **)** and **isDefault()**

Marks the button as the default button in a dialog, meaning it will be triggered when Enter is pressed.

Connecting Buttons to Callback Functions

In PyQt, buttons such as QPushButton are interactive widgets designed to trigger actions in response to user interaction. These actions are implemented using **callback functions—** functions that are automatically called when a specific signal (like a click or press) is emitted by the button.

Common Signal or Event Types in QPushButton

QPushButton provides several built-in signals for connecting to callback functions:

- **clicked** – Emitted when the button is clicked (pressed and released).
- **pressed** – Emitted the moment the button is pressed down.
- **released** – Emitted when the button is released after being pressed.
- **toggled** – Emitted when the button is toggled (applicable if the button is checkable).

Connecting Functions to Button Signals

You can connect functions (slots) to these signals in multiple ways:

① Direct Connection (for argument-less functions)

Connect the signal directly to a function without parentheses:

```
#clicked event
button.clicked.connect(function)

#pressed event
button.pressed.connect(function)

#released event
button.released.connect(function)

#toggled event
button.toggled.connect(function)
```

Example

```
</> Python
import sys
from PyQt6.QtWidgets import *

class MyApp(QMainWindow):
  def __init__(self):
     super().__init__()

     self.setWindowTitle("My Calculator")
     self.setProperty("setGeometry", (100, 100, 400, 200))
     self.setStyleSheet("background:#ebebeb")

     self.button = QPushButton( self )
     self.button.setGeometry(100, 50, 100, 50)
     self.button.setText("Click")
     self.button.clicked.connect(self.myFunc)


  def myFunc(self):
     self.button.setStyleSheet("background:#FF6700")

app = QApplication(sys.argv)
window = MyApp()
window.show()
sys.exit(app.exec())
```

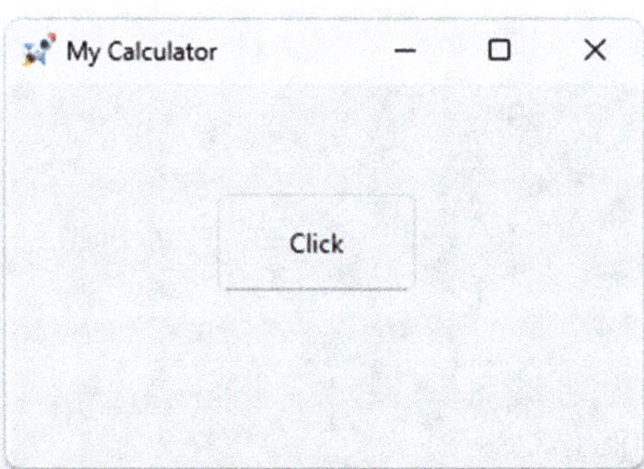

Before clicking

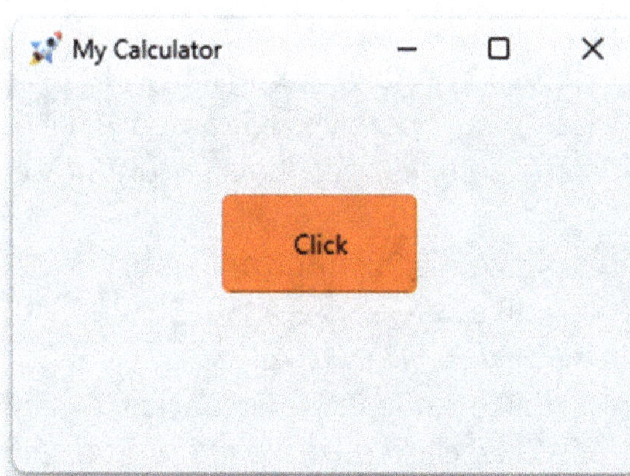

After clicking

② Using **lambda** (for functions with arguments)

If your function requires parameters, use a lambda expression to pass arguments:

```
button.clicked.connect(lambda: callback_function(arg1, arg2) )

button.pressed.connect(lambda: callback_function(arg) )

button.released.connect(lambda: callback_function(arg) )

button.toggled.connect(lambda: callback_function(arg) )
```

Example

</> Python

```python
import sys
from PyQt6.QtWidgets import *
from datetime import datetime

class MyApp(QMainWindow):
    def __init__(self):
        super().__init__()

        time = datetime.now().hour

        self.setWindowTitle("My Calculator")
        self.setProperty("setGeometry", (100, 100, 400, 200))
        self.setStyleSheet("background:#ebebeb")

        self.like = QPushButton( self )
        self.like.setGeometry(50, 50, 200, 40)
        self.like.setText("Like")
        self.like.setStyleSheet("background:#45553D;border-radius:20px; color:white")
        self.like.clicked.connect(lambda: self.likedFunc())

        self.submit = QPushButton( self )
        self.submit.setGeometry(50, 110, 200, 40)
        self.submit.setText("Submit")
```

```
        self.submit.setStyleSheet("border:2px solid #45553D; border-radius:20px")
        self.submit.clicked.connect(lambda: self.submitFunc(time))


    def likedFunc(self):
        self.like.setText("Liked")

    def submitFunc(self, message):
        self.submit.setText(f"Submitted at {message}h ago")


app = QApplication(sys.argv)
window = MyApp()
window.show()
sys.exit(app.exec())
```

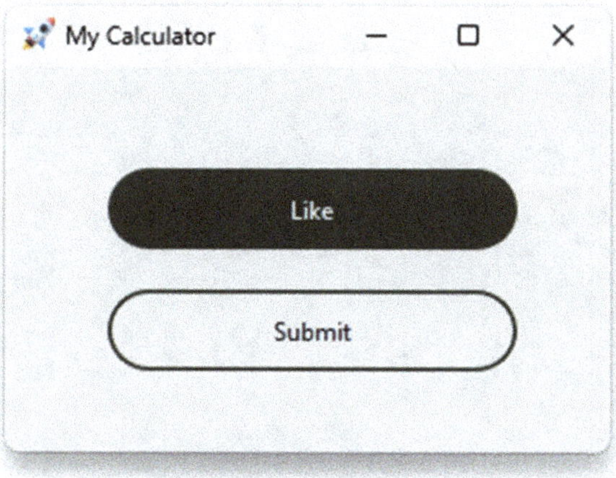

Before clicking

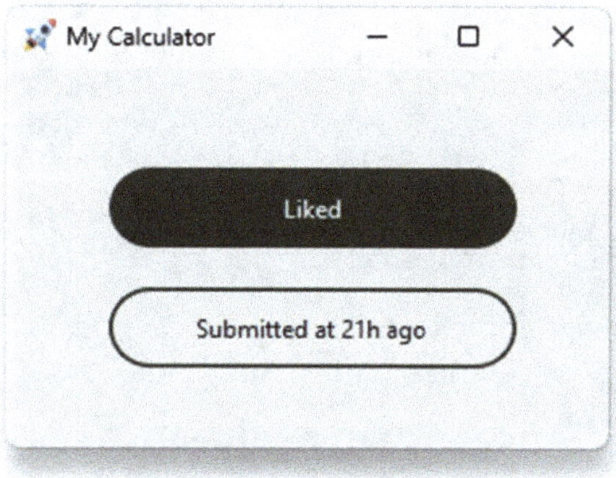

After clicking

③ Using **lambda** for Inline Statements

```
button.clicked.connect(lambda: print("You've clicked me"))
```

Example

</> Python

```python
import sys
from PyQt6.QtWidgets import *

class MyApp(QMainWindow):
    def __init__(self):
        super().__init__()

        self.setWindowTitle("My Calculator")
        self.setProperty("setGeometry", (100, 100, 400, 200))
        self.setStyleSheet("background:#ebebeb")

        self.button = QPushButton( self )
        self.button.setGeometry(100, 50, 100, 50)
        self.button.setText("Click")
        self.button.pressed.connect(lambda: print("Heya!, I'm pressed"))


app = QApplication(sys.argv)
window = MyApp()
window.show()
sys.exit(app.exec())
```

Disconnecting Signals

To remove a previously connected function from a signal, use the **disconnect()** method:

</> Python

```python
button.clicked.disconnect(callback_function)
```

setDown(bool **)** and **isDown()**

Sets or checks whether the button appears visually pressed.

```python
button = QPushButton( parent )
button.setDown(True)
```

setShortcut(string **)** and **shortcut()**

Sets or returns the keyboard shortcut that activates the button.

```python
button = QPushButton( parent )
button.setShortcut("V")
```

isChecked() and **setChecked(** bool **)**

Indicates whether the button is in a checked (on) state. Useful for toggle buttons.

```python
button = QPushButton( parent )
button.setChecked(True)
```

isCheckable( ) and **setCheckable(** bool **)**

Enables the button to maintain a toggled state—checked or unchecked—like a toggle switch.

```python
button = QPushButton( parent )
button.setCheckable(True)
```

toggle() and **nextCheckState(** bool **)**

Programmatically switches the button between checked and unchecked states.

setAutoDefault(bool **)** and **autoDefault()**

Determines whether the button automatically becomes the default when it receives focus.

setMenu(QMenu **)**, **menu()** and **showMenu()**

Associates a drop-down menu with the button, turning it into a menu button.

click() and **animateClick()**

Simulates a button click programmatically. *animateClick* includes visual feedback.

setAutoExclusive() and **autoExclusive()**

When used within a button group, ensures only one button can be checked at a time.

setAutoRepeat() and **autorepeat()**

Allows the button to send repeated click signals when held down.

setAutoRepeatDelay() and **autoRepeatDelay()**

Sets the initial delay before repeating click signals when the button is held.

setAutoRepeatInterval() and **autoRepeatInterval()**

Determines the interval at which the button continues to emit repeated click signals.

checkStateSet()

A low-level method invoked internally when the button's check state changes—often overridden in subclasses.

initStyleOption()

Initializes the button's appearance parameters, often used for custom styling in QStyle-based rendering.

group

Returns the button group to which the button belongs, if any.

Layout Management

The arrangement and dynamic resizing of widgets in response to window resizing is a crucial aspect of any responsive GUI application. In PyQt, layouts manage the positioning, alignment and scaling of widgets, ensuring that the user interface remains organized and responsive across different screen sizes and window states.

In every PyQt application, the interface typically follows a hierarchical structure:

- A **parent widget** (commonly the main window) contains a **layout**.
- The layout manages multiple child widgets.
  This layout hierarchy determines how widgets are displayed and how they adapt to changes in the window size.

Significance of Layouts

Layouts play a vital role in user interface design by:

1. Positioning child widgets within the parent container.
2. Automatically expanding or shrinking widgets based on the window size (UI responsiveness).
3. Providing consistent alignment for widgets.
4. Managing spacing and margins between widgets.
5. Supporting nesting of multiple layouts for complex UI designs.

Proper Application Structure for UI Responsiveness

When building PyQt desktop applications, a recommended structure ensures both organization and responsiveness:

- The main application window is typically a **QMainWindow**.
- Although *QMainWindow* has its own layout, adding widgets directly to it results in absolute positioning—which means widgets won't respond to window resizing.

❖ To enable responsiveness:

1. **Set a central widget**, usually an instance of **QWidget** on the QMainWindow using **setCentralWidget()**.
2. **Apply a layout** to the central widget (e.g., QVBoxLayout, QGridLayout, etc.).
3. **Add all child widgets** to this layout. The layout manages widget resizing and alignment automatically.

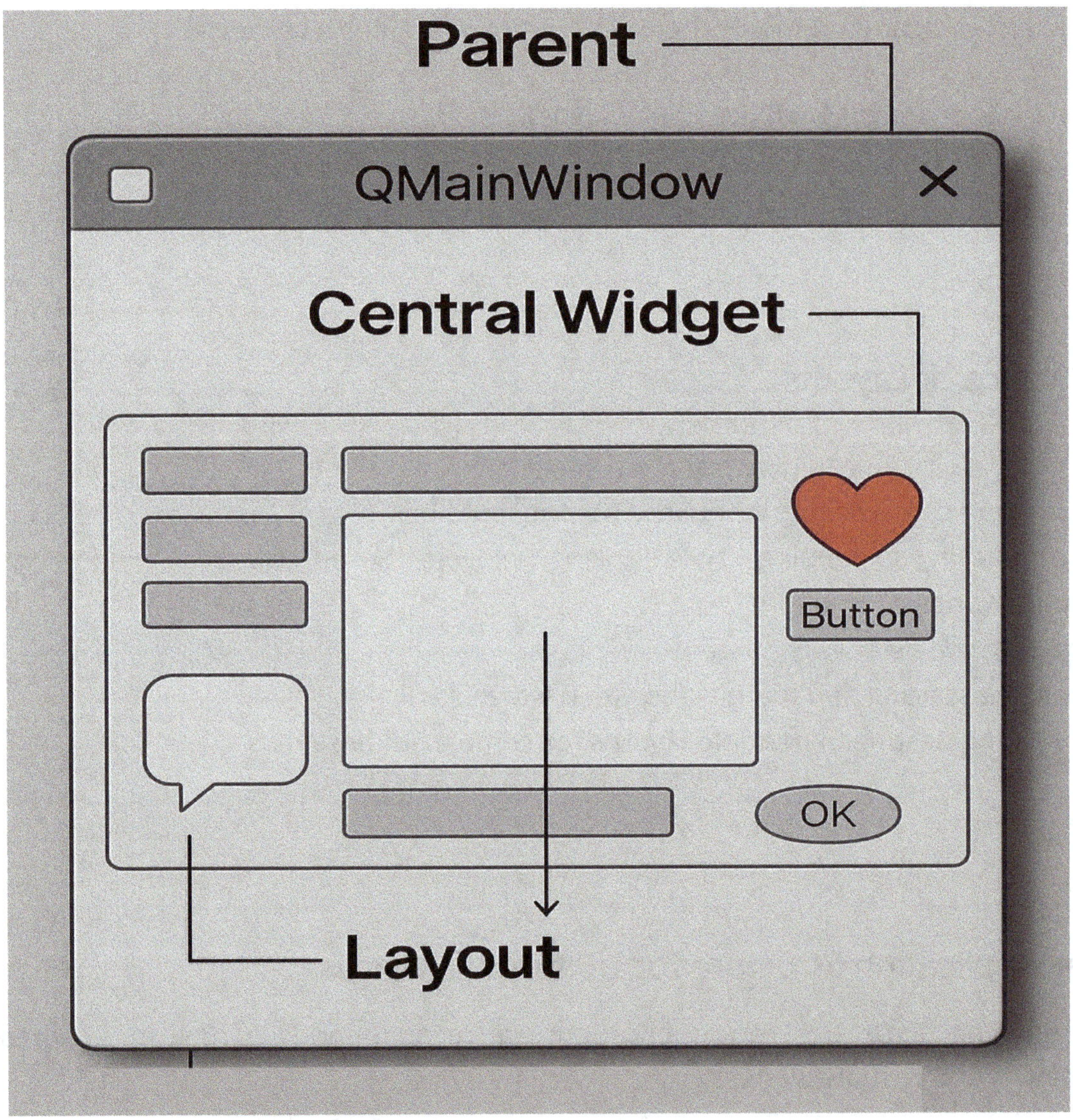

Figure 5.0 : PyQt Application structure

Types of Layouts in PyQt

PyQt provides seven primary layout classes, each with unique features and organizational behavior. Despite their differences, all layouts share core properties such as alignment control, automatic resizing, and support for nested layouts.

List of Layouts in PyQt

1. **QHBoxLayout**
2. **QVBoxLayout**
3. **QGridLayout**
4. **QStackedLayout**
5. **QFormLayout**
6. **QLayout**
7. **QBoxLayout**

Common Properties and Methods in Layouts

These properties and methods are **inherited from QLayout or its subclasses** and are available across all layout types:

addWidget	spacing	insertSpacing	activate
addSpacing	controlTypes	insertLayout	Direction
addSpacerItem	sizeConstraint	expandingDirections	closestAcceptableSize
addChildLayout	addStretch	setAlignment	setSizeConstraint
addStrut	totalMinimumSize	count	spacerItem
addChildWidget	direction	totalMaximumSize	indexOf
addItem	unsetContentsMargins	removeWidget	setSpacing
addLayout	replaceWidget	totalSizeHint	alignment
insertWidget	insertItem	setDirection	totalHeightForWidth
widgetEvent	removeItem	setStretch	SizeConstraint
itemAt	insertStretch	alignmentRect	takeAt
minimumHeightForWidth	isEmpty	getContentsMargins	setStrecthFactor
stretch	insertSpacerItem		

QHBoxLayout

Arranges widgets **horizontally** (left to right).

Figure 5.1 : QHBoxLayout structure

addWidget(widget)

Adds a widget to the layout.

```
layout = QHBoxLayout()
layout.addWidget( widget1 )
layout.addWidget( widget2 )
layout.addWidget( widget3 )
```

Example

</> Python

```
import sys
from PyQt6.QtWidgets import *

class MyApp(QMainWindow):
    def __init__(self):
        super().__init__()

        self.setWindowTitle("My Calculator")
        self.setProperty("setGeometry", (100, 100, 400, 200))
        self.setStyleSheet("background:#ebebeb")

        self.mainPage = QWidget()
        self.setCentralWidget(self.mainPage)              #Setting central widget

        self.lay = QHBoxLayout()
        self.mainPage.setLayout(self.lay)                  #Setting central widget layout

        self.lay.addWidget(QPushButton("button1"))         #Adding children to layout
        self.lay.addWidget(QPushButton("button2"))
        self.lay.addWidget(QPushButton("button3"))

app = QApplication(sys.argv)
window = MyApp()
window.show()
sys.exit(app.exec())
```

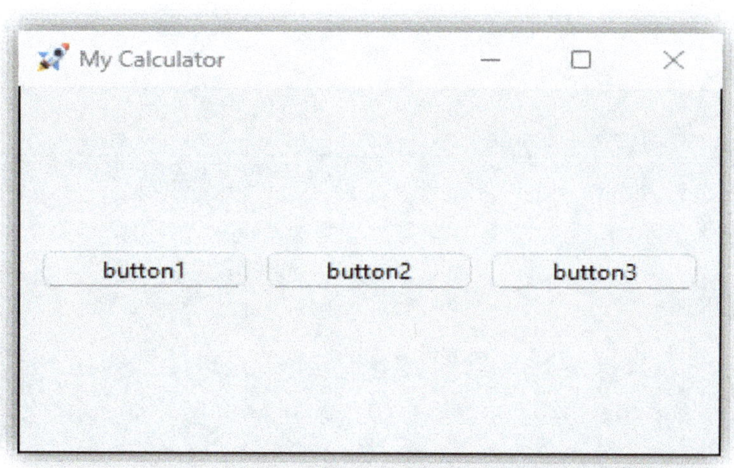

insertWidget(index, widget)

Inserts a widget at a specific index.

</> Python

```
lay = QHBoxLayout( )
button = QPushButton("button3")
button.setStyleSheet("background:orange")

lay.insertWidget(1, button)
```

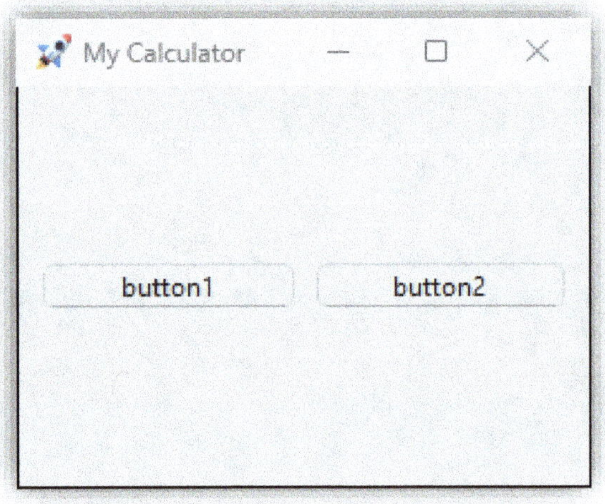

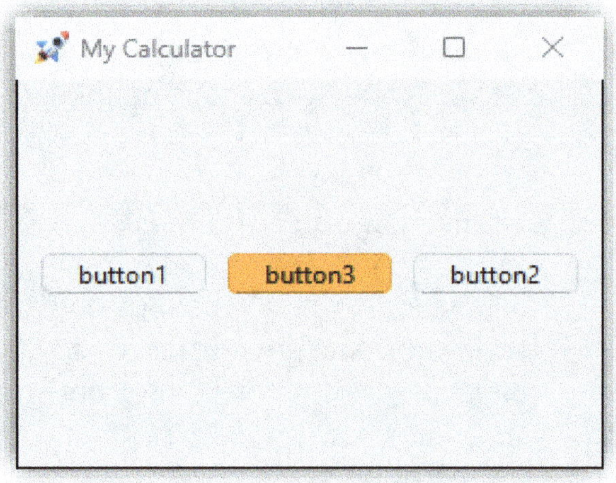

removeWidget(widget)

Removes a widget from the layout.

</> Python

```
lay = QHBoxLayout( )

button1 = QPushButton("button1")
button2 = QPushButton("button2")
button3 = QPushButton("button3")

lay.removeWidget(button2)
```

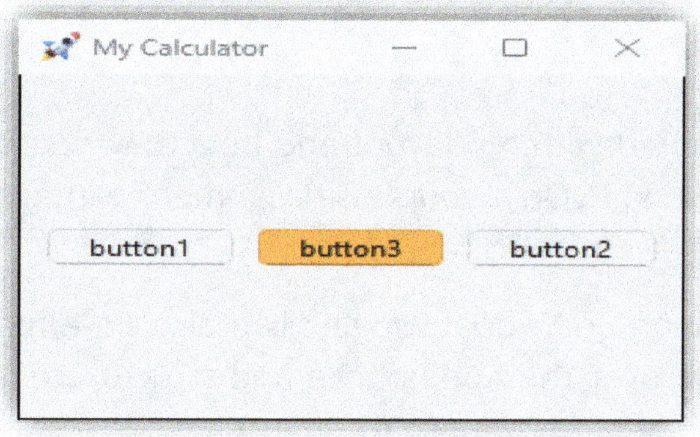

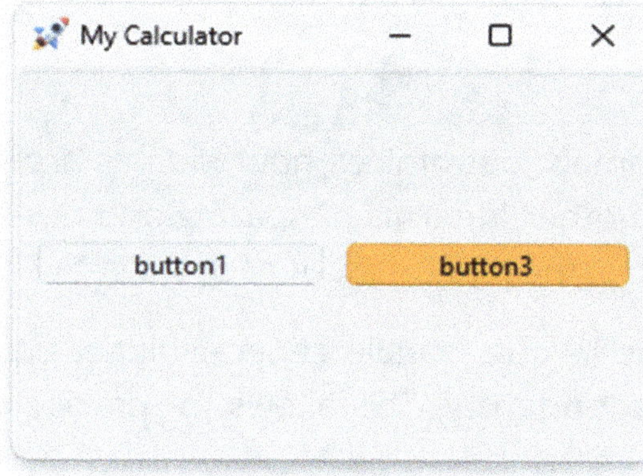

setSpacing(int)

Sets the space between widgets.

</> Python

```python
lay = QHBoxLayout( )
lay.setSpacingt(50)
```

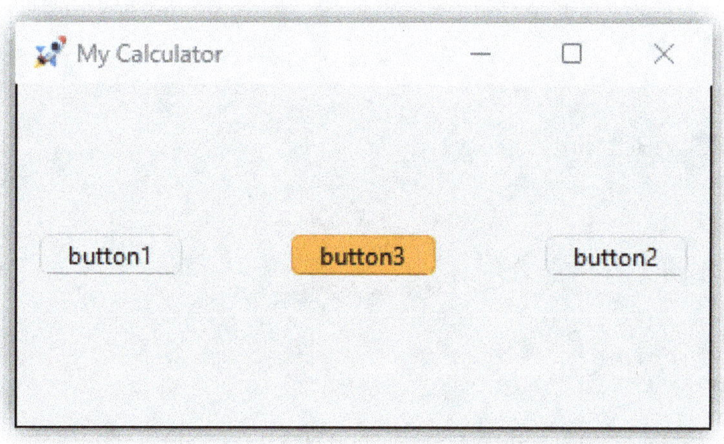

Alignment

Alignment determines how widgets are positioned within a layout and how they relate to each other in terms of spacing and orientation. In PyQt, layouts use alignment settings to control the placement of each widget within its layout cell or area.

While layouts handle general widget organization, individual widgets can also be **aligned independently**. This allows for precise control over the appearance and structure of the user interface.

By default, PyQt aligns widgets to the **center** within their layout space. However, developers can override this using predefined alignment flags provided by the Qt.AlignmentFlag class.

Common Alignment Flags

AlignCenter	AlignJustify	AlignHCenter	AlignBottom	AlignBaseline
AlignLeft	AlignLeading	AlignHorizontal_Mask	AlignTop	AlignAbsolute
AlignRight	AlignTrailing	AlignVCenter	AlignVertical_Mask	

setAlignment(Qt.AlignmentFlag **)**

Sets the alignment of widgets.

</> Python

```
lay = QHBoxLayout( )
lay.setAlignment(Qt.AlignmentFlag.AlignBottom)
```

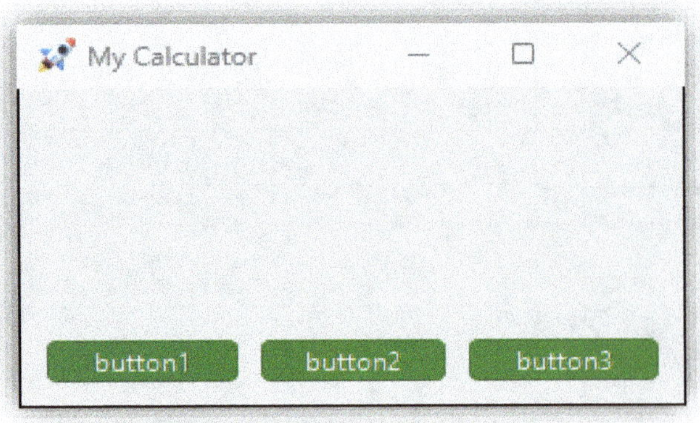

QVBoxLayout

Arranges widgets vertically (top to bottom).

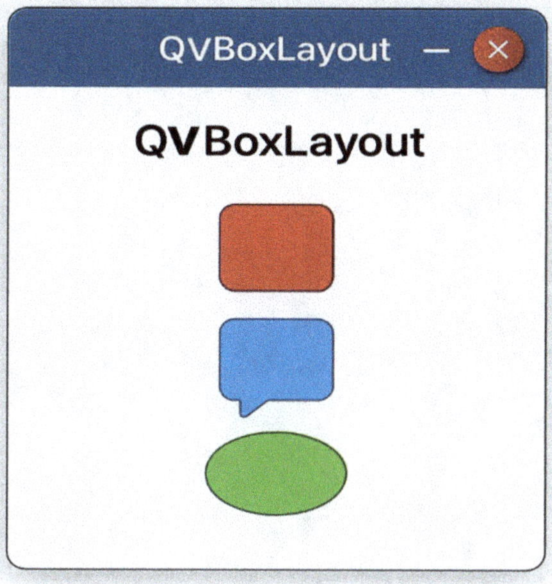

Figure 5.2 : QVBoxLayout structure

addWidget(widget)

Adds a widget to the layout.

```
layout = QVBoxLayout()
layout.addWidget( widget1 )
layout.addWidget( widget2 )
layout.addWidget( widget3 )
```

Example 1

</> Python

```
import sys
from PyQt6.QtWidgets import *

class MyApp(QMainWindow):
    def __init__(self):
        super().__init__()

        self.setWindowTitle("My Calculator")
        self.setProperty("setGeometry", (100, 100, 400, 200))
        self.setStyleSheet("background:#ebebeb")

        self.mainPage = QWidget()
        self.setCentralWidget(self.mainPage)                    #Setting central widget

        self.vlay = QVBoxLayout()
        self.mainPage.setLayout(self.vlay)                      #Setting central widget layout

        self.vlay.addWidget(QPushButton("button1"))             #Adding children to layout
        self.vlay.addWidget(QPushButton("button2"))
        self.vlay.addWidget(QPushButton("button3"))

app = QApplication(sys.argv)
window = MyApp()
window.show()
sys.exit(app.exec())
```

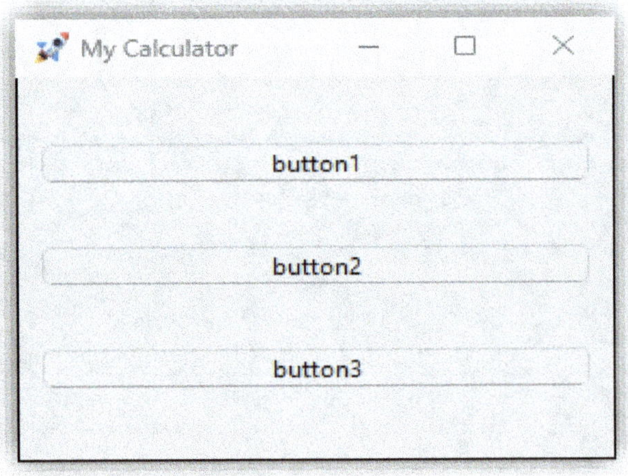

Example 2

</> Python

```python
import sys
from PyQt6.QtWidgets import *

class MyApp(QMainWindow):
    def __init__(self):
        super().__init__()

        self.setWindowTitle("My Calculator")
        self.setProperty("setGeometry", (100, 100, 400, 200))
        self.setStyleSheet("background:#ebebeb")

        self.main = QWidget()
        self.setCentralWidget(self.main)

        self.mainLay = QHBoxLayout()
        self.main.setLayout(self.mainLay)

        self.frame1 = QFrame()
        self.frame2 = QFrame()
        self.mainLay.addWidget(self.frame1, stretch=4)
        self.mainLay.addWidget(self.frame2, stretch=10)

        self.frame1Lay = QVBoxLayout()
        self.frame1.setLayout(self.frame1Lay)
        self.frame1.setStyleSheet("background:teal;")

        self.dashboard = QPushButton("Dashboard")
        self.dashboard.resize(100, 20)
        self.dashboard.setSizePolicy(QSizePolicy.Policy.Expanding,QSizePolicy.Policy.Expanding )
        self.dashboard.setStyleSheet("background:#F0F0F0")
        self.frame1Lay.addWidget(self.dashboard, stretch=1)

        self.food = QPushButton("Food")
        self.food.resize(100, 20)
        self.food.setSizePolicy(QSizePolicy.Policy.Expanding, QSizePolicy.Policy.Expanding )
        self.food.setStyleSheet("background:#F0F0F0")
        self.frame1Lay.addWidget(self.food, stretch=1)

        self.cocktail = QPushButton("Cocktail")
        self.cocktail.resize(100, 20)
        self.cocktail.setSizePolicy(QSizePolicy.Policy.Expanding,QSizePolicy.Policy.Expanding )
        self.cocktail.setStyleSheet("background:#F0F0F0")
        self.frame1Lay.addWidget(self.cocktail, stretch=1)
```

```
        self.frame2Lay = QHBoxLayout()
        self.frame2.setLayout(self.frame2Lay)
        self.frame2.setStyleSheet("background: teal;")

        self.labelBurger = QLabel()
        self.labelBurger.setPixmap(QPixmap("burg.jpg"))
        self.frame2Lay.addWidget(self.labelBurger)

        self.labelSalad = QLabel()
        self.labelSalad.setPixmap(QPixmap("salad.jpg"))
        self.frame2Lay.addWidget(self.labelSalad)

        self.labelPizza = QLabel()
        self.labelPizza.setPixmap(QPixmap("pizza.jpg"))
        self.frame2Lay.addWidget(self.labelPizza)


app = QApplication(sys.argv)
window = MyApp()
window.show()
sys.exit(app.exec())
```

replaceWidget(old, new **)**

Replaces one widget with another.

```
</> Python

vlay = QVBoxLayout( )

button4 = QPushButton("button4")
button4.setStyleSheet("background:blue; color:white")

lay.replaceWidget(button2, button4)
```

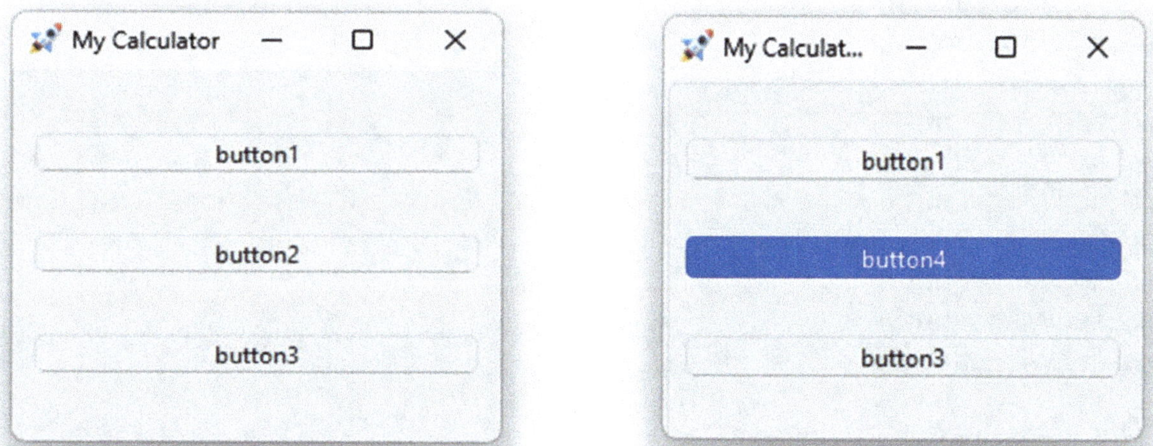

takeAt(index **)**

Removes and returns the layout item at the index.

```
</> Python

lay = QVBoxLayout( )
lay.takeAt( 2 )
```

addLayout(layout)

Nests another layout inside the current one.

```python
lay = QVBoxLayout( )

but1 = QPushButton("button1")
but2 = QPushButton("button2")
but3 = QPushButton("button3")
but4 = QPushButton("button4")
but5 = QPushButton("button5")
but6 = QPushButton("button6")

hbox1 = QHBoxLayout()
hbox2 = QHBoxLayout()

hbox1.addWidget(but1)
hbox1.addWidget(but2)
hbox1.addWidget(but3)

hbox2.addWidget(but4)
hbox2.addWidget(but5)
hbox2.addWidget(but6)

lay.addLayout(hbox1)        #Adding layout to main layout
lay.addLayout(hbox2)
```

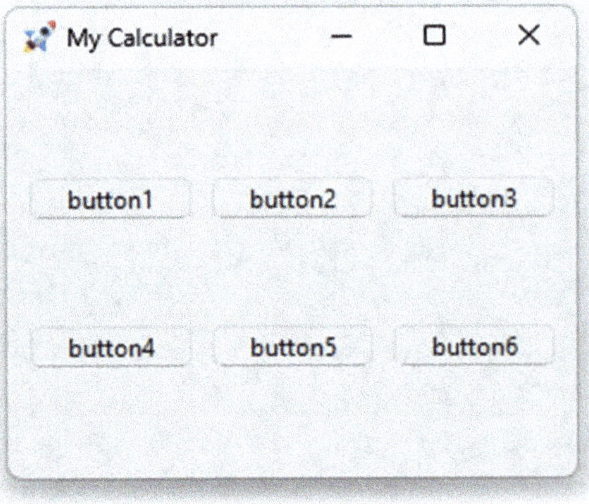

setContentMargins(left, top, right, bottom **)**

Creates a space between the items and its boundary.

```python
lay = QVBoxLayout( )
lay.setContentMargins(30, 50, 30, 50)
```

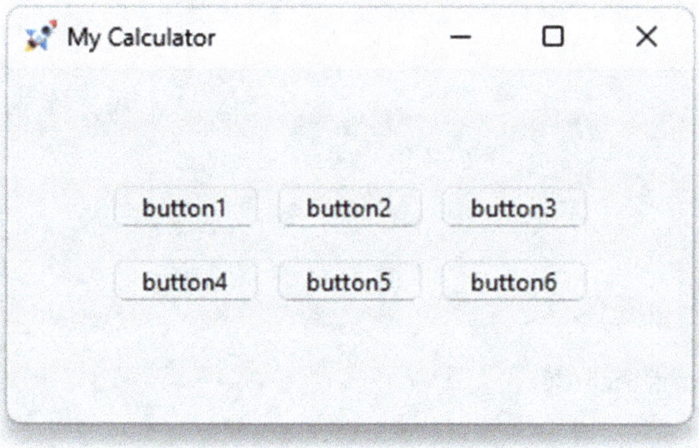

setDirection(QBoxLayout.Direction **)**

Sets horizontal or vertical layout direction. The various directions include

Up	LeftToRight	TopToBottom
Down	RightToLeft	BottomToTop

```python
lay = QVBoxLayout( )
lay.setDirection(QBoxLayout.Direction.BottomToTop)
```

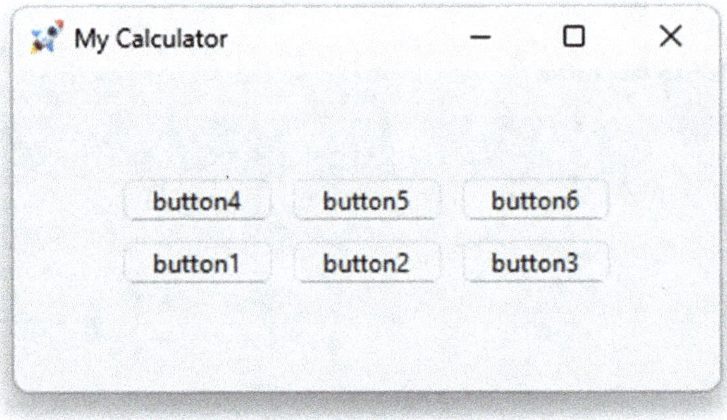

setSizeConstraints(QLayout.SizeConstraint **)**

Controls layout resizing behavior. Options include:

- SetDefaultConstraint
- SetFixedSize
- SetMinimumSize
- SetMaximumSize
- SetNoConstraint

</> **Python**

```
lay = QVBoxLayout( )
lay.setSizeConstraint(QLayout.SizeConstraint.SetFixedSize)
```

QGridLayout

Organizes widgets in a grid (rows and columns).

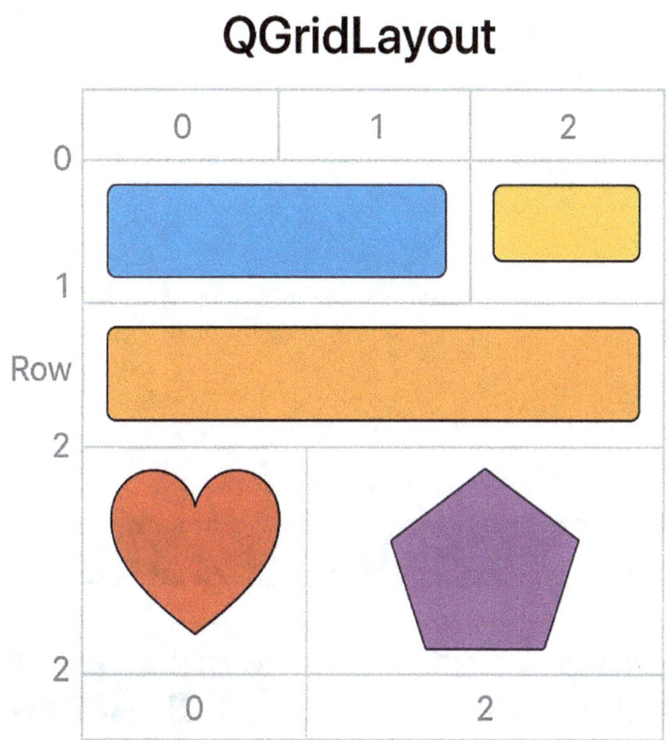

Figure 5.3 : QGridLayout structure

Key Properties and Methods

setVerticalSpacing	setColumnMinimumWidth	cellRect	setHorizontalSpacing
horizontalSpacing	setDefaultPositioning	getItemPosition	setRowStretch
columnCount	columnMinimumWidth	rowCount	rowMinimumHeight
verticalSpacing	setColumnStretch	setOriginCorner	rowStretch
originCorner	setRowMinimumHeight	columnStretch	itemAtPosition

addWidget(widget, row, column)

Adds a widget to the layout by specifying row (int) and column (int).

```
lay = QGridLayout( )
lay.addWidget( widgetA, 0, 0 )          #First row and first column
lay.addWidget( widgetB, 0, 1 )          #First row and second column
lay.addWidget( widgetC, 1, 2 )          #Second row and third column
lay.addWidget( widgetD, 2, 2, 2,4  )    #Spans 1 row and 4 columns
```

Example

Layout Structure

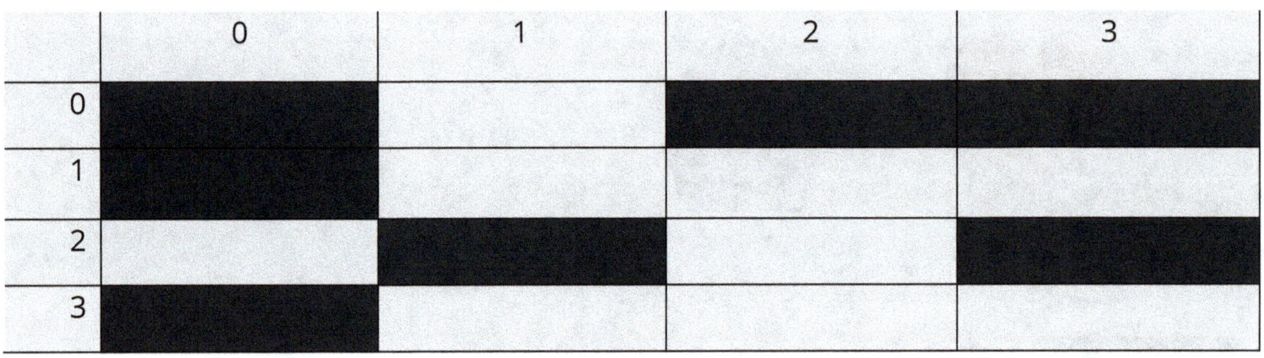

</> Python

```
import sys
from PyQt6.QtWidgets import *

class MyApp(QMainWindow):
   def __init__(self):
       super().__init__()
       self.setWindowTitle("My Calculator")
       self.setProperty("setGeometry", (100, 100, 400, 200))
       self.setStyleSheet("background:#ebebeb")

       self.mainPage = QWidget()
       self.setCentralWidget(self.mainPage)            #Setting central widget
```

```
        self.grid = QGridLayout()
        self.mainPage.setLayout(self.grid)                    #Setting central widget layout

        self.butA = QPushButton("button1")
        self.butB = QPushButton("button2")
        self.butC = QPushButton("button3")
        self.butD = QPushButton("button4")
        self.butE = QPushButton("button5")
        self.butF = QPushButton("button6")
        self.butG = QPushButton("button7")

        self.grid.addWidget(self.butA, 0, 0)
        self.grid.addWidget(self.butB, 1, 0)
        self.grid.addWidget(self.butC, 3, 0)
        self.grid.addWidget(self.butD, 2, 1)
        self.grid.addWidget(self.butE, 0, 2)
        self.grid.addWidget(self.butF, 0, 3)
        self.grid.addWidget(self.butG, 2, 3)

app = QApplication(sys.argv)
window = MyApp()
window.show()
sys.exit(app.exec())
```

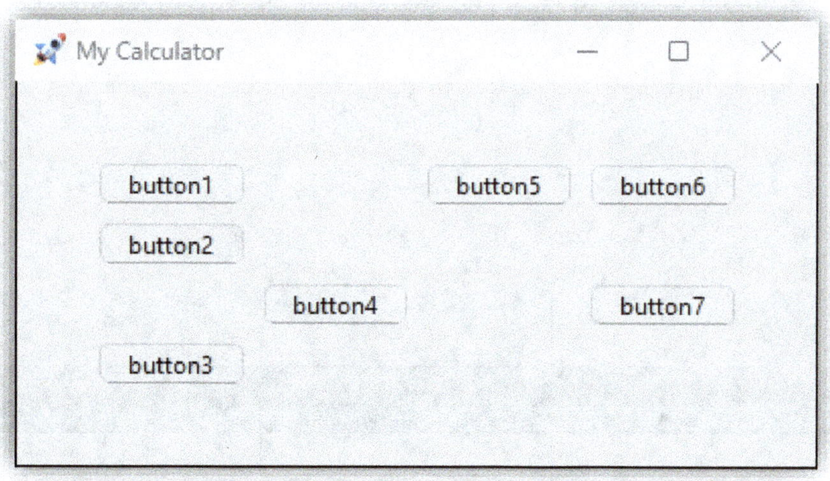

Spanning

In PyQt's QGridLayout, widgets are normally placed in a single cell defined by a specific row and column. However, in certain design cases, you may want a widget to **span across multiple rows or columns** — for example, to create a larger area for a label, text box, or button.

This is known as **spanning**, and it allows a widget to occupy more space in the layout grid.

Syntax

```
layout.addWidget( widget, row, column, rowSpan, columnSpan )
```

Parameters:

- widget: The widget you want to add.
- row: The starting row index (zero-based).
- column: The starting column index.
- rowSpan: How many **rows** the widget should span (default is 1).
- columnSpan: How many **columns** the widget should span (default is 1).

Example

Layout Structure

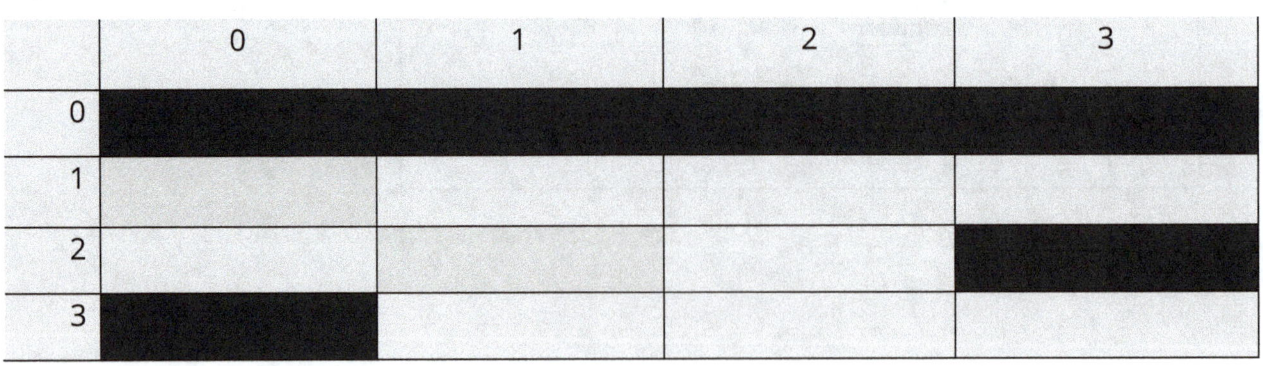

```
</> Python
import sys
from PyQt6.QtWidgets import *

class MyApp(QMainWindow):
    def __init__(self):
        super().__init__()
        self.setWindowTitle("My Calculator")
        self.setProperty("setGeometry", (100, 100, 400, 200))
        self.setStyleSheet("background:#ebebeb")

        self.mainPage = QWidget()
        self.setCentralWidget(self.mainPage)            #Setting central widget

        self.grid = QGridLayout()
        self.mainPage.setLayout(self.vlay)              #Setting central widget layout

        self.butA = QPushButton("button1")
        self.butB = QPushButton("button2")
        self.butC = QPushButton("button3")

        self.grid.addWidget(self.butA, 0,  0, 0, 3)     #spanning  1row and 3 column
        self.grid.addWidget(self.butB, 3,  0)
        self.grid.addWidget(self.butC, 2,  2)

app = QApplication(sys.argv)
window = MyApp()
window.show()
sys.exit(app.exec())
```

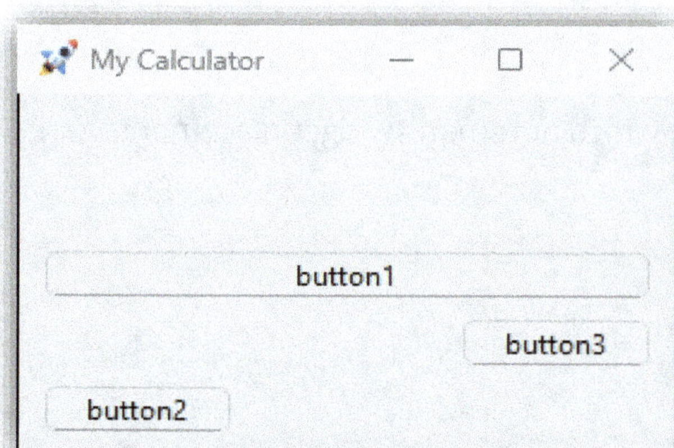

setHorizontalSpacing(int)

Sets the **horizontal** space (in pixels) between columns in the layout.

```python
lay = QGridLayout( )
lay.setHorizontalSpacing(34)
```

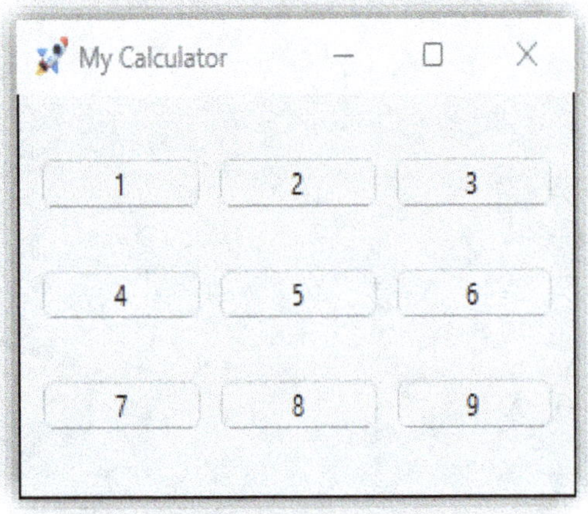

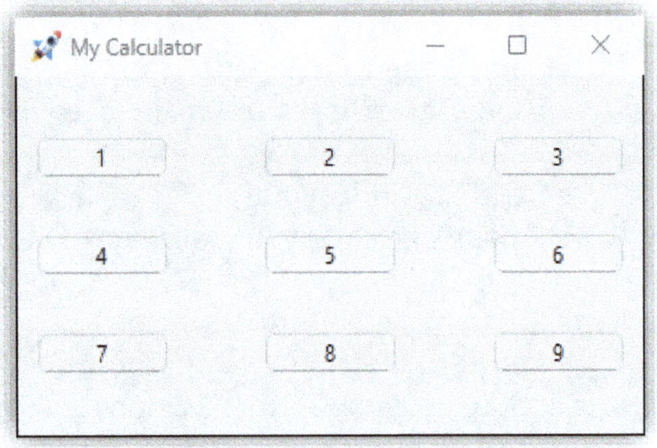

setVerticalSpacing(int)
Sets the **vertical** space between rows.

horizontalSpacing(int)
Returns the current **horizontal spacing** between columns.

setDefaultPositioning(row, column)
Sets a **default** row and column position from which automatic widget placements can begin (rarely used manually).

rowCount( )
Returns the **number of rows** in the grid layout.

setColumnStretch(int column, int stretch **)**
Sets the **stretch factor** for a column, affecting how it expands relative to other columns. Higher values stretch more.

</> Python

```python
lay = QGridLayout( )
lay.setColumnStretch(0, 20)
lay.setColumnStretch(1, 30)
lay.setColumnStretch(2, 50)
```

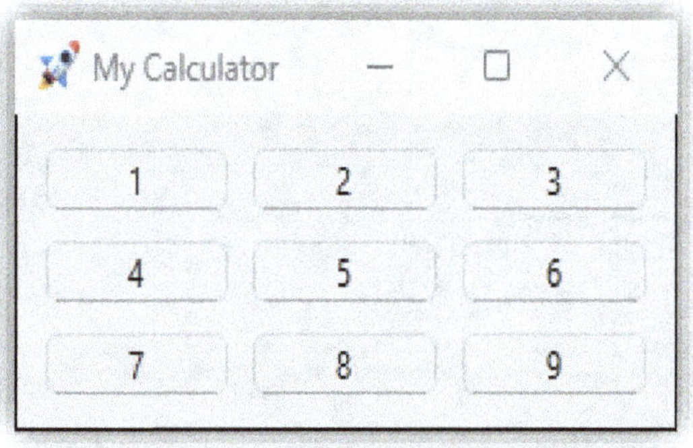

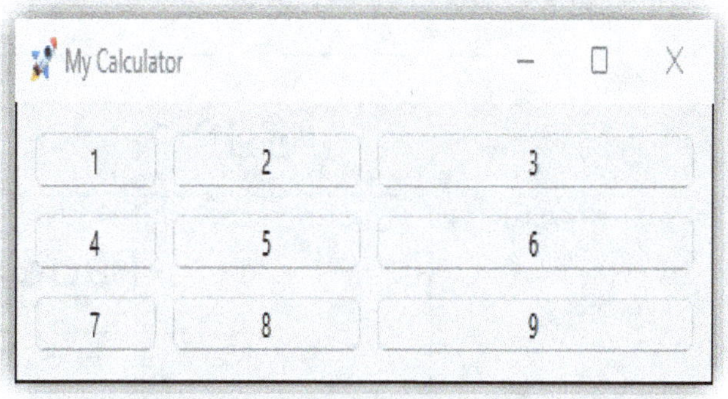

columnStretch(int column**)**
Returns the **stretch factor** of a given column.

setRowStretch(int row, int stretch **)**
Sets the **stretch factor** for a row.

setColumnMinimumWidth(int column, int minWidth**)**
Sets the **minimum width** for a column in pixels.

setRowMinimumHeight(int row, int minHeight**)**
Sets the **minimum height** for a specific row.

rowMinimumHeight(int**)**
Returns the **minimum height** of a row.

QStackedLayout

Displays only one widget at a time, like a deck of cards. At any given time, only **one widget is visible,** and the others are hidden. This is useful for implementing **tab interfaces**, **wizard pages** or **multi-step forms**.

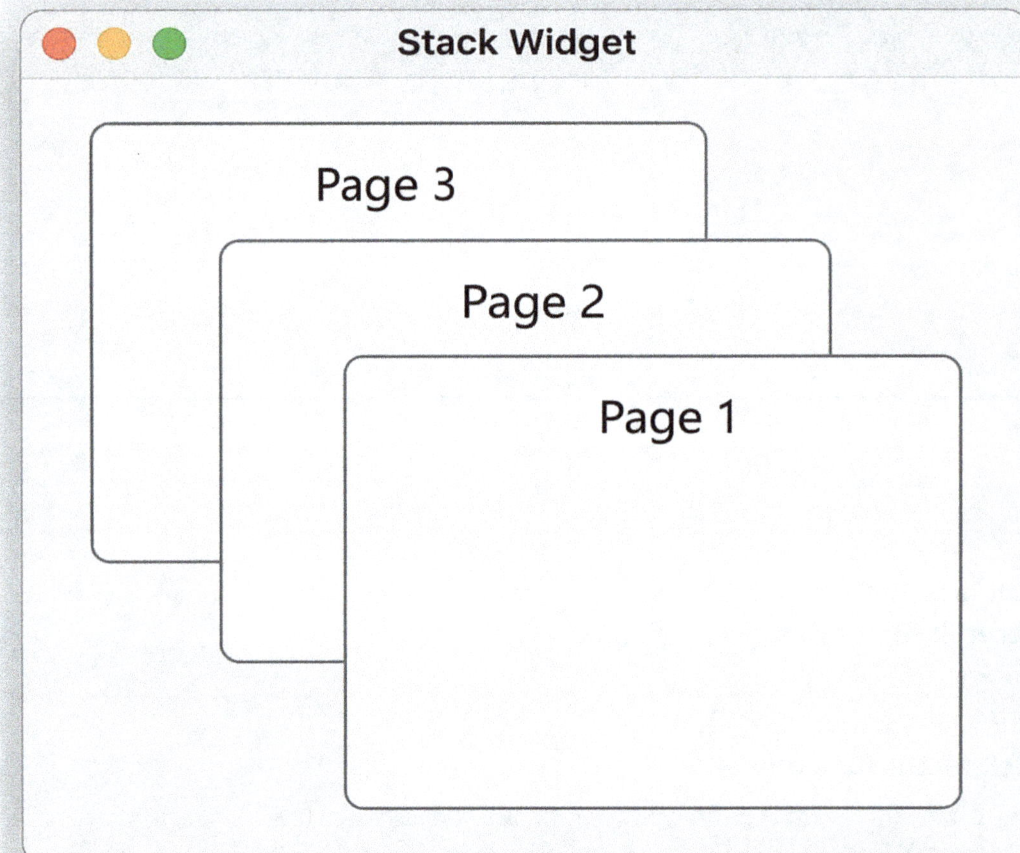

Figure 5.4 : Stack Layout structure

Key Properties and Methods

currentChanged	StackingMode	currentWidget	setCurrentWidget
setCurrentIndex	stackingMode	widgetRemoved	currentIndex
setStackingMode			

setCurrentIndex(int index**)**

Makes the widget at the specified index visible. Widget becomes the topmost child.

```python
import sys
from PyQt6.QtWidgets import *

class MyApp(QMainWindow):
    def __init__(self):
        super().__init__()
        self.setWindowTitle("My Calculator")
        self.setProperty("setGeometry", (100, 100, 400, 200))
        self.setStyleSheet("background:#ebebeb")

        self.mainPage = QWidget()
        self.setCentralWidget(self.mainPage)              #Setting central widget

        self.stack = QStackedLayout()
        self.mainPage.setLayout(self.stack)               #Setting central widget layout

        self.page1 = QWidget()                            #Creating pages
        self.page1.setStyleSheet("background: #b1bde2")
        self.stack.addWidget(self.page1)

        self.page2 = QWidget()
        self.page2.setStyleSheet("background: #78A6C9")
        self.stack.addWidget(self.page2)

        self.page3 = QWidget()
        self.page3.setStyleSheet("background: #908CA4")
        self.stack.addWidget(self.page3)

        self.butA = QPushButton("Go to Page 2", self.page1)
        self.butB = QPushButton("Go to Page 3", self.page2)
        self.butC = QPushButton("Go to Page 1", self.page3)
```

```
        #Functions to change pages
        self.butA.clicked.connect(lambda: self.stack.setCurrentIndex(1))
        self.butB.clicked.connect(lambda: self.stack.setCurrentIndex(2))
        self.butC.clicked.connect(lambda: self.stack.setCurrentIndex(0))

app = QApplication(sys.argv)
window = MyApp()
window.show()
sys.exit(app.exec())
```

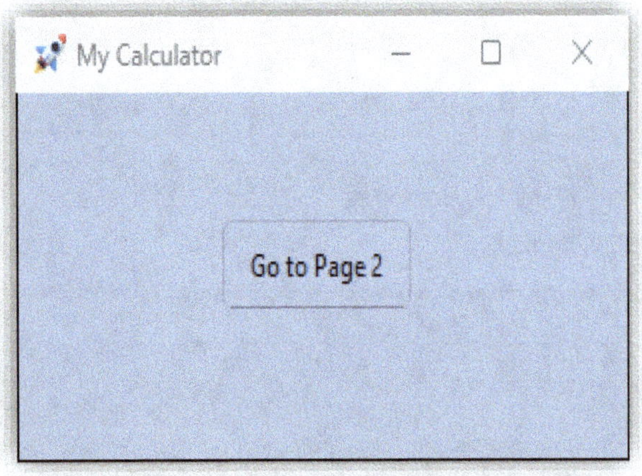

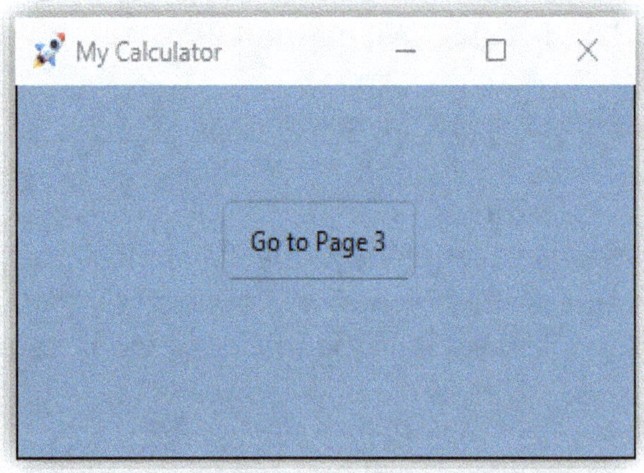

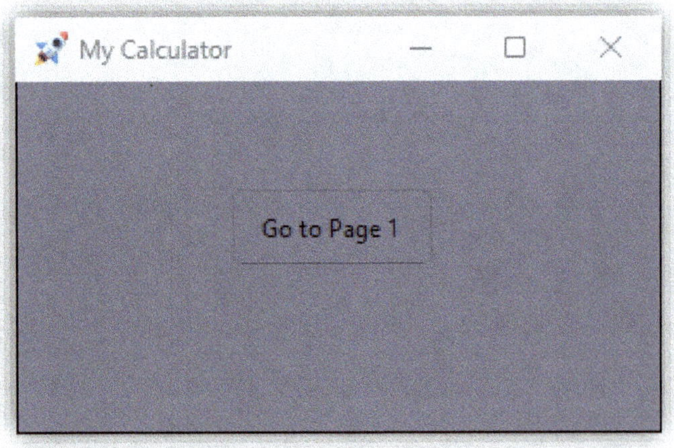

currentIndex()
Returns the index (position) of the currently visible widget. Index starts at **0** for the first widget added.

currentWidget()
Returns the actual widget (not just the index) that is currently visible in the layout.

setCurrentWidget(QWidget)
Sets the given widget as the current visible widget (instead of using its index).

currentChanged
Signal that is emitted when the current visible widget changes (i.e., a different page is shown). Useful for triggering actions when the user navigates between widgets.

</> Python

```python
lay = QStackedLayout( )
lay.currentChanged.connect(yourFunction)
```

setStackingMode(QStackedLayout.StackingMode)
Defines how widgets are stacked. There are two modes:
StackOne (default): Only the current widget is visible.
StackAll: All widgets are visible and stacked on top of each other (rarely used).

</> Python

```python
lay = QStackedLayout( )
lay.setStackingMode(QStackedLayout.StackingMode.StackAll)
```

stackingMode()
Returns the current stacking mode of the layout.

Use of QBoxLayout and QLayout

Both QBoxLayout and QLayout serve as **base layout classes** in PyQt. These classes are **not used directly** to arrange widgets in a window like QVBoxLayout, QHBoxLayout, or QGridLayout. Instead, they are typically **used indirectly** by being passed into higher-level layout containers through methods such as:

```
layout = QVBoxLayout()
box = QBoxLayout()
layout.addWidget(box)
```

This means that to use QBoxLayout, you typically instantiate a subclass like QHBoxLayout or QVBoxLayout.

Size Behavior of Widgets in Layouts

When widgets are added to a layout using *addWidget()*, the layout system takes full control of their positioning and sizing. As a result:

- Manual sizing with methods like **resize()** or **setGeometry()** has no effect.
- The layout adjusts the widget size automatically based on available space and layout rules.

Enforcing Widget Size Control with setSizePolicy()

To influence how a widget behaves when the parent window is resized, PyQt provides the *setSizePolicy()* method:

```
widget.setSizePolicy(horizontal QSizePolicy, vertical QSizePolicy)
```

horizontalPolicy(QSizePoliy.Policy.Fixed): defines how the widget behaves horizontally.
verticalPolicy(QSizePoliy.Policy.Fixed): defines how the widget behaves vertically.

Common QSizePolicy Flags

Flag	Behavior
Fixed	The widget keeps a constant size. It neither expands nor shrinks.

Minimum	The widget keeps at least its minimum size and may shrink if needed.
Maximum	The widget can grow but not below its preferred size.
Preferred	The widget prefers its size hint but may grow or shrink.
Expanding	The widget expands to fill the available space.
MinimumExpanding	The widget will expand but prioritize its minimum size.
Ignored	The widget ignores the size hint and layout constraints.

Table: 5.1 – Size Policy flags

Tips

setSizePolicy() is essential when you want widgets to behave independently of the layout's default resizing rules.
Combining setSizePolicy() with spacers or stretch factors can help you design responsive and dynamic interfaces.

QLabel

QLabel is a widget used to display **text**, **images**, or **both** on the interface. It is commonly used for **labels**, **titles**, **descriptions**, or **static information** that the user doesn't interact with directly. A *QLabel* can also render HTML content and can be customized with font styles, colors, and alignment.

It is a versatile widget that serves as a visual output element in GUIs and plays a vital role in designing clean and informative user interfaces.

Key Properties and Methods

setMidLineWidth	setFrameShape	setTextInteractionFlags	setAlignment
frameShadow	setFrameShadow	Shadow	setFrameStyle
setResourceProvider	setPixmap	movie	frameShape
setOpenExternalLinks	selectionStart	setPicture	hasSelectedText
setLineWidth	wordWrap	textFormat	buddy
drawFrame	setIndent	linkActivated	alignment
setMovie	setTextFormat	frameWidth	indent
frameRect	setMargin	Shape	initStyleOption
hasScaledContents	setFrameRect	margin	frameStyle
pixmap	setNum	setScaledContents	picture
linkHovered	StyleMask	setWordWrap	resourceProvider
textInteractionFlags	setText	clear	openExternalLinks
midLineWidth	setSelection	lineWidth	setBuddy
selectedText	text		

Tips

To discover the complete list of available properties, methods, and attributes of the QLabel class in PyQt, you can use Python's built-in dir() function.

```
>>> from PyQt5.QtWidgets import QLabel
>>> print(dir(QLabel))
.....[ ]
```

setText(text) and text()

The setText() sets the label text and text() returns the current label text.

Example,

```python
import sys
from PyQt6.QtWidgets import *

class MyApp(QMainWindow):
    def __init__(self):
        super().__init__()

        self.setWindowTitle("My Calculator")
        self.setProperty("setGeometry", (100, 100, 400, 200))
        self.setStyleSheet("background:#ebebeb")

        text = '''
         <h2 style="color:red">The Coder's Joy</h2>
          The best feeling in the world is sipping your coffee alone<br>
          in your quiet room while cracking code.<br>
          Others may call it boredom — but I call it freedom.<br><br>

          Coding is life.<br>
          Keep cracking.
        '''
        self.label = QLabel(self)

        self.label.setText(text)
        self.label.setGeometry(50,20, 350, 150)
        self.label.setMargin(5)


app = QApplication(sys.argv)
window = MyApp()
window.show()
sys.exit(app.exec())
```

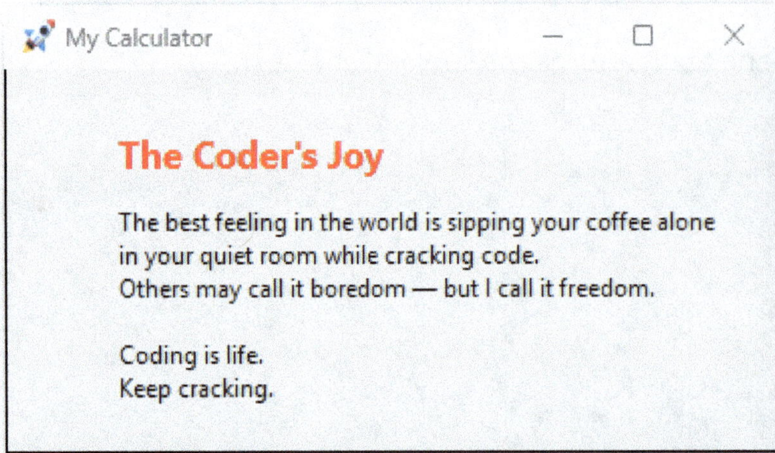

setMargin(int) and margin()

The setMargin() sets the margin around the contents and margin() returns the margin size.

</> Python

```
label = QLabel( )
label.setMargin(20)

label.setStyleSheet("border: 2px solid green; border-radius:50px")
```

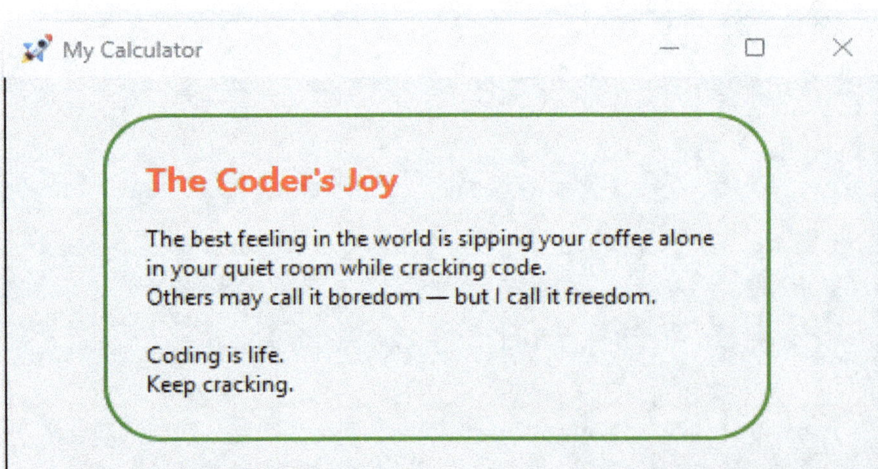

setAlignment(Qt.AlignmentFlag) and **alignment()**
Sets the horizontal and vertical alignment of text or content and get the current alignment.

</> Python

```
label = QLabel( )
label.setAlignment(Qt.AlignmentFlag.AlignRight)

label.setStyleSheet("background:#0e121A;color:white; border-radius:50px")
```

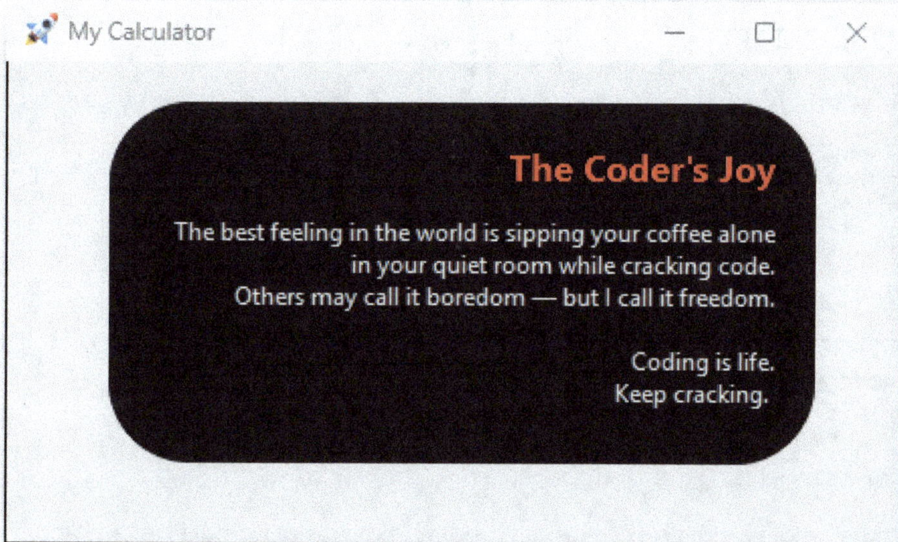

Alignment Flags

AlignCenter	AlignJustify	AlignHCenter	AlignBottom	AlignBaseline
AlignLeft	AlignLeading	AlignHorizontal_Mask	AlignTop	AlignAbsolute
AlignRight	AlignTrailing	AlignVCenter	AlignVertical_Mask	

clear()
Clears all text and content from the label.

setFrameShape(QFrame.Shape) and **frameShape()**

Sets the frame's shape and returns the current frame shape.

```python
label = QLabel( )
label.setFrameShape(QFrame.Shape.WinPanel)
```

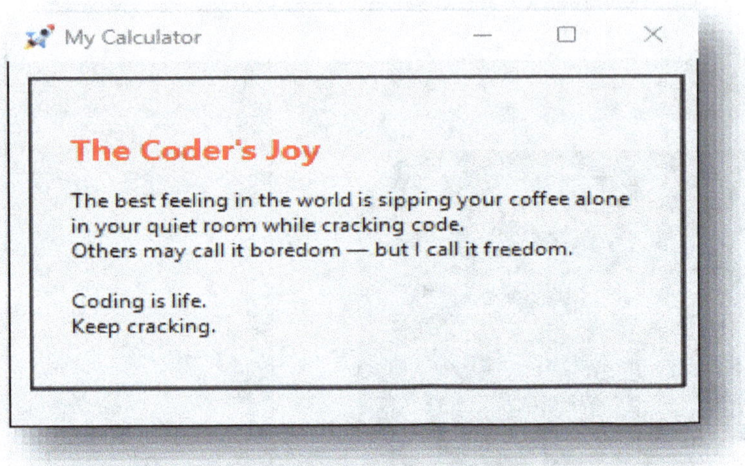

QFrame Shapes

NoFrame	No visible border
Box	A simple rectangular box
Panel	A raised or sunken panel (often used for grouping)
WinPanel	A Window style panel
StyledPanel	A panel with the look based on the current style.
HLine	A horizontal line (great for separators)
VLine	A vertical line (for vertical separation)

Table: 5.2 – Some Frame shapes

setFrameShadow(QFrame.Shadow) and **frameShadow()**

Sets the frame's shadow type and returns the current shadow type of the frame. Frame shadow is mostly visible when the frame shape is set. The frame shadows are ***Raised***, ***Sunken*** and ***Plain***

</> Python

```
label = QLabel( )
label.setFrameShape(QFrame.Shape.Panel)
label.setFrameShadow(QFrame.Shadow.Raised)
```

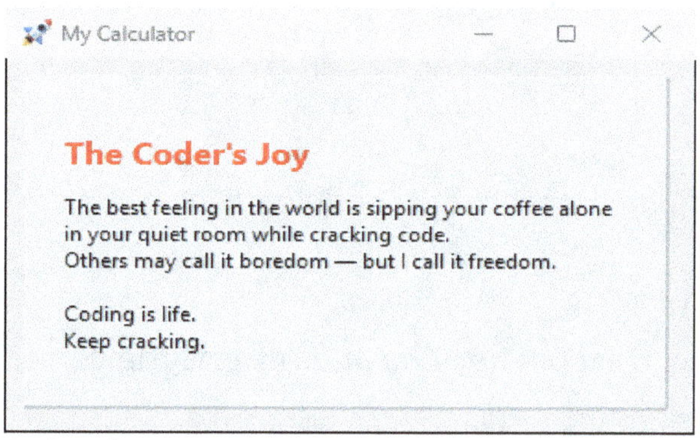

Raised

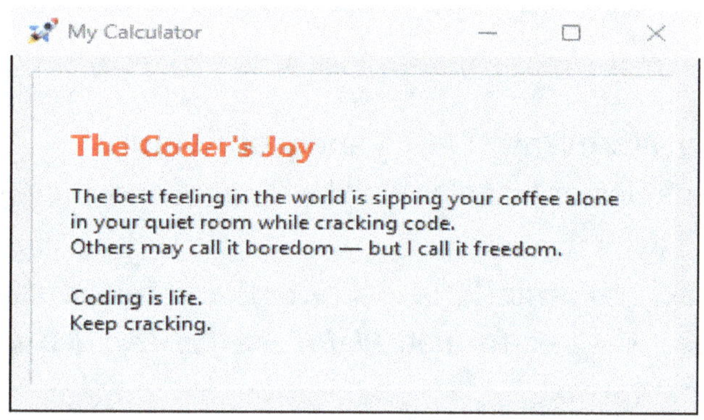

Sunken

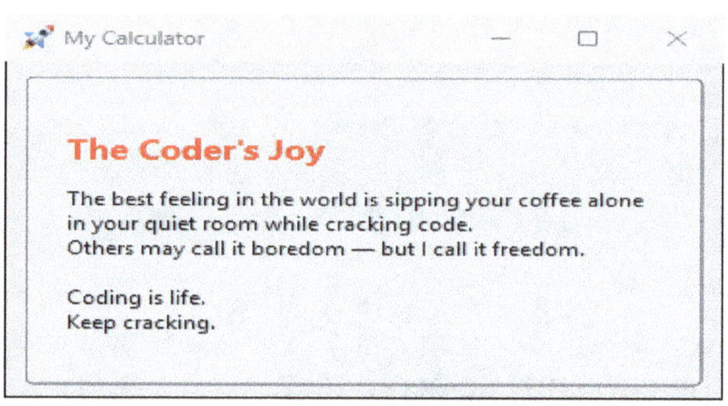

Plain

Raised

Sunken

Plain

setFrameStyle(int) and **frameStyle()**

Sets the frame style using a combination of *QFrame.Shape* and *QFrame.Shadow* and Returns the current frame style as an integer.

</> Python

```
label = QLabel( )
label.setFrameStyle(2)
```

setWordWrap(bool) and **wordWrap()**

Enables or disables word wrapping and checks if word wrapping is enabled.

setTextFormat(Qt.TextFormat) and **textFormat()**

Sets the text format: ***PlainText***, ***RichText***, ***MarkdownText*** or ***AutoText*** and returns the current text format.

</> Python

```
label = QLabel( )
label.setTextFormat(Qt.TextFormat.RichText)
```

setSelection(start, length) and **selectedText()**

Selects a substring of the label text and returns the currently selected text.

</> Python

```
label = QLabel("Coding is life, creativity is fun", parent )
label.setSelection(7, 20)
text = label.selectedText()

print(text)
```

selectionStart()

Returns the index of the selected text start.

hasSelectedText()
Returns whether any text is selected.

setNum(number)
Sets the label text as a stringified number.

setPixmap(QPixmap()) and pixmap()
The *setPixmap()* sets a raster image for the label and *pixmap()* returns the current QPixmap image set in the label.

```python
label = QLabel( )
label.setPixmap(QPixmap("rockect_launch.jpg"))
```

setMovie(QMovie)
Sets a movie (GIF or other animated format) to be displayed in the label.

movie()
Returns the current QMovie assigned to the label.

QFrame

The QFrame widget acts as a **container** that can hold and organize other widgets within it. It is commonly used to visually group related elements together or to create structured layouts. A QFrame can have different **frame styles**, **shapes** and **shadow effects** to improve the appearance and separation of UI components. It is a module of the QtWidgets class.

Key Features:

- ❖ Acts as a parent container for other widgets.
- ❖ Can be styled with different frames and shadows.
- ❖ Useful for creating sections or bordered areas within a window.
- ❖ Supports customization through properties like frameShape, *frameShadow*, *linewidth* and *midLineWidth*.
- ❖ Can be enhanced with CSS for more advanced styling.

Key Properties and Methods

frameRect	StyleMask	frameShadow	setFrameShape
frameShape	drawFrame	setLineWidth	setFrameShadow
initStyleOption	Shadow	setFrameRect	setMidLineWidth
frameWidth	frameStyle	midLineWidth	setFrameStyle
linewidth	Shape	setlayout	

setLayout(layout)

Assigns a layout manager (like QVBoxLayout, QHBoxLayout, etc.) to the frame. This is necessary for adding child widgets inside the frame in a structured way.

Example 1

</> Python

```python
import sys
from PyQt6.QtWidgets import *

class MyApp(QMainWindow):
    def __init__(self):
        super().__init__()

        self.setWindowTitle("My Calculator")
        self.setProperty("setGeometry", (100, 100, 400, 200))
        self.setStyleSheet("background:#ebebeb")

        self.frame = QFrame(self)
        self.frame.setGeometry(10, 10, 400, 480)
        self.frame.setStyleSheet("background:#24252b;border-radius:10px")

        self.box = QVBoxLayout()
        self.frame.setLayout(self.box)

        self.pizza = QLabel()
        self.pizza.setPixmap(QPixmap("pizzaimg.jpg"))
        self.pizza.resize(400,200)
        self.box.addWidget(self.pizza)

        self.pizzaTitle = QLabel(
         '''<h1 style='color:orange'><b>
        🍕 Chicago Deep-Dish Pizza</b></h1>
         <p><b style='color:green'><h4>Tasty in flamming hot</h4></b>
         Stacks of    Cheese, Rivers of Sauce,
         and a Crust That Bites Back<br>This Is Deep-Dish Done Right!"</p>
         ''')
        self.pizzaTitle.resize(400,200)
        self.pizzaTitle.setStyleSheet("color:white")
        self.box.addWidget(self.pizzaTitle)

        self.button = QPushButton("Order now")
        self.button.resize(100, 40)
        self.button.setSizePolicy(QSizePolicy.Policy.Expanding,QSizePolicy.Policy.Expanding)
        self.button.setStyleSheet("background:#6693EB; color:white;font-size:20px")
        self.box.addWidget(self.button)
```

```
app = QApplication(sys.argv)
window = MyApp()
window.show()
sys.exit(app.exec())
```

Example 2

</> Python

```
import sys
from PyQt6.QtWidgets import *

class MyApp(QMainWindow):
    def __init__(self):
        super().__init__()

        self.setWindowTitle("My Calculator")
        self.setProperty("setGeometry", (100, 100, 400, 200))
        self.setStyleSheet("background:#ebebeb")

        self.container1 = QFrame(self)
        self.container1.setGeometry(10,10, 150, 150)
        self.container1.setContentsMargins(20,20,20,20)
        self.container1.setStyleSheet('''
                background:#0C3B2E; border-radius:2px; border:5px solid tomato
                ''')
        self.container2 = QFrame(self)
        self.container2.setGeometry(170,10, 150, 150)
        self.container2.setStyleSheet('''
                background:#F7C846; border-radius:75px; border:5px dotted tomato''')

        self.container3 = QFrame(self)
        self.container3.setGeometry(330,10, 150, 150)
        self.container3.setStyleSheet('''
                background:#8AE98D; border-radius:30px; border:5px dashed tomato''')

        self.label1 = QLabel("<h4>Deep green</h4>", self.container1)
        self.label1.setGeometry(40,50,100,50)
        self.label1.setStyleSheet("color:white;border:0px")

        self.label2 = QLabel("<h4>Yellow</h4>", self.container2)
        self.label2.setGeometry(40,50,100,50)
        self.label2.setStyleSheet("color:black;border:0px")

        self.label3 = QLabel("<h4>Lemon green</h4>", self.container3)
        self.label3.setGeometry(40,50,100,50)
        self.label3.setStyleSheet("color:black;border:0px")

app = QApplication(sys.argv)
window = MyApp()
window.show()
sys.exit(app.exec())
```

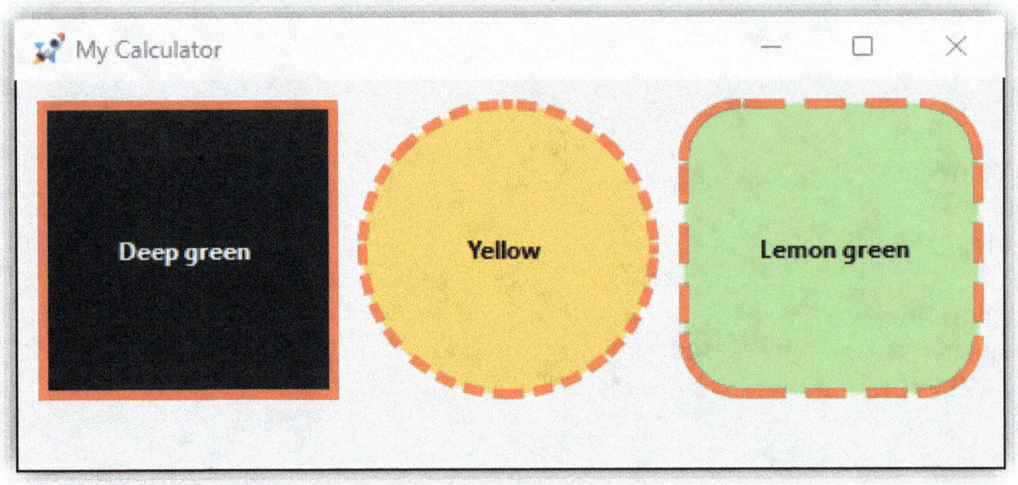

setFrameRect(QRect(int aleft, int atop, int awidth, int aheight **))**

Sets the rectangle area that defines where the frame's content will be drawn.

```python
frame = QFrame( )
frame.setFrameRect(QRect(30,50, 200, 300))
```

frameRect( )

Returns a ***QRect*** representing the internal rectangle (excluding the frame's borders) used to draw the frame's content.

```python
frame = QFrame( )
rect = frame.frameRect()
```

setFrameShape(QFrame.Shape)

Sets the shape of the frame using one of the predefined *QFrame.Shape* enums.

</> Python

```python
frame = QFrame( )
frame.setFrameShape(QFrame.Shape.Box)
```

QFrame Shapes

NoFrame	No visible border
Box	A simple rectangular box
Panel	A raised or sunken panel (often used for grouping)
WinPanel	A Window style panel
StyledPanel	A panel with the look based on the current style.
HLine	A horizontal line (great for separators)
VLine	A vertical line (for vertical separation)

Table: 5.3 – Some Frame Shapes

setFrameShadow(QFrame.Shadow)

Sets the visual shadow effect of the frame. Available shadows include ***Plain***, ***Raised*** and ***Sunken***.

</> Python

```python
frame = QFrame( )
frame.setFrameShadow(QFrame.Shadow.Plain)
```

setFrameStyle(int) and **frameStyle()**

Combines shape and shadow into a single value and returns a combined integer value representing both the Shape and Shadow of the frame.

</> Python

```python
frame = QFrame( )
frame.setFrameStyle( 2 )
```


setMidLineWidth(int **)** and **midLineWidth()**

Sets the width of the inner (middle) line for styles like *QFrame.Panel*.

</> **Python**

```
frame = QFrame( )
frame.setMidLineWidth( 10 )
```

setLineWidth(int **)** and **lineWidth()**

Sets the width of the main border line of the frame and returns the width of the frame's main line (outer border). It can be set using *setLineWidth()*.

</> **Python**

```
frame = QFrame( )
frame.setLineWidth( 5 )
```

QPainter

QPainter is a fundamental PyQt class that provides low-level painting capabilities for drawing shapes, images, text, gradients, and other graphical effects. It is essential for creating custom UIs, artistic visuals, game elements, and non-standard widgets.
Unlike regular widgets, which are added to layouts, QPainter works by overriding the paintEvent() of a widget and drawing directly onto it. This gives developers full control over the appearance and aesthetics of their applications.

Use Cases

- Drawing custom backgrounds or borders
- Designing non-rectangular widgets or buttons
- Creating visualizations like graphs, charts, and meters
- Implementing games with 2D graphics
- Drawing watermarks, signs, or overlays
- Painting text or images with transformations
- Building canvas-like applications (e.g. paint, diagrams)

Key Properties and Methods

beginNativePainting	testRenderHint	end	worldMatrixEnabled
fillRect	drawPoints	isActive	transform
worldTransform	setRenderHints	drawGlyphRun	setClipPath
hasClipping	PixmapFragmentHint	setWindow	drawEllipse
clipPath	setBrush	drawLine	setClipRect
setTransform	setClipping	device	begin
drawPixmapFragments	setRenderHint	drawLines	drawStaticText
backgroundMode	compositionMode	drawImage	drawPicture
translate	drawChord	clipRegion	endNativePainting
setBackground	setViewport	pen	restore
viewport	setClipRegion	setViewTransformEnabled	setCompositionMode
drawConvexPolygon	drawRects	viewTransformEnabled	strokePath
brush	drawArc	scale	drawPixmap
drawText	renderHints	setBackgroundMode	drawPoint
resetTransform	setPen	clipBoundingRect	drawPath
save	shear	opacity	boundingRect
drawRoundedRect	drawTiledPixmap	setWorldMatrixEnabled	deviceTransform
PixmapFragment	drawPolyline	setWorldTransform	CompositionMode
background	setBrushOrigin	brushOrigin	RenderHint
setOpacity	drawRect	fillPath	drawPie
combinedTransform	drawPolygon	rotate	eraseRect

QPen(color, width, style, cap, join)

QPen is used to define how lines, outlines, and shapes are drawn using *QPainter*. It controls the **color**, **thickness**, and style of **strokes**.

color → The color of the pen. Accepts a QColor, color name (e.g., "red"), or hex code (e.g., "#ff0000").

width → The thickness of the pen stroke. Default is 1.

style → The line style. Options include:
- Qt.PenStyle.SolidLine (default)
- Qt.PenStyle.DashLine
- Qt.PenStyle.DotLine
- Qt.PenStyle.DashDotLine
- Qt.PenStyle.NoPen

cap → The shape of the line **endpoints**:
- Qt.PenCapStyle.FlatCap
- Qt.PenCapStyle.SquareCap (default)
- Qt.PenCapStyle.RoundCap

join → The shape used where two lines **meet**:
- Qt.PenJoinStyle.BevelJoin (default)
- Qt.PenJoinStyle.MiterJoin
- Qt.PenJoinStyle.RoundJoin

setPen(QPen)

Set the line color, width, and style.

</> Python

```python
def paintEvent(parent, event):
    painter = QPainter( parent )

    pen = QPen(QColor("red"), 2, Qt.PenStyle.DotLine)
    painter.setPen( pen )
```

QBrush(color, style)

QBrush is used to **fill shapes and areas** drawn with QPainter, such as rectangles, circles, or polygons. It defines the **color, pattern, or texture** used for filling.

color → The fill color can be a QColor, name, or hex code.

style → The pattern or texture used for the fill. Common styles:
- Qt.BrushStyle.SolidPattern (default)
- Qt.BrushStyle.Dense1Pattern to Qt.BrushStyle.Dense7Pattern
- Qt.BrushStyle.HorPattern
- Qt.BrushStyle.VerPattern
- Qt.BrushStyle.CrossPattern
- Qt.BrushStyle.BDiagPattern
- Qt.BrushStyle.ConicalGradientPattern
- Qt.BrushStyle.DiagCrossPattern
- Qt.BrushStyle.FDiagPattern
- Qt.BrushStyle.LinearPattern
- Qt.BrushStyle.RadialGradientPattern
- Qt.BrushStyle.TexturePattern
- Qt.BrushStyle.NoBrush for no fill

setBrush(QBrush)

Set the fill color or gradient.

</> Python

```python
def paintEvent(parent, event):
    painter = QPainter( parent )

    brush = QBrush(QColor("red"), Qt.BrushStyle.CrossPattern)
    painter.setBrush( brush )
```

Basic Drawing

drawRect(x, y, width, height **)**

Draw a rectangle.

</> Python

```
import sys
from PyQt6.QtCore import *
from PyQt6.QtWidgets import *
from PyQt6.QtGui import *

class MyApp(QMainWindow):

    def __init__(self):
        super().__init__()

        self.setWindowTitle("Calculator")
        self.resize(300,150)
        self.setWindowIcon(QIcon("images/rocket.png"))
        self.setStyleSheet("background:#ebebeb")

        self.label = QLabel(self)
        self.label.setText("""
        <h1 style="color:#00334c"><b>Do you know!</b></h1>
        <p>With <b style="color:green;font-size:14px">QPainter</b>,
         you can do more than just drawing.Code to give the best UI.</p>""")
        self.label.setGeometry(50,50, 300, 100)
        self.label.setWordWrap(True)
        self.label.setStyleSheet("padding: 10px; border-radius:10px;background:#8eb2eb")


    def paintEvent(self, a0):
        painter = QPainter(self)
        painter.setPen(QPen(QColor("#C086EA"), 3))
        painter.setBrush(QBrush(QColor("#5c8bdc")))

        painter.drawRect(30, 30 , 340, 140)


app = QApplication([])
myapp = MyApp()
myapp.show()
sys.exit(app.exec())
```

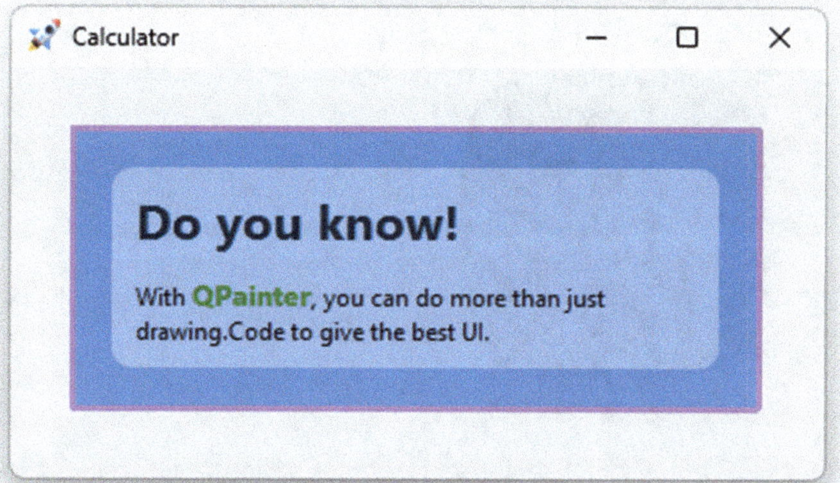

drawRoundedRect(x, y, width, height, xRadius, yRadius**)**

Draw a rectangle with rounded corners

</> Python

```
QLabel("""<h1 style="color:#0C3B2E">72%</h1><h4>Efficiency Score</h4>
        """, self).setGeometry(40,40, 100, 100)

QLabel("""<h1 style="color:#FF8E2B;background:#0C3B2E">$4,500.<sub>00</sub></h1>
        """, self).setGeometry(220,70, 105, 30)

def paintEvent(self, event):
    rect1 = QPainter(self)
    rect1.setPen(QPen(QColor("orange"), 2, Qt.PenStyle.DotLine))
    rect1.drawRoundedRect(10,10, 150, 150,20, 20)

    rect2 = QPainter(self)
    rect2.setPen(QPen(QColor("#0C3B2E"), 2, ))
    rect2.setBrush(QBrush(QColor("#0C3B2E"), Qt.BrushStyle.Dense1Pattern))
    rect2.drawRoundedRect(QRect(200,10, 150, 150), 40, 40)
```

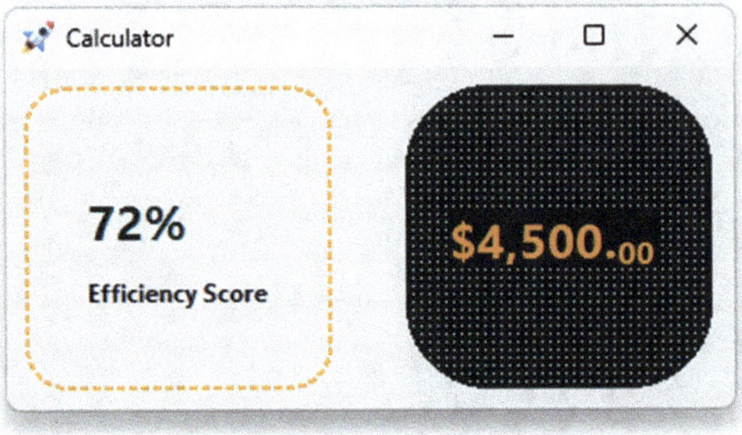

drawLine(x1, y1, x2, y2 **)**

Draw a line.

</> Python

```
def paintEvent(self, a0):
    painter = QPainter(self)
    painter.setPen(QPen(QColor("#00334c"), 3))

    painter.drawLine(30, 50, 300, 50)
    painter.drawLine(30, 150, 300, 150)
    painter.drawLine(50, 10, 50, 180)
    painter.drawLine(280, 10, 280, 180)
```

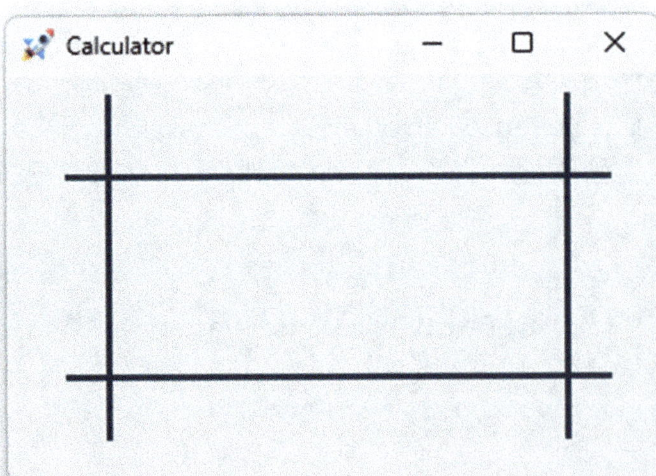

drawEllipse(x, y, width, height **)**

Draw an ellipse or circle.

</> Python

```
def paintEvent(self, a0):
    ellipse1 = QPainter(self)
    ellipse1.setPen(QPen(QColor("orange"), 2))
    ellipse1.setBrush(QBrush(QColor("orange"), Qt.BrushStyle.SolidPattern))
    ellipse1.drawEllipse(10, 10, 50, 50)

    ellipse2 = QPainter(self)
    ellipse2.setPen(QPen(QColor("green"), 10))
    ellipse2.setBrush(QBrush(QColor("green"), Qt.BrushStyle.FDiagPattern))
    ellipse2.drawEllipse(250, 150, 50, 50)

    ellipse3 = QPainter(self)
    ellipse3.setPen(QPen(QColor("red"), 20))
    ellipse3.drawEllipse(50, 100, 100, 100)

    ellipse4 = QPainter(self)
    ellipse4.setPen(QPen(QColor("#3a6ea5"), 40))
    ellipse4.setBrush(QBrush(QColor("#3a6ea5"), Qt.BrushStyle.CrossPattern))
    ellipse4.drawEllipse(200, -50, 150, 150)
```

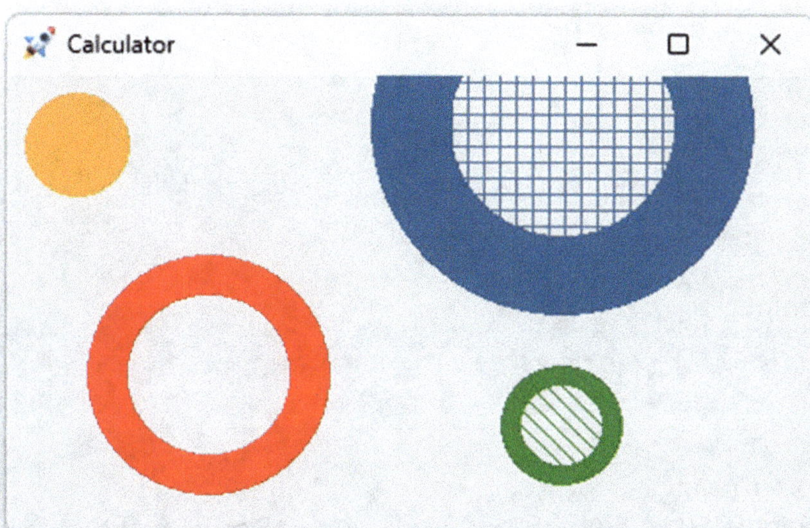

drawPolygon([QPoints*] **)**

Draw a polygon from a list of points.

Python

```python
def paintEvent(self, a0):
    hexagon = QPainter(self)
    hexagon.setPen(QPen(QColor("orange"), 2))
    hexagon.setBrush(QBrush(QColor("orange"), Qt.BrushStyle.Dense1Pattern))
    hexagon.drawPolygon([QPoint(100, 50), QPoint(200, 50), QPoint(250, 150),
                QPoint(200, 250),QPoint(100, 250),QPoint(50, 150)])
```

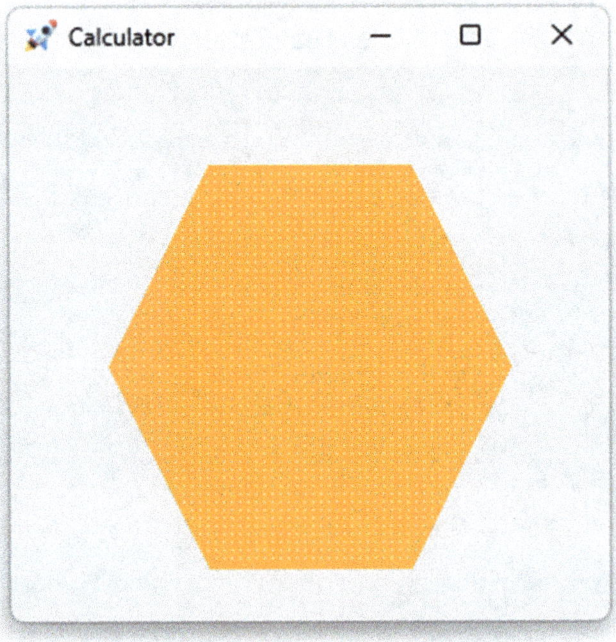

drawPolyline([QPoints*] **)**

Draw shapes by connecting points.

Python

```python
def paintEvent(self, event):
    painter = QPainter(self)
    painter.setPen(QPen(QColor("orange"), 5,))
    painter.drawPolyline([QPoint(0, 50,), QPoint(50, 100), QPoint(100, 50),
        QPoint(150, 100), QPoint(200, 50), QPoint(250, 100), QPoint(300, 50)])
```

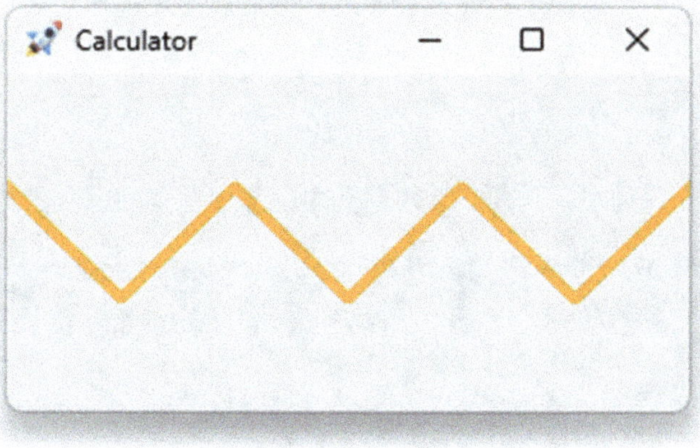

drawArc(QRect, int a, int alen **)**, **drawPie(** QRect, int a, int alen **)** and **drawChord(**QRect, int a, int alen **)**

Draw arc-shaped elements.

</> Python

```
def paintEvent(self, event):
    painter = QPainter(self)
    painter.setPen(QPen(QColor("red"), 10,))
    painter.setBrush(QBrush(QColor("#0C3B2E")))
    painter.drawChord(QRect(10,10,250,250), 100, 3000)
```

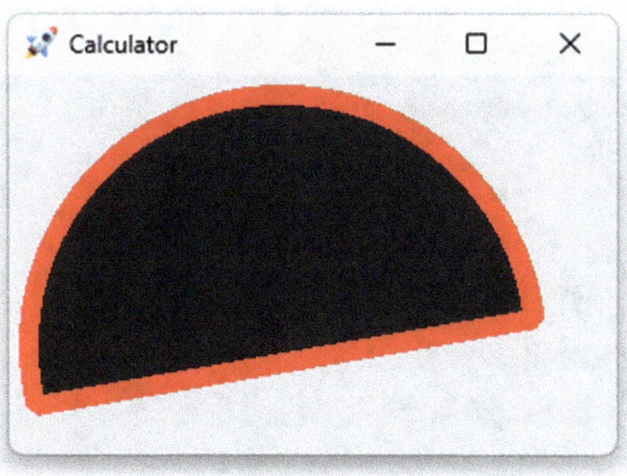

Drawing Text and Image

drawText(x, y, text **)**

Draw text at position.

</> Python

```
import sys
from PyQt6.QtCore import *
from PyQt6.QtWidgets import *
from PyQt6.QtGui import *

class PracticalApp(QMainWindow):

    def __init__(self):
        super().__init__()

        self.setWindowTitle("Calculator")
        self.setFixedSize(380,200)
        self.setWindowIcon(QIcon("images/rocket.png"))
        self.setStyleSheet("background:#ebebeb")

        QPushButton("Upgrade Now", self).move(20, 70)


    def paintEvent(self, a0):

        bigbox = QPainter(self)
        bigbox.setBrush(QBrush(QColor("#0C3B2E"),))
        bigbox.setPen(QPen(QColor("#0C3B2E"), 2,))
        bigbox.drawRoundedRect(QRect(10, 10, 350, 100 ), 10, 10)
        bigbox.setBrush(QBrush(QColor("orange"),Qt.BrushStyle.BDiagPattern))
        bigbox.drawEllipse(QRect(250, 10, 100,100))
        bigbox.setPen(QPen(QColor("white"), 2,))

        bigbox.drawText(20, 30, "Upgrade Your Plan to Premium")
        bigbox.drawText(20, 50, "and Get unlimited access")
        bigbox.drawText(290, 70, "PyQt")

app = QApplication([])
myapp = PracticalApp()
myapp.show()
sys.exit(app.exec())
```

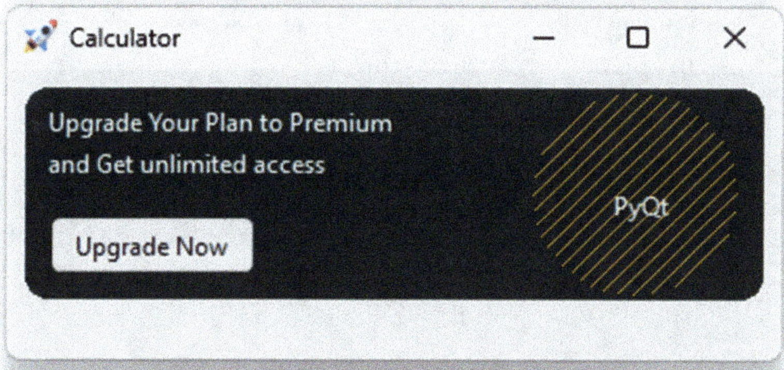

drawPixmap(QRect, QPixmap **)**

Draw an image at a position.

</> Python

```
import sys
from PyQt6.QtCore import *
from PyQt6.QtWidgets import *
from PyQt6.QtGui import *

class PracticalApp(QMainWindow):

 def __init__(self):
     super().__init__()

     self.setWindowTitle("Calculator")
     self.setFixedSize(400,400)
     self.setWindowIcon(QIcon("images/rocket.png"))
     self.setStyleSheet("background:#ebebeb")

     lab = QLabel("<h2>Do you know you can own a car today?</h2><h4>Why wait untill you get
     enough money to buy your own car.<br>Just pay part and get one for yourself!</h4>", self)
     lab.setGeometry(80,10, 350, 100)
     lab.setWordWrap(True)
     lab.setStyleSheet("background:#1D2330;color:white")

     QPushButton("Get a car", self).move(20,120)


 def paintEvent(self, a0):
```

```
        bigbox = QPainter(self)
        bigbox.setBrush(QBrush(QColor("#1D2330"),))
        bigbox.setPen(QPen(QColor("#0E121A"), 2,))
        bigbox.drawRoundedRect(QRect(10, 10, 450, 150 ), 10, 10)

        bigbox.drawPixmap(QRect(10, 10, 50, 50), QPixmap("images/sport-car.png"))
        bigbox.drawPixmap(QRect(400, 100, 50, 50), QPixmap("images/performance.png"))
        bigbox.drawPixmap(QRect(80, 150, 300, 300), QPixmap("images/luxury-car.png"))
        bigbox.drawPixmap(QRect(10, 170, 80, 80), QPixmap("images/pie-chart.png"))


app = QApplication([])
myapp = PracticalApp()
myapp.show()
sys.exit(app.exec())
```

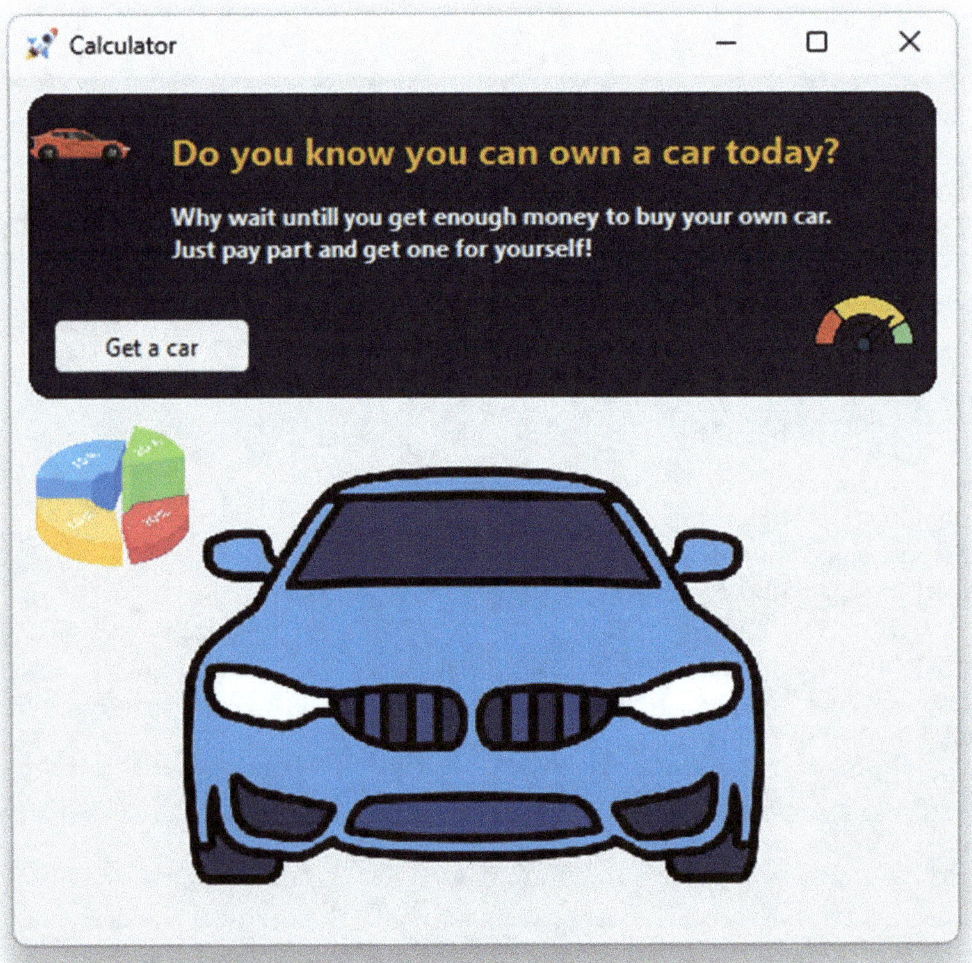

drawImage(QRect, QImage)
Draw from a *QImage*.

</> Python

```
        google = QPushButton(self)
        google.setGeometry(10, 100, 100, 100)
        google.setIcon(QIcon("images/google.png"))

        apple = QPushButton(self)
        apple.setGeometry(140, 100, 100, 100)
        apple.setIcon(QIcon("images/apple.png"))

        facebook = QPushButton(self)
        facebook.setGeometry(270, 100, 100, 100)
        facebook.setIcon(QIcon("images/facebook.png"))


    def paintEvent(self, event):
        painter = QPainter(self)
        painter.drawImage(QRect(-5, -5, 400, 300), QImage("images/background.jpg"))
```

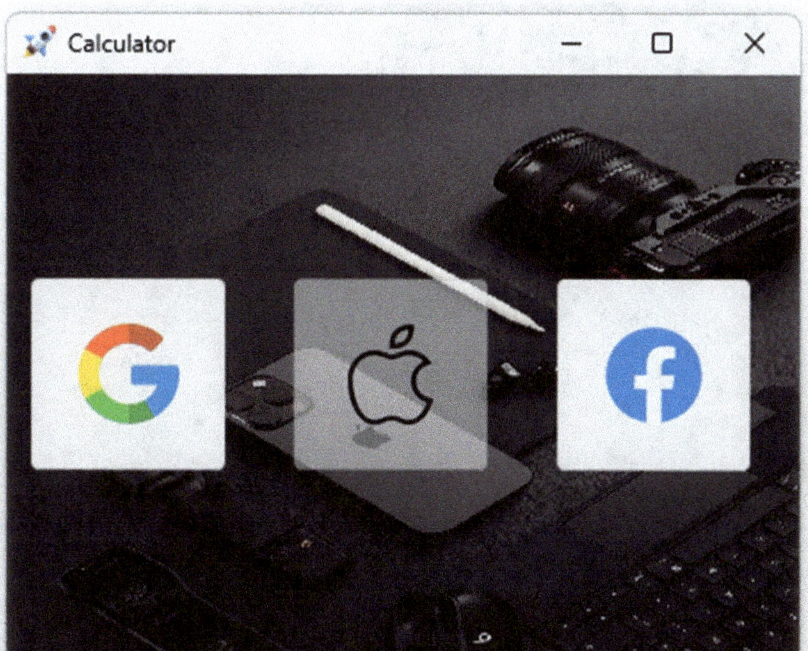

setOpacity(float **)**

Set transparency (**0.0 – 1.0**).

</> Python

```
def paintEvent(self, event):
    painter = QPainter(self)
    painter.setOpacity(0.5)
    painter.drawImage(QRect(-5, -5, 400, 300), QImage("images/background.jpg"))
```

setBackground(QColor **)**

Set background fill color.

setBackgroundMode(Qt.BGMode **)**

Set background behavior (*OpaqueMode* or *TransparentMode*).

</> Python

```
def paintEvent(self, event):
    painter = QPainter(self)
    painter.setBackgroundMode(Qt.BGMode.TransparentMode)
```

Transformation

translate(dx, dy**)**

Move the object.

</> Python

```
def paintEvent(self, event):
    painter = QPainter(self)
    painter.translate(10, 50)
```

shear(sx, sy**)**

Skew the coordinates.

</> Python

```
def paintEvent(self, event):
    painter = QPainter(self)
    painter.shear(0.2, 0.1)
    painter.drawPixmap(QRect(100, 10, 150, 150 ), QPixmap("images/person.jpg"))
```

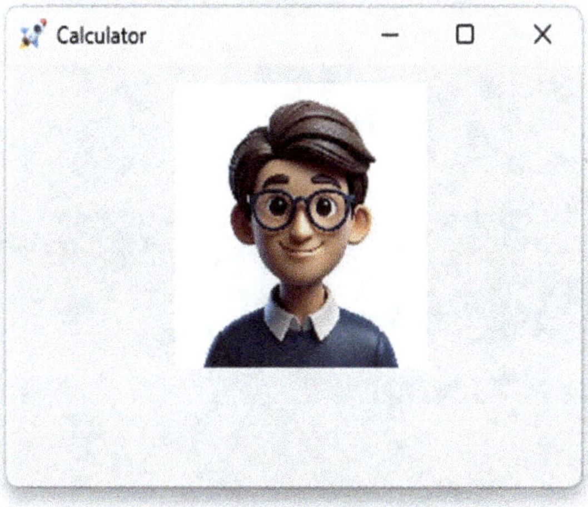

scale(sx, sy**)**

Scale x and y axes.

</> Python

```python
def paintEvent(self, event):
    painter = QPainter(self)
    painter.scale(2, 0.9)
    painter.drawPixmap(QRect(100, 10, 150, 150 ), QPixmap("images/person.jpg"))
```

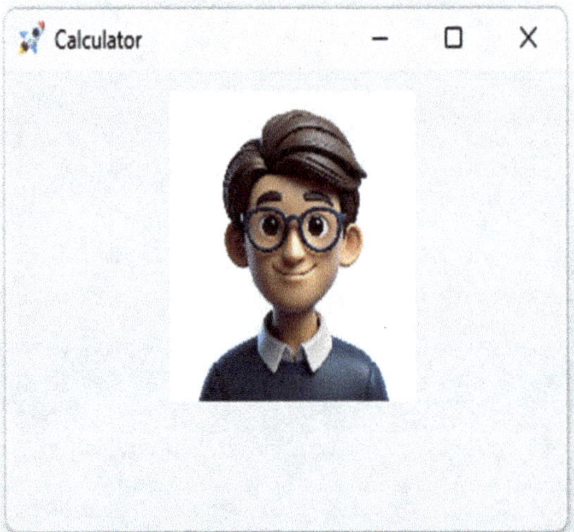

rotate(angle**)**

Rotate the coordinate system.

</> Python

```python
def paintEvent(self, event):
    painter = QPainter(self)
    painter.rotate(45)
    painter.drawPixmap(QRect(100, -10, 150, 150 ), QPixmap("images/person.jpg"))
```

fillPath(QPointF, QColor **)**
Fill a path with color.

setClipRect(), setClipPath() and **clipRegion(), clipBoundingRect()**

setClipRect()	→	Define clipping area with rectangle coordinates.
setClipPath()	→	Define clipping area with path.
clipRegion()	→	Get the current clip bounds.
clipBoundingRect()	→	Get the current clip bounds.

save(), restore() and **isActive()**

save()	→	Save current painter state.
restore()	→	Restore last saved state.
isActive()	→	Check if the painter is active.

Gradients

Gradients are a way to **smoothly blend multiple colors** across an area. Instead of filling a shape with a solid color, you can use a gradient for more depth, realism, or style. PyQt makes this easy with *QBrush* and gradient classes.

Common Use Cases

- Buttons with shiny highlights
- Backgrounds with color fade
- Charts with gradient fills
- Progress bars with dynamic colors
- Custom dials and knobs

Kinds of Gradients

① QLinearGradient(xstart, ystart, xstop, ystop)

A gradient that blends colors in a straight line between two points.

Example

</> Python

```python
def paintEvent(self, event):

    painter = QPainter(self)

    gradient = QLinearGradient(0, 0, 300, 200)
    gradient.setColorAt(0.0, QColor("orange"))
    gradient.setColorAt(0.5, QColor("red"))
    gradient.setColorAt(1.0, QColor("blue"))

    painter.setBrush(gradient)
    painter.drawRect(10, 10, 300, 200)
```

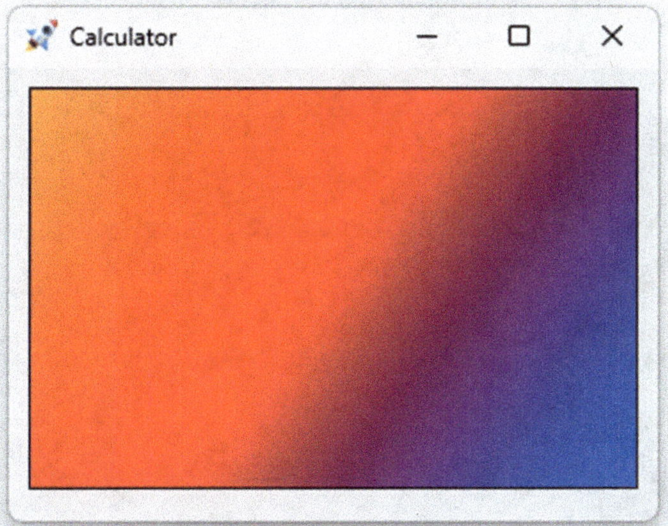

② **QRadialGradient(** centerx, centery, radius **)**

A gradient that radiates outward in a circle or ellipse from a center point.

Example

</> Python

```
def paintEvent(self, event):

    painter = QPainter(self)

    gradient = QRadialGradient(150, 100, 200)
    gradient.setColorAt(0.0, QColor("yellow"))
    gradient.setColorAt(0.2, QColor("orange"))
    gradient.setColorAt(0.4, QColor("red"))
    gradient.setColorAt(0.6, QColor("green"))
    gradient.setColorAt(0.8, QColor("blue"))
    gradient.setColorAt(1.0, QColor("white"))

    painter.setBrush(gradient)
    painter.drawRect(10, 10, 300, 200)
```

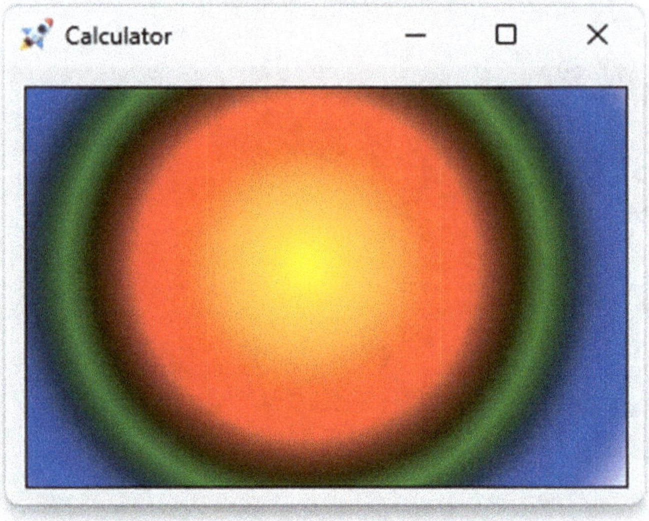

③ QConicalGradient(cx, cy, startAngle)

A gradient that spins around a center point like a color wheel.

Example

</> Python

```
def paintEvent(self, event):
    painter = QPainter(self)

    gradient = QConicalGradient(200, 200, 200)
    gradient.setColorAt(0.0, QColor("yellow"))
    gradient.setColorAt(0.2, QColor("orange"))
    gradient.setColorAt(0.4, QColor("red"))
    gradient.setColorAt(0.6, QColor("green"))
    gradient.setColorAt(0.8, QColor("blue"))
    gradient.setColorAt(1.0, QColor("white"))

    painter.setBrush(gradient)
    painter.drawRect(10, 10, 350, 250)
```

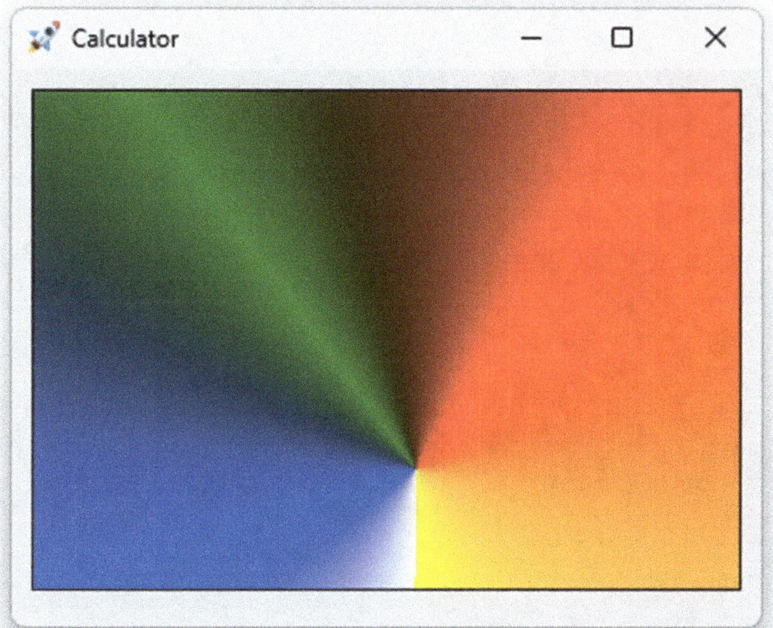
Calculator

Finalizing Project - Building Calculator

</> Python

```python
import sys
from PyQt6.QtWidgets import *
from PyQt6.QtCore import *
from PyQt6.QtGui import *

class MyApp(QMainWindow):
    def __init__(self):
        super().__init__()

        self.setWindowTitle("My Calculator")
        self.setProperty("setGeometry", (100, 100, 400, 200))
        self.setStyleSheet("background:#ebebeb")

        self.setContentsMargins(10,10,10,10)

        self.main = QWidget()
        self.setCentralWidget(self.main)

        self.lay = QVBoxLayout()
        self.main.setLayout(self.lay)

        self.input = QLabel()
        self.input.resize(self.width(), 50)
        self.input.setStyleSheet("color:teal;font-size:25px")
        self.input.setSizePolicy(QSizePolicy.Policy.Expanding, QSizePolicy.Policy.Expanding)
        self.lay.addWidget(self.input)

        self.output = QLabel()
        self.output.resize(self.width(), 50)
        self.output.setContentsMargins(10,5,5,5)
        self.output.setStyleSheet("background:#24252B;color:white;font-size:25px")
        self.output.setSizePolicy(QSizePolicy.Policy.Expanding, QSizePolicy.Policy.Expanding)
        self.lay.addWidget(self.output)

        self.grid = QGridLayout()
        self.lay.addLayout(self.grid)

        self.cleanButton = QPushButton("C")
        self.cleanButton.resize(100,50)
        self.cleanButton.setSizePolicy(QSizePolicy.Policy.Expanding, QSizePolicy.Policy.Expanding)
        self.cleanButton.setStyleSheet("color:white; font-size:20px;background:tomato")
        self.cleanButton.clicked.connect(self.clear)
        self.grid.addWidget(self.cleanButton,0,0)

        self.exponetialButton = QPushButton("exp")
        self.exponetialButton.resize(100,50)
```

```
self.exponetialButton.setSizePolicy(QSizePolicy.Policy.Expanding, QSizePolicy.Policy.Expanding)
self.exponetialButton.setStyleSheet("color:white;font-size:20px;background:#424349")
self.exponetialButton.clicked.connect(lambda: self.addCharacter('**'))
self.grid.addWidget(self.exponetialButton,0,1)

self.moduloButton = QPushButton("%")
self.moduloButton.resize(100,50)
self.moduloButton.setSizePolicy(QSizePolicy.Policy.Expanding, QSizePolicy.Policy.Expanding)
self.moduloButton.setStyleSheet("color:white;font-size:20px;background:#424349")
self.moduloButton.clicked.connect(lambda: self.addCharacter('%'))
self.grid.addWidget(self.moduloButton,0,2)

self.diviButton = QPushButton("/")
self.diviButton.resize(100,50)
self.diviButton.setSizePolicy(QSizePolicy.Policy.Expanding, QSizePolicy.Policy.Expanding)
self.diviButton.setStyleSheet("color:white;font-size:20px;background:#424349")
self.diviButton.clicked.connect(lambda: self.addCharacter('/'))
self.grid.addWidget(self.diviButton,0,3)

self.sevenButton = QPushButton("7")
self.sevenButton.resize(100,50)
self.sevenButton.setSizePolicy(QSizePolicy.Policy.Expanding, QSizePolicy.Policy.Expanding)
self.sevenButton.setStyleSheet("color:white; font-size:20px;background:#424349")
self.sevenButton.clicked.connect(lambda: self.addCharacter('7'))
self.grid.addWidget(self.sevenButton,1,0)

self.eightButton = QPushButton("8")
self.eightButton.resize(100,50)
self.eightButton.setSizePolicy(QSizePolicy.Policy.Expanding, QSizePolicy.Policy.Expanding)
self.eightButton.setStyleSheet("color:white;font-size:20px;background:#424349")
self.eightButton.clicked.connect(lambda: self.addCharacter('8'))
self.grid.addWidget(self.eightButton,1,1)

self.nineButton = QPushButton("9")
self.nineButton.resize(100,50)
self.nineButton.setSizePolicy(QSizePolicy.Policy.Expanding, QSizePolicy.Policy.Expanding)
self.nineButton.setStyleSheet("color:white;font-size:20px;background:#424349")
self.nineButton.clicked.connect(lambda: self.addCharacter('9'))
self.grid.addWidget(self.nineButton,1,2)

self.multiplicationButton = QPushButton("x")
self.multiplicationButton.resize(100,50)
self.multiplicationButton.setSizePolicy(QSizePolicy.Policy.Expanding, QSizePolicy.Policy.Expanding)
self.multiplicationButton.setStyleSheet("color:white;font-size:20px;background:#424349")
self.multiplicationButton.clicked.connect(lambda: self.addCharacter('*'))
self.grid.addWidget(self.multiplicationButton,1,3)

self.fourButton = QPushButton("4")
self.fourButton.resize(100,50)
self.fourButton.setSizePolicy(QSizePolicy.Policy.Expanding, QSizePolicy.Policy.Expanding)
self.fourButton.setStyleSheet("color:white; font-size:20px;background:#424349")
self.fourButton.clicked.connect(lambda: self.addCharacter('4'))
```

```
self.grid.addWidget(self.fourButton,2,0)

self.fiveButton = QPushButton("5")
self.fiveButton.resize(100,50)
self.fiveButton.setSizePolicy(QSizePolicy.Policy.Expanding, QSizePolicy.Policy.Expanding)
self.fiveButton.setStyleSheet("color:white;font-size:20px;background:#424349")
self.fiveButton.clicked.connect(lambda: self.addCharacter('5'))
self.grid.addWidget(self.fiveButton,2,1)

self.sixButton = QPushButton("6")
self.sixButton.resize(100,50)
self.sixButton.setSizePolicy(QSizePolicy.Policy.Expanding, QSizePolicy.Policy.Expanding)
self.sixButton.setStyleSheet("color:white;font-size:20px;background:#424349")
self.sixButton.clicked.connect(lambda: self.addCharacter('6'))
self.grid.addWidget(self.sixButton,2,2)

self.subtractionButton = QPushButton("-")
self.subtractionButton.resize(100,50)
self.subtractionButton.setSizePolicy(QSizePolicy.Policy.Expanding, QSizePolicy.Policy.Expanding)
self.subtractionButton.setStyleSheet("color:white;font-size:20px;background:#424349")
self.subtractionButton.clicked.connect(lambda: self.addCharacter('-'))
self.grid.addWidget(self.subtractionButton,2,3)

self.oneButton = QPushButton("1")
self.oneButton.resize(100,50)
self.oneButton.setSizePolicy(QSizePolicy.Policy.Expanding, QSizePolicy.Policy.Expanding)
self.oneButton.setStyleSheet("color:white; font-size:20px;background:#424349")
self.oneButton.clicked.connect(lambda: self.addCharacter('1'))
self.grid.addWidget(self.oneButton,3,0)

self.twoButton = QPushButton("2")
self.twoButton.resize(100,50)
self.twoButton.setSizePolicy(QSizePolicy.Policy.Expanding, QSizePolicy.Policy.Expanding)
self.twoButton.setStyleSheet("color:white;font-size:20px;background:#424349")
self.twoButton.clicked.connect(lambda: self.addCharacter('2'))
self.grid.addWidget(self.twoButton,3,1)

self.threeButton = QPushButton("3")
self.threeButton.resize(100,50)
self.threeButton.setSizePolicy(QSizePolicy.Policy.Expanding, QSizePolicy.Policy.Expanding)
self.threeButton.setStyleSheet("color:white;font-size:20px;background:#424349")
self.threeButton.clicked.connect(lambda: self.addCharacter('3'))
self.grid.addWidget(self.threeButton,3,2)

self.additionButton = QPushButton("+")
self.additionButton.resize(100,50)
self.additionButton.setSizePolicy(QSizePolicy.Policy.Expanding, QSizePolicy.Policy.Expanding)
self.additionButton.setStyleSheet("color:white;font-size:20px;background:#424349")
self.additionButton.clicked.connect(lambda: self.addCharacter('+'))
self.grid.addWidget(self.additionButton,3,3)

self.zeroButton = QPushButton("0")
```

```
        self.zeroButton.resize(100,50)
        self.zeroButton.setSizePolicy(QSizePolicy.Policy.Expanding, QSizePolicy.Policy.Expanding)
        self.zeroButton.setStyleSheet("color:white; font-size:20px;background:#424349")
        self.zeroButton.clicked.connect(lambda: self.addCharacter('0'))
        self.grid.addWidget(self.zeroButton,4,0)

        self.decimalButton = QPushButton(".")
        self.decimalButton.resize(100,50)
        self.decimalButton.setSizePolicy(QSizePolicy.Policy.Expanding, QSizePolicy.Policy.Expanding)
        self.decimalButton.setStyleSheet("color:white;font-size:20px;background:#424349")
        self.decimalButton.clicked.connect(lambda: self.addCharacter('.'))
        self.grid.addWidget(self.decimalButton,4,1)

        self.deleteButton = QPushButton("<-")
        self.deleteButton.resize(100,50)
        self.deleteButton.setSizePolicy(QSizePolicy.Policy.Expanding, QSizePolicy.Policy.Expanding)
        self.deleteButton.setStyleSheet("color:white;font-size:20px;background:#424349")
        self.deleteButton.clicked.connect(self.delete)
        self.grid.addWidget(self.deleteButton,4,2)

        self.equalButton = QPushButton("=")
        self.equalButton.resize(100,50)
        self.equalButton.setSizePolicy(QSizePolicy.Policy.Expanding, QSizePolicy.Policy.Expanding)
        self.equalButton.setStyleSheet("color:white;font-size:20px;background:#424349")
        self.equalButton.clicked.connect(self.answer)
        self.grid.addWidget(self.equalButton,4,3)


    def addCharacter(self, item):
        self.input.setText(self.input.text() + item )

    def clear(self):
        self.output.clear()
        self.input.clear()

    def delete(self):
        currentText = self.input.text()
        length = len(currentText)
        newInput = str(currentText[0:length-1])
        self.input.setText(newInput)

    def answer(self):
        try:
            currentText = self.input.text()
            result = eval(currentText)
            self.output.setText(str(result))
        except:
            self.output.setText("Error")


app = QApplication(sys.argv)
window = MyApp()
```

```
window.show()
sys.exit(app.exec())
```

Chapter 6

PyQt Widgets - Set B (Inputs)

Chapter Objectives

- ◈ Work with text editors
- ◈ Use QSize
- ◈ Implement QRadioButton
- ◈ Group buttons with QButtonGroup
- ◈ Use QCheckBox
- ◈ Apply QComboBox
- ◈ Integrate QCalendarWidget
- ◈ Use QColorDialog
- ◈ Work with QSlider
- ◈ Explore QDial

Project B – Creating a Login Page

Login pages are an essential part of modern applications, commonly used by services that require account creation or secure user access. These pages are designed to collect user credentials, such as usernames and passwords, to either register new users or authenticate existing ones.

In this project, we will focus on building a functional login interface using **PyQt**. The purpose is to reinforce your understanding of input-handling widgets and layouts covered in previous chapters.

You will gain practical experience working with:

- **Input fields** for username and password
- **Push buttons** for user interaction
- **Layouts** for organizing the interface neatly
- **Basic validation** and logic control

This hands-on project serves as a foundation for building more advanced user interfaces and managing user input within a structured application flow.

💡 **Note**: The widgets and techniques used here are based on the concepts previously introduced—this is your opportunity to put them into practice in a real-world scenario.

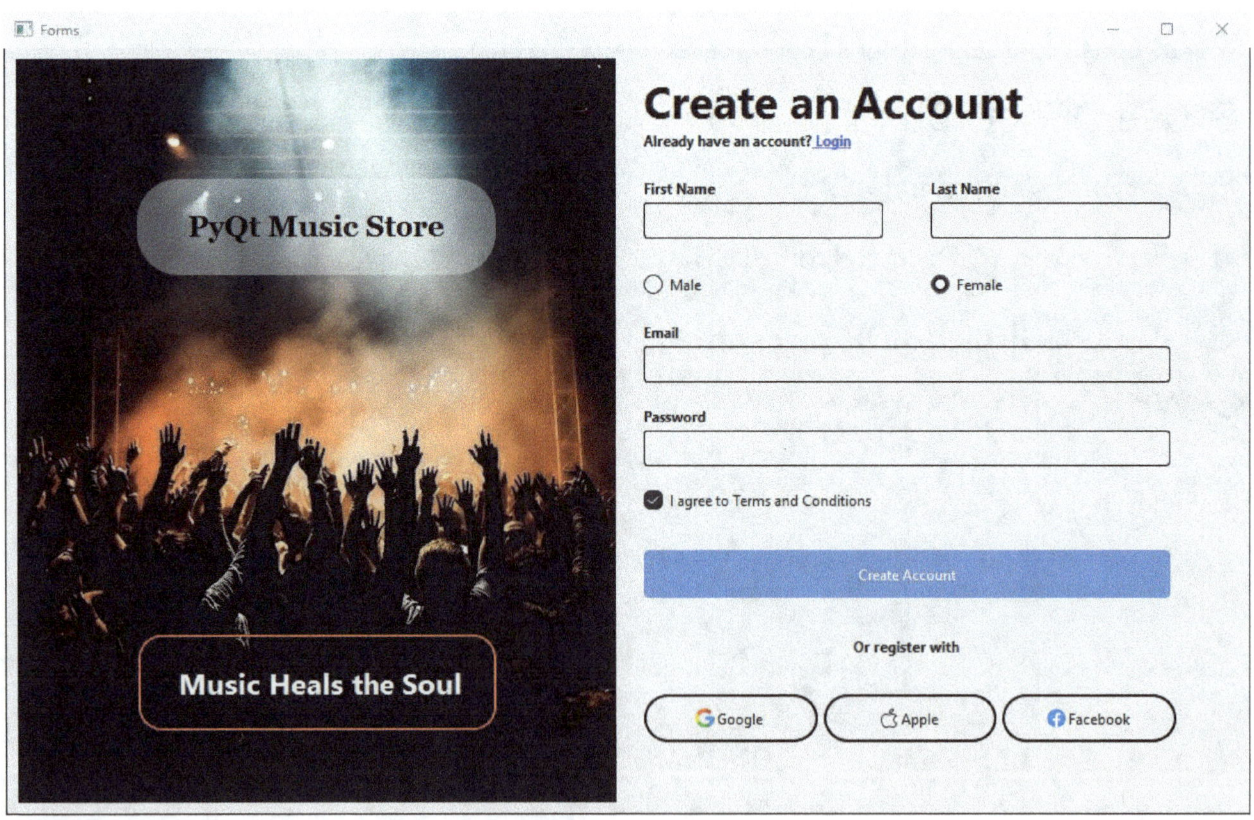

TextEditors

Text editors in GUI applications are essential widgets used for receiving, displaying, and formatting textual data. They play a crucial role in user input and data interaction within an application. Formatting text enhances visual appeal and aligns with input expectations, improving both usability and readability.

Common text formatting operations include:

- Copying, cutting, and pasting
- Text alignment (left, center, right, justified)
- Font styling (bold, italic, underline)
- Text decorations (strikethrough, subscript, superscript)
- Bulleting and numbering
- Font and background coloring
- Highlighting and painting
- Paragraph formatting (spacing, indentation, justification)
- Undo and redo actions
- Text searching and replacing

Text editors are commonly used for both data entry (e.g., messages, emails, usernames, passwords, dates of birth, etc.) and data display.

Use Cases of Text Editors

Text editors are frequently used for:

- User login and sign-up forms (username, email, password, date of birth, etc.)
- Message composition (emails, comments, chat inputs)
- Data display and editing (logs, notes, descriptions)
- Code editors or terminals
- Rich text document editing

Text Editors in PyQt

PyQt provides several widgets that function as text editors, each with distinct features and capabilities for handling either plain text or rich text. The most commonly used text editor widgets in PyQt include:

1. **QLineEdit** – Ideal for single-line text input.
2. **QTextEdit** – Supports rich text formatting and multi-line input.
3. **QPlainTextEdit** – Optimized for handling large amounts of plain text efficiently.

Common Methods and Properties

While each of these widgets has unique features tailored to its intended use case, they also share a range of common properties and methods. These include methods for setting and retrieving text, modifying alignment, managing clipboard operations (copy, cut, paste), and connecting to signals for text changes.

setCursorWidth	canInsertFromMimeData	tabStopDistance	setMarkdown
undoAvailable	paste	lineWrapColumnOrWidth	initStyleOption
viewportSizeHint	copyAvailable	setCornerWidget	setupViewport
fontFamily	textChanged	frameWidth	textColor
textInteractionFlags	toMarkdown	createStandardContextMenu	setViewport
sizeAdjustPolicy	setSizeAdjustPolicy	textBackgroundColor	fontItalic
fontPointSize	toHtml	documentTitle	setLineWidth
loadResource	frameShadow	redoAvailable	extraSelections
fontUnderline	mergeCurrentCharFormat	tabChangesFocus	scrollBarWidgets
setLineWrapMode	alignment	setReadOnly	isReadOnly
setFrameShape	cursorForPosition	setLineWrapColumnOrWidth	ensureCursorVisible
drawFrame	setFrameStyle	horizontalScrollBar	LineWrapMode
insertFromMimeData	setFontFamily	verticalScrollBarPolicy	undo
setTextCursor	setVerticalScrollBar	placeholderText	frameRect
viewportMargins	selectAll	setAlignment	setUndoRedoEnabled
cut	setAcceptRichText	setOverwriteMode	setCurrentFont
cursorWidth	zoomOut	zoomIn	print
SizeAdjustPolicy	toPlainText	setDocumentTitle	scrollToAnchor
copy	horizontalScrollBarPolicy	canPaste	textCursor
setFontItalic	setCurrentCharFormat	lineWrapMode	setAutoFormatting
viewport	cursorPositionChanged	frameStyle	acceptRichText
insertHtml	moveCursor	setTabStopDistance	setFontUnderline
frameShape	wordWrapMode	document	setText
cornerWidget	viewportEvent	autoFormatting	redo
maximumViewportSize	cursorRect	fontWeight	setHorizontalScrollBar
setTextColor	setHorizontalScrollBarPolicy	createMimeDataFromSelection	Shape
midLineWidth	lineWidth	setFrameRect	setTextBackgroundColor
setPlainText	Shadow	overwriteMode	setFontPointSize
selectionChanged	ExtraSelection	currentCharFormat	AutoFormattingFlag
setViewportMargins	setDocument	setVerticalScrollBarPolicy	setFontWeight
setPlaceholderText	currentCharFormatChanged	scrollContentsBy	setExtraSelections
setTextInteractionFlags	currentFont	isUndoRedoEnabled	verticalScrollBar
StyleMask	setMidLineWidth	setHtml	anchorAt
addScrollBarWidget	append	setWordWrapMode	setFrameShadow
clear	insertPlainText	setTabChangesFocus	

QLineEdit

QLineEdit is a PyQt widget that provides a single-line text box for user input. It's widely used in GUI applications for taking inputs such as names, email addresses, search queries, or passwords.

Key Features of QLineEdit:

- Accepts **single-line text input** (unlike QTextEdit which supports multi-line).
- Allows setting **input masks**, **placeholders**, and **password modes**.
- Supports **text validation**, **auto-completion**, and **signals** for real-time input monitoring.

Key Properties and Methods

displayText	cursorPosition	cursorWordForward	isModified
EchoMode	completer	setDragEnabled	home
hasSelectedText	end	backspace	maxLength
selectionEnd	text	validator	cursorMoveStyle
selectedText	isUndoAvailable	isClearButtonEnabled	selectionLength
inputMask	insert	del_	setInputMask
setMaxLength	textMargins	editingFinished	isRedoAvailable
textEdited	setSelection	selectionStart	dragEnabled
cursorBackward	returnPressed	ActionPosition	setClearButtonEnabled
setCompleter	setModified	cursorPositionAt	deselect
setEchoMode	setValidator	setFrame	cursorWordBackward
setTextMargins	echoMode	setCursorPosition	hasFrame
cursorForward	inputRejected	setCursorMoveStyle	hasAcceptableInput

setText(text **) and text()**

The *setText()* sets the content of the line edit and *text()* gets the current text from the line edit.

</> Python

```
import sys
from PyQt6.QtCore import *
```

```
from PyQt6.QtWidgets import *
from PyQt6.QtGui import *
from PyQt6.QtGui import QIcon

class MyApp(QMainWindow):

    def __init__(self):
        super().__init__()

        self.setWindowTitle("Forms")
        self.setProperty("resize", (1000, 800))
        self.setWindowIcon(QIcon("images/rocket.png"))
        self.setStyleSheet("background:#ebebeb")

        QLabel('Whats your name',self).move(10,10)
        self.input = QLineEdit(self)
        self.input.setGeometry(10,50, 200, 30),
        self.input.setStyleSheet("border:1px solid; border-radius:3px")

        QLabel('Output', self).move(10,90)
        self.output = QLineEdit(self)
        self.output.setGeometry(10,120, 200, 30),
        self.output.setStyleSheet("border:1px solid; border-radius:3px")

        self.submit = QPushButton('Submit',self)
        self.submit.setGeometry(10,170, 100,40)
        self.submit.clicked.connect(self.greetings)


    def greetings(self):
        userInput = self.input.text()                #Getting text
        self.output.setText(f"Hello {userInput}")    #Setting text


app = QApplication([])
myapp = MyApp()
myapp.show()
sys.exit(app.exec())
```

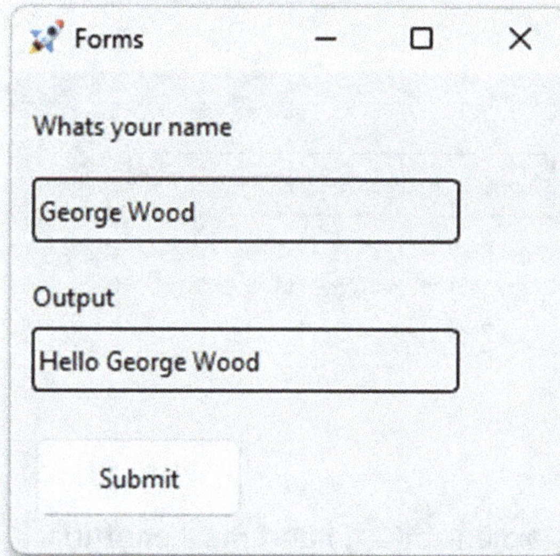

clear( )
Clears all content.

```python
textEdit = QLineEdit( )
textEdit.clear( )
```

setPlaceholderText(text **)** and **placeholderText()**
Shows grayed-out text when empty and returns the placeholder string.

```python
textEdit = QLineEdit( )
textEdit.setPlaceholderText("Enter your surname here...")
```

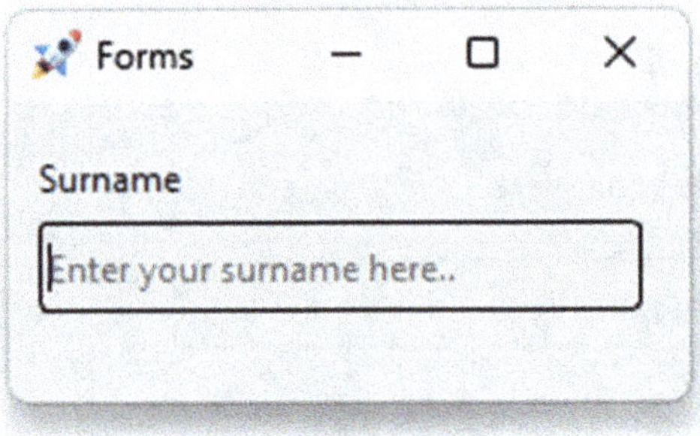

setMaxLength(int **)** and **maxLength()**

Limits the number of characters and gets the set limit.

```python
textEdit = QLineEdit( )
textEdit.setMaxLength(6)
```

setAlignment(Qt.AlignmentFlag **)** and **alignment()**

The *setAlignment()* aligns the text within the text box and the *alignment()* returns the current paragraph alignment (e.g., left, right, center).

```python
textEdit = QLineEdit( )
textEdit.setAlignment(Qt.AlignmentFlag.AlignRight)
```

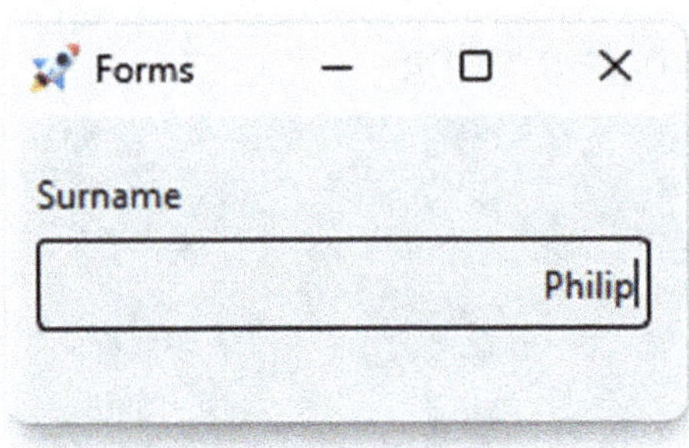

Alignment Flags

AlignCenter	AlignJustify	AlignHCenter	AlignBottom	AlignBaseline
AlignLeft	AlignLeading	AlignHorizontal_Mask	AlignTop	AlignAbsolute
AlignRight	AlignTrailing	AlignVCenter	AlignVertical_Mask	

setReadOnly(bool **)**

Makes the editor non-editable.

</> Python

```python
line_edit = QLineEdit( )
line_edit.setReadOnly(True)
```

setEchoMode(QLineEdit.EchoMode**)** and **echoMode()**

The *setEchoMode()* adds password masking and the *echoMode()* returns the current mode.

</> Python

```python
line_edit = QLineEdit( )
line_edit.setEchoMode( QLineEdit.EchoMode.Password)
```

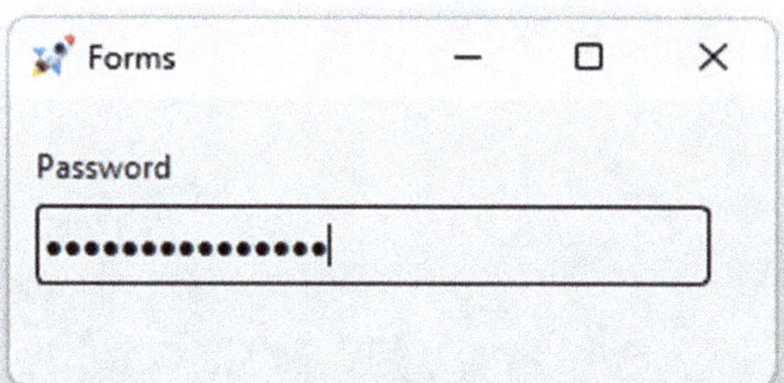

EchoMode

Password	Masks characters (e.g., ●●●●).
Normal	Shows typed characters.
NoEcho	Displays nothing while typing.
PasswordEchoOnEdit	Masks input but shows actual characters during editing.

Table 6.0 : Text editor echo modes

setValidator(QIntValidator**)**
Accepts only valid text (e.g., only integers).

```
line_edit = QLineEdit( )
line_edit.setValidator( QIntValidator() )
```

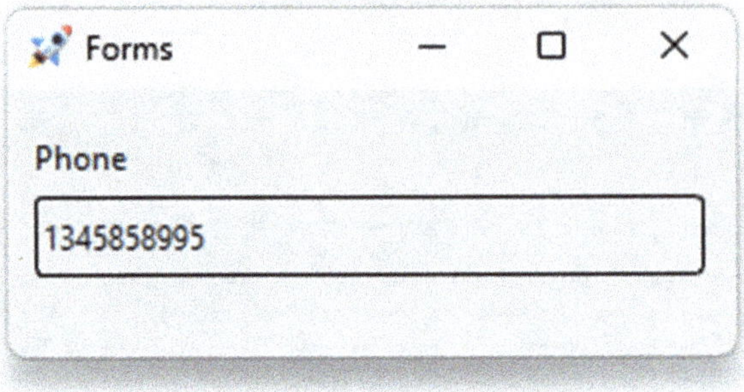

setTextMargins(int left, int top, int right, int bottom**)** and **textMargins()**
The *setTextMargins()* adds spaces around text and *textMargins()* returns the margin size.

```
line_edit = QLineEdit( )
line_edit.setTextMargins( 45, 0, 0, 0)
```

textChanged

Emitted when the text changes.

```python
line_edit = QLineEdit( )
line_edit.textChanged.connect(callback)

def callback():
    pass
```

editingFinished

Triggered when editing is done (focus lost or enter).

```python
line_edit = QLineEdit( )
line_edit.editingFinished.connect(callback)

def callback():
    pass
```

returnPressed

Emitted when Enter or Return is pressed.

```python
line_edit = QLineEdit( )
line_edit.returnPressed.connect(lambda: print("Return button has been pressed"))
```

textEditted

Emitted only when user manually edits the text.

```python
line_edit = QLineEdit( )
line_edit.textEditted.connect(lambda: print("Text modified"))
```

Search Bars

Search bars are common features in GUI applications that allow users to enter a query and search a database or list for matching items. They typically use text editor widgets like **QLineEdit** to capture user input.
Modern search bars often include features such as auto-completion and predictive typing. As the user types, the search bar can suggest possible matches. If a suggestion matches what the user intends to type, they can accept it to auto complete the input.

PyQt provides a powerful widget called **QCompleter**, which integrates seamlessly with text editors such as *QLineEdit* and *QTextEdit* to enable these predictive features.

To use *QCompleter*, all possible suggestions (or search options) are added to a list, which serves as the completer's data model. As the user types, *QCompleter* searches through this list and displays matching suggestions in real time.

Example,

</> Python

```python
from PyQt5.QtWidgets import QCompleter

completer = QCompleter(["New York", "London", "New Jersey", "Ontario", "Paris"])
line_edit = QLineEdit()
line_edit.setCompleter(completer)
```

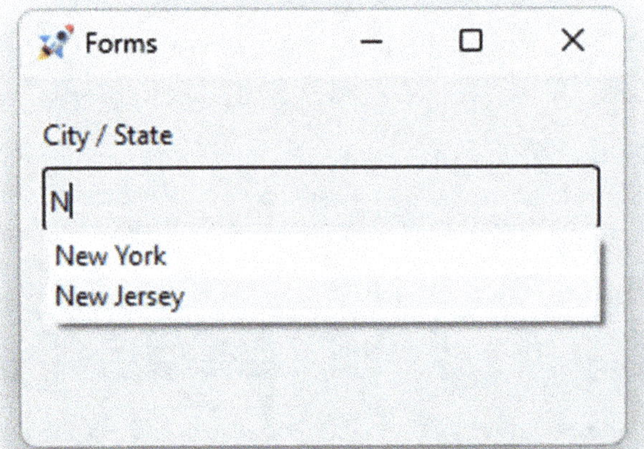

QTextEdit

QTextEdit is a versatile PyQt widget designed to accept and display multi-line text input from users. It typically appears as a rectangular or square box and can be visually customized using style options to match the application's design.

This widget is particularly useful in scenarios where extended or formatted text input is required, such as entering emails, passwords, user messages, names, or other textual content. With rich text support, it also allows formatting such as bold, italics, and underlining, making it suitable for both plain and styled text inputs.

setTextColor(QColor) and **textColor()**
Sets or retrieves the color of the text.

- **QColor**("color_name") → QColor("red")
- **QColor**("#hex") → QColor("#b1bed2")

</> Python

```
import sys
from PyQt6.QtCore import *
from PyQt6.QtWidgets import *
from PyQt6.QtGui import *

class MyApp(QMainWindow):

    def __init__(self):
        super().__init__()

        self.setWindowTitle("Forms")
        self.setProperty("resize", (1000, 800))
        self.setWindowIcon(QIcon("images/rocket.png"))
        self.setStyleSheet("background:#ebebeb")

        QLabel('Comment',self).move(10,10)
        self.input = QTextEdit(self)
        self.input.setGeometry(10,40, 300, 200),
        self.input.setTextColor(QColor("green"))
```

```
        self.input.setStyleSheet("border:1px solid; border-radius:5px")

app = QApplication([])
myapp = MyApp()
myapp.show()
sys.exit(app.exec())
```

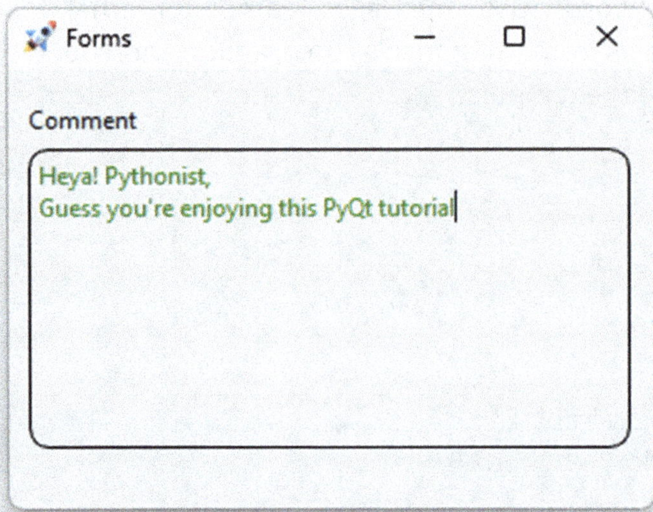

setFontFamily(family **)** and **fontFamily()**
Sets or returns the current font family.

```
Python
text_edit = QTextEdit( )
text_edit.setFontFamily("Georgia")
```

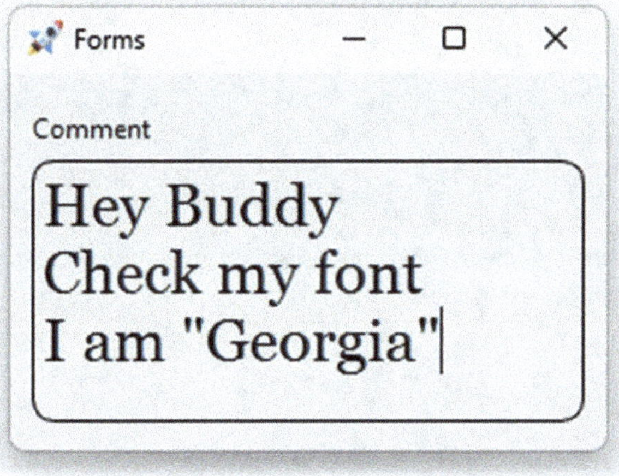

Georgia

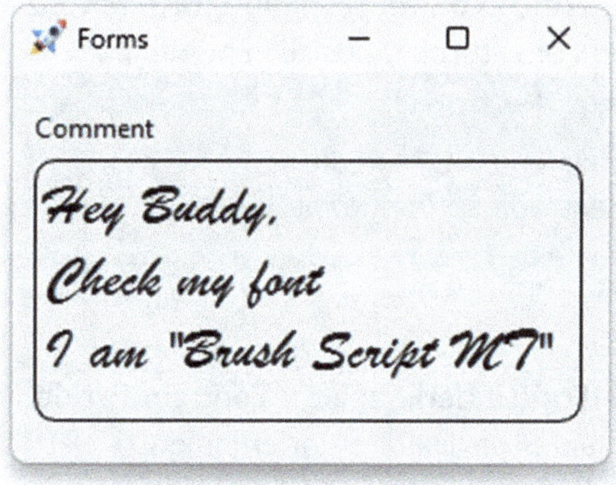

Brush Script MT

Available Font-Family

Georgia	Cursive	Trebuchet MS	Comic Sans MS
Times New Roman	fantasy	Courier New	Brush Script MT
Arial	Garamond	Consolas	Tahoma
Serif	Helvetica	Lucida Console	Mono-space
Sans-serif	Verdana	Monaco	

Table 6.1 : Accepted font families

setFontItalic(bool **)** and **fontItalic**

Sets or returns italic styling.

</> Python

```
text_edit = QTextEdit( )
text_edit.setFontItalic(True)
```

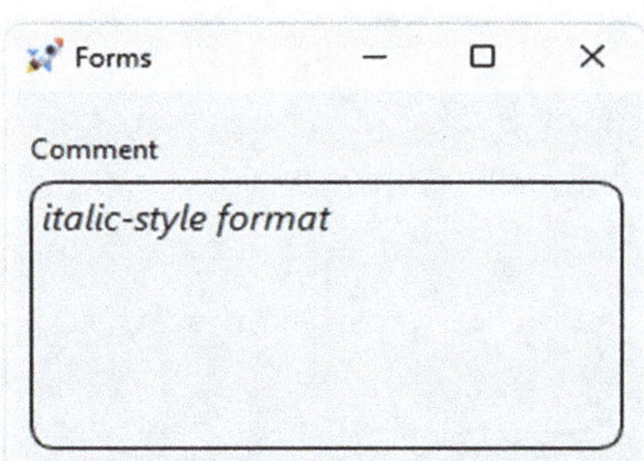

setFontPontSize(size **) and fontPointSize()**

Sets or returns font size in points.

```python
text_edit = QTextEdit( )
text_edit.setFontPointSize(20)
```

setFontUnderline(bool **) and fontUnderline()**

Enables or disables underlining.

```python
text_edit = QTextEdit( )
text_edit.setFontUnderline(True)
```

setFontWeight(int **) and fontWeight()**

Controls text boldness using predefined weights.

```python
text_edit = QTextEdit( )
text_edit.setFontWeight( 20 )
```

setTextBackgroundColor(QColor **) and textBackgroundColor()**

Controls the background color of the text.

```python
text_edit = QTextEdit( )
text_edit.setTextBackgroundColor(QColor("red"))
```

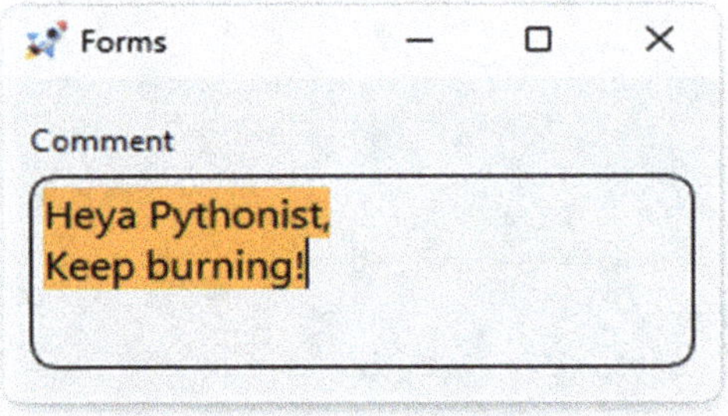

Selection and Clipboard

setSelectAll( )

This method selects all text.

</> Python

```
text_edit = QTextEdit( )
text_edit.selectAll()
```

hasSelectedText()

Returns True if any text is selected.

</> Python

```
text_edit = QTextEdit( )
status = text_edit.hasSelectedText()
```

copy(), **cut()** and **paste()**

copy()	→	This copies the selected text to the clipboard.
cut()	→	It moves the selected text to the clipboard.
paste()	→	Paste the copied or cut content from the clipboard.

</> Python

```
text_edit = QTextEdit( )
text_edit.copy()
text_edit.cut()
text_edit.paste()
```

undo() and **redo()**

undo()	→	Reverses changes
redo()	→	Re-applies changes

```python
text_edit = QTextEdit( )
text_edit.clear()
text_edit.undo()      #reverse clean
text_edit.redo()      #re-clean text
```

zoomIn(int) and zoomOut()

zoomIn()	→	Zooms text in by a specific range
zoomOut()	→	Zooms text out by a specific level

```python
text_edit = QTextEdit( )
text_edit.zoomIn( 10 )     #Zoom in by 10
text_edit.zoomOut( 10 )    #Zoom out by 10
```

setHtml(html) and toHtml()

setHtml()	→	Sets the rich text (HTML).
toHtml()	→	Returns the rich text (HTML) representation of the content.

```python
text_edit = QTextEdit( )
text_edit.setText( "This is a raw text" )
html = text_edit.toHtml( )

print(html)
```

```
#Output
<!DOCTYPE HTML PUBLIC "-//W3C//DTD HTML 4.0//EN" "http://www.w3.org/TR/REC-html40/strict.dtd">
<html><head><meta name="qrichtext" content="1" /><meta charset="utf-8" /><style type="text/css">
p, li { white-space: pre-wrap; }
hr { height: 1px; border-width: 0; }
li.unchecked::marker { content: "\2610"; }
li.checked::marker { content: "\2612"; }
</style></head><body style=" font-family:'Segoe UI'; font-size:9pt; font-weight:400; font-style:normal;">
<p style=" margin-top:0px; margin-bottom:0px; margin-left:0px; margin-right:0px; -qt-block-indent:0; text-indent:0px;">This is a raw text</p></body></html>
```

setMarkdown(markdown) and toMarkdown()

setMarkdown()	→	Sets the markdown content.
toMarkdown()	→	Returns the markdown.

setPlainText(text) and toPlainText()

setPlainText()	→	Sets the text content as plain text, removing any rich formatting.
toPlainText()	→	Returns the current text as plain text.

```python
html = "<html><body>Hello, Pythonist!</body></html>"

text_edit = QTextEdit( )
text_edit.setHtml( html )
plaintext = text_edit.toPlainText( )

print(plaintext)
```

```
#Output
Hello, Pythonist!
```

insertPlainText(text)
Inserts plain text at the current cursor.

insertHtml(html)
Inserts HTML-formatted text at the current cursor.

append(text)
Adds text as a new paragraph at the end.

QPlainTextEdit

QPlainTextEdit is a PyQt widget used for displaying and editing large, plain (non-rich) text content. Unlike *QTextEdit*, which handles rich text (HTML/Markdown), QPlainTextEdit is optimized for handling plain text with better performance, especially for large files or logs.

Key Properties and Methods

setCenterOnScroll	centerOnScroll	appendPlainText	contentOffset
modificationChanged	setMaximumBlockCount	centerCursor	maximumBlockCount
getPaintContext	backgroundVisible	appendHtml	blockBoundingGeometry
blockCount	blockBoundingRect	setBackgroundVisible	blockCountChanged
firstVisibleBlock	updateRequest	setPlainText	toPlainText

setPlainText(text **)** and **toPlainText( )**

setPlainText()	→	Sets the entire content as plain text.
toPlainText()	→	Gets the current content as plain text.

</> **Python**

```python
import sys
from PyQt6.QtCore import *
from PyQt6.QtWidgets import *
from PyQt6.QtGui import *

class MyApp(QMainWindow):

    def __init__(self):
        super().__init__()

        self.setWindowTitle("Forms")
        self.setProperty("resize", (1000, 800))
        self.setWindowIcon(QIcon("images/rocket.png"))
        self.setStyleSheet("background:#ebebeb")

        QLabel('Your Bio', self).move(10,10)
        self.plain = QPlainTextEdit(self)
```

```
        self.plain.setGeometry(10, 40, 250, 150)
        self.plain.setReadOnly(True)
        self.plain.setPlainText('Eg: I am a Computer Science graduate from Harvard ...')

app = QApplication([])
myapp = MyApp()
myapp.show()
sys.exit(app.exec())
```

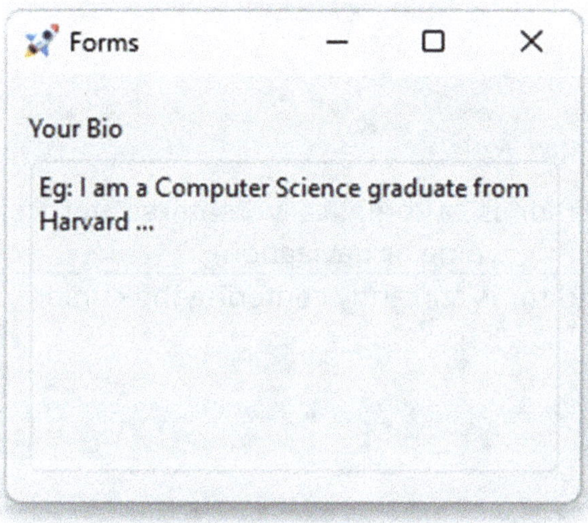

appendHtml(html**)** and **appendPlainText(** text **)**

appendHtml()	→	Adds html content at the end of the document.
appendPlainText()	→	Appends a new line of text at the end.

</> Python

```python
html = "<html><body style='color:red'>Hello, Pythonist!</body></html>"

plain_edit = QPlainTextEdit( )
plain_edit.appendHtml( html )
plain_edit.appendPlainText( "Have a nice day" )
```

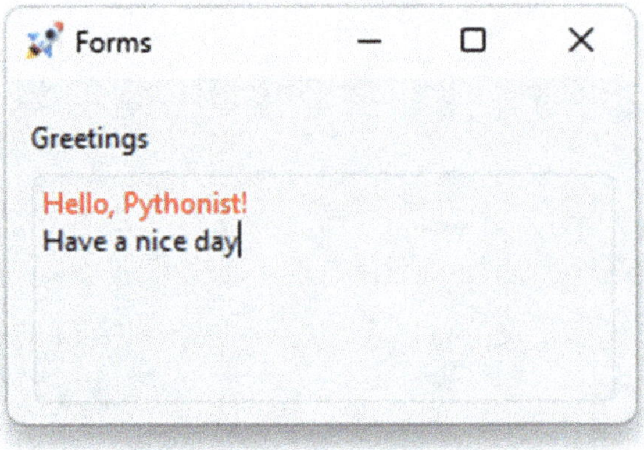

setCenterOnScroll(bool **)**

setCenterOnScroll()	→	If set to True, the cursor is automatically centered vertically when it moves (like during typing or navigation).
centerOnScroll()	→	Returns whether the editor is currently centering the cursor when scrolling.

</> Python

```python
plain_edit = QPlainTextEdit( )
plain_edit.setCenterOnScroll( True )
```

modificationChanged

Emitted whenever the modification state of the document changes. Useful to detect unsaved changes.

</> Python

```python
plain_edit = QPlainTextEdit( )
plain_edit.modificationChanged.connect( lambda: print("text modified!") )
```

setMaximumBlockCount(int **), maximumBlockCount()** and **blockCount()**

setMaximumBlockCount()	→	Limits the number of text blocks (lines). Older lines will be automatically removed once the limit is reached. Useful for log viewers.

maximumBlockCount()	→	Returns the current limit set for the number of blocks in the document.
blockCount()	→	Returns the total number of text blocks (usually lines or paragraphs) in the editor.

</> Python

```
plain_edit = QPlainTextEdit( )
plain_edit.setMaximumBlockCount( 10 )
```

setBackgroundVisible(bool **)** and **backgroundVisible()**

setBackgroundVisible()	→	Shows or hides the background when no text is present.
backgroundVisible()	→	Returns whether the editor's background is drawn when there is no text.

</> Python

```
plain_edit = QPlainTextEdit( )
plain_edit.setBackgroundVisible( True )
```

Tips

Exploring Methods and Properties of TextEditors

You can explore the full list of methods and properties available for each PyQt text editor widget using Python's built-in dir() and help() functions.
For example,

```
>>> line = QLineEdit()

# Get a list of all methods and properties
>>> print(dir(line))

# Get the full documentation of the QLineEdit object
>>> help(line)

# Get documentation for a specific method (e.g., text())
>>> help(line.text)
```

QRadioButton

The QRadioButton widget in PyQt is used to present mutually exclusive options to users. It appears as a small circular button accompanied by a descriptive label. When grouped together, only one radio button can be selected at a time, making it ideal for choosing one option from a defined set.

Each radio button has two states:

- **Checked (True):** The option is selected.
- **Unchecked (False):** The option is not selected.

This makes QRadioButton perfect for collecting precise and singular user input in a structured form.

Common Use Cases

- Selecting gender (e.g., Male / Female / Other)
- Choosing an application theme (e.g., Light / Dark / System Default)
- Selecting payment method (e.g., Credit Card / PayPal / Bank Transfer)
- Setting user role in a form (e.g., Admin / Editor / Viewer)
- Choosing subscription plan (e.g., Free / Standard / Premium)
- Picking default file format (e.g., PDF / DOCX / TXT)
- Selecting preferred language
- Determining level of access (e.g., Read-Only / Read & Write)

Key Properties and Methods

icon	setCheckable	setAutoRepeatInterval	setAutoRepeatDelay
setIcon	autoRepeat	group	pressed
autoExclusive	setShortcut	autoRepeatInterval	isCheckable
nextCheckState	released	hitButton	setChecked
clicked	autoRepeatDelay	setText	click
shortcut	initStyleOption	text	setAutoRepeat
checkStateSet	setDown	toggled	setAutoExclusive
toggle	isDown	animateClick	isChecked

setText(text) and text()

setText()	→	Sets the text label on the button.
text()	→	Returns the current text of the button.

</> Python

```
import sys
from PyQt6.QtCore import *
from PyQt6.QtWidgets import *
from PyQt6.QtGui import *

class MyApp(QMainWindow):

    def __init__(self):
        super().__init__()

        self.setWindowTitle("Forms")
        self.setProperty("resize", (1000, 800))
        self.setWindowIcon(QIcon("images/rocket.png"))
        self.setStyleSheet("background:#ebebeb")

        QLabel("<h1>Choose a theme</h1>", self).setGeometry(10,10, 200, 50)

        self.lightRadio = QRadioButton(self)
        self.lightRadio.setText("Light")
        self.lightRadio.setGeometry(10,60, 250, 40)
        self.lightRadio.setStyleSheet('''background:rgba(112,173,71,150);
                border-radius:5px; padding-left:10px''')

        self.darkRadio = QRadioButton(self)
        self.darkRadio.setText("Dark")
        self.darkRadio.setGeometry(10,110, 250, 40)
        self.darkRadio.setStyleSheet('''background:rgba(112,173,71,150);
                border-radius:5px; padding-left:10px''')

app = QApplication([])
myapp = MyApp()
myapp.show()
sys.exit(app.exec())
```

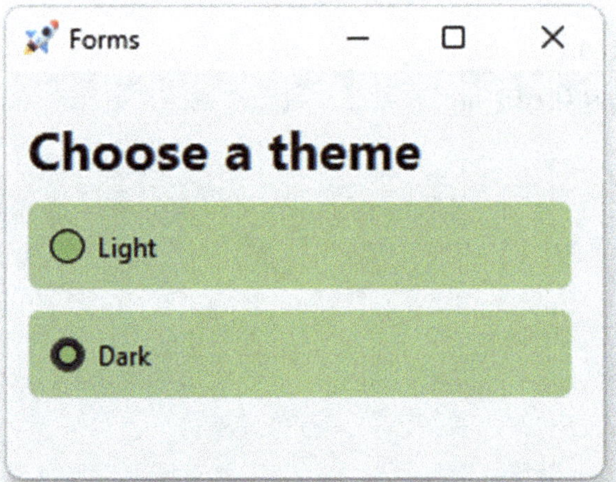

setIcon(QIcon**)** and **icon( )**

setIcon()	→	Sets an icon (image) to appear alongside the button's text.
icon()	→	Returns the ***QIcon*** currently set for the button.

</> Python

```
google = QRadioButton( )
google.setText("Google")
google.setIcon( QIcon("images/google.png") )

facebook = QRadioButton( )
facebook.setIcon( QIcon("images/facebook.png") )
```

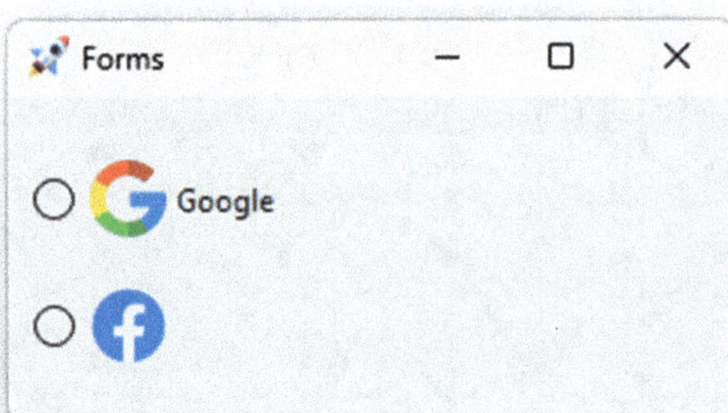

setShortCut(key **)** and **icon( )**

setShortCut()	→	Sets a keyboard shortcut to activate the button.
shortcut()	→	Returns the keyboard shortcut associated with the button.

</> Python

```
radio = QRadio( )
radio.setShortCut("m")
```

setDown(bool **)** and **isDown( )**

setDown()	→	Manually sets whether the button appears pressed.
isDown()	→	Returns True if the button is currently being pressed down.

</> Python

```
radio = QRadio( )
radio.setDown(True)
```

setChecked(bool **)** and **isChecked( )**

setChecked()	→	Sets the button's state to checked or unchecked.
isChecked()	→	Returns True if the button is currently checked.

</> Python

```
radio = QRadio( )
radio.setText("US residence")
radio.setChecked(True)
```

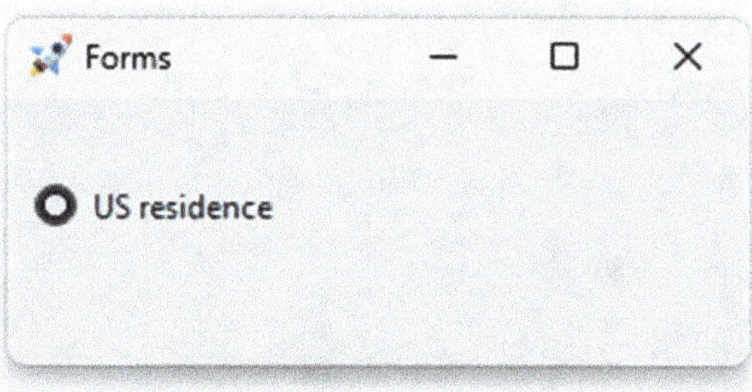

setCheckable(bool **)** and **isCheckable( )**

setCheckable()	→	Enables or disables the button's checkable state (i.e., makes it toggleable like a checkbox or radio button).
isCheckable()	→	Returns True if the button is checkable.

```
</> Python
radio = QRadio( )
radio.setCheckable(True)
```

clicked, pressed, released and **toggled**

clicked	→	Signal emitted when the button is clicked.
pressed	→	Signal emitted when the button is pressed down.
released	→	Signal emitted when the button is released after being pressed.
toggled	→	Signal emitted when the button's checked state changes.

```
</> Python
radio = QRadio( )
radio.clicked.connect(lambda: print("radio is clicked"))
radio.pressed.connect(lambda: print("radio is pressed"))
radio.released.connect(lambda: print("radio has been released"))
radio.toggled.connect(lambda: print("radio is toggled"))
```

click( ) and **toggle( )**

click()	→	Programmatically clicks the button (emits pressed, released, and clicked).
toggle()	→	Toggles the button's state (checked ↔ unchecked).

```
</> Python
radio = QRadio( )

button = QPushButton("Press me")
button.pressed.connect(lambda: self.radio.click() )
```

Grouping Buttons

When designing software applications, there are often scenarios where multiple buttons need to trigger the same action or be handled by the same callback function. This is especially common when a group of buttons represents a set of related options or tasks.

Manually assigning each button to the same function can quickly become cumbersome—particularly when dealing with a large pool of buttons. A more efficient and organized approach is to group the buttons based on their functionality.

QButtonGroup

PyQt provides the QButtonGroup class to simplify this process. It allows you to:

- Group related buttons logically (without affecting their layout)
- Assign unique IDs to buttons in the group
- Handle signals like *buttonClicked* from any button in the group
- Route all button interactions through a single function or slot
- Track which button is checked

Key Methods and Properties of QButtonGroup

Method/Property	Function
addButton(button)	Adds a button to the group. Optionally assigns a unique ID.
removeButton(button)	Removes a button from the group.
button(id)	Returns the button associated with a given ID.
buttons()	Returns a list of all buttons in the group.
checkedButtons()	Returns the currently checked button (if any).
checkedId()	Returns the ID of the checked button.
setExclusive(bool)	If True, only one button in the group can be checked at a time (like radio buttons).
exclusive	Returns True if the group is in exclusive mode.
setId(button, id)	Assigns a unique integer ID to a button in the group.
id(button)	Returns the ID of the given button.
buttonClicked	Emitted when any button in the group is clicked.
idClicked	Emitted when a button with a specific ID is clicked.
buttonPressed	Emitted when a button is pressed.
idPressed	Emitted when a button (by ID) is pressed.
buttonReleased	Emitted when a button is released.
idReleased	Emitted when a button (by ID) is released.
buttonToggled	Emitted when a button's checked state changes.
idToggled	Emitted when a button (by ID) is toggled.

Table 6.2 : Properties and methods of the QButtonGroup

Grouping Radio Buttons

By default, when multiple QRadioButton widgets are added to the same parent widget (e.g., QMainWindow() or QWidget()), they automatically behave as a group. This means that only one radio button can be selected at a time within that parent.
However, in more complex user interfaces, you may need to create multiple independent groups of radio buttons. For instance, a form might ask users to select:

- **Gender** (Male / Female / Other)
- **Country** (USA / Canada / UK)
- **Race** (Asian / African / Caucasian / Other)

Each of these sections must allow only one selection within their own group but should not interfere with selections in other groups.

To achieve this behavior, PyQt provides the QButtonGroup() class, which allows you to explicitly define custom groups of buttons, regardless of their parent widget. Using QButtonGroup, you can:

- Group related QRadioButtons logically.
- Ensure only one button in each group can be checked at a time.
- Retrieve which button (or button ID) is selected in each group.
- Connect signals from grouped buttons to shared callbacks efficiently.

Example

</> Python

```
import sys
from PyQt6.QtCore import *
from PyQt6.QtWidgets import *
from PyQt6.QtGui import *

class MyApp(QMainWindow):

    def __init__(self):
        super().__init__()

        self.setWindowTitle("Forms")
        self.setProperty("resize", (1000, 800))
        self.setWindowIcon(QIcon("images/rocket.png"))
        self.setStyleSheet("background:#ebebeb")

        QLabel("Select your gender", self).setGeometry(10, 10, 100, 30)
        self.maleRadio = QRadioButton(self)
        self.maleRadio.setText("Male")
```

```
        self.maleRadio.setGeometry(10, 50, 100, 30)

        self.femaleRadio = QRadioButton(self)
        self.femaleRadio.setText("Female")
        self.femaleRadio.setGeometry(10, 80, 100, 30)

        QLabel("Residence information",self).setGeometry(10, 110, 150, 30)
        self.usRadio = QRadioButton(self)
        self.usRadio.setText("US")
        self.usRadio.setGeometry(10, 140, 100, 30)

        self.nonUsRadio = QRadioButton(self)
        self.nonUsRadio.setText("Non US residence")
        self.nonUsRadio.setGeometry(10, 170, 100, 30)

        self.gender = QButtonGroup(self)
        self.gender.addButton(self.maleRadio)
        self.gender.addButton(self.femaleRadio)

        self.residence = QButtonGroup(self)
        self.residence.addButton(self.usRadio)
        self.residence.addButton(self.nonUsRadio)

app = QApplication([])
myapp = MyApp()
myapp.show()
sys.exit(app.exec())
```

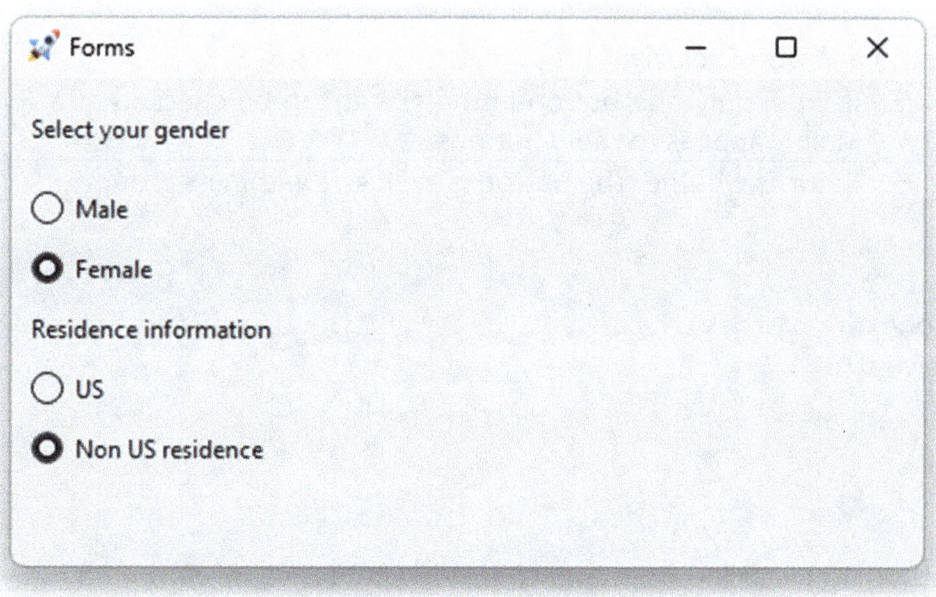

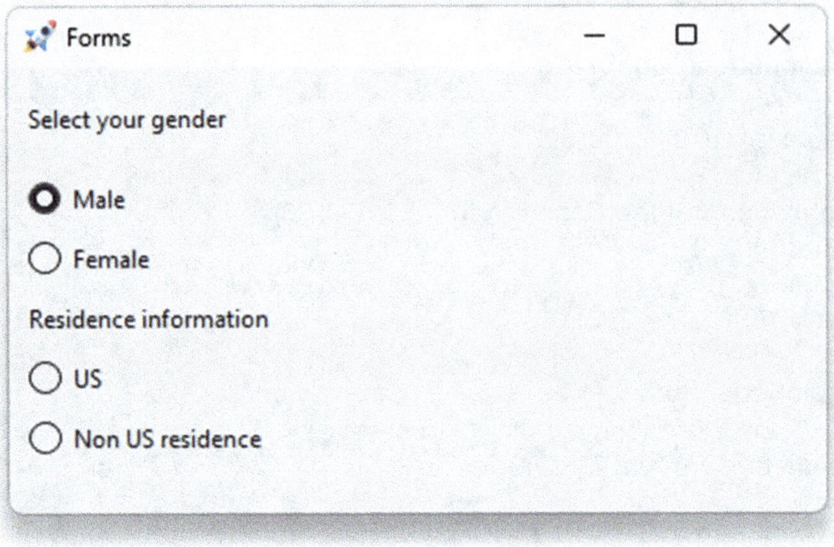

Before grouping buttons

group( )

Returns the *QButtonGroup* the button belongs to (if any).

```python
radio = QRadioButton( )
group = radio.group()
```

setAutoExclusive(bool **)** and **autoExclusive( )**

setAutoExclusive()	→	If True, only one button in the group can be checked at a time. Mainly applies to radio buttons.
autoExclusive()	→	Returns whether the button is exclusive within its group.

```python
radio = QRadioButton( )
radio.setAutoExclusive( True )
```

checkStateSet()

Protected virtual method that is called whenever the check state is set programmatically.

animateClick()

Simulates a button click visually for a specified time in milliseconds.

setAutoRepeat(bool **)** and **autoRepeat( )**

setAutoRepeat()	→	Enables/disables auto-repeat behavior on press and hold.
autoRepeat()	→	If True, the button will repeatedly emit clicked when held down.

</> Python

```
radio = QRadioButton( )
radio.setAutoRepeat( True )
```

hitButton(QPoint **)**

Returns True if the button should react to a press at position pos (used in custom styling).

QPoint(x, y)	→	QPoint(20, 30)

</> Python

```
radio = QRadioButton( )
isHit = radio.hitButton( QPoint(10, 60))
```

QCheckBox

The QCheckBox is a type of button displayed as a small box that can be checked or unchecked. It is commonly used when users need to select multiple options from a list, whether the options are related or unrelated.
Unlike radio buttons, which allow only one selection in a group, checkboxes support multiple simultaneous selections.

States

QCheckBox operates in two basic states:

- True → Checked (selected)
- False → Unchecked (not selected)

Typical Use Cases

- Accepting terms and conditions
- Selecting preferences (e.g., Enable notifications, Remember me)
- Choosing multiple items from a list (e.g., hobbies, skills, filters)

Key Properties and Methods

released	click	checkState	nextCheckState
stateChanged	shortcut	isChecked	setTristate
setCheckable	autoRepeatInterval	autoRepeatDelay	hitButton
initStyleOption	setDown	setAutoRepeat	isDown
setIcon	setShortcut	autoRepeat	pressed
checkStateSet	clicked	toggle	setCheckState
checkStateChanged	autoExclusive	isCheckable	text
isTristate	setAutoRepeatDelay	setText	setAutoRepeatInterval
toggled	setChecked	icon	animateClick
setAutoExclusive	group		

setText(text) and text()

setText()	→	Sets the label text beside the checkbox.
text()	→	Returns the current label text.

</> Python

```
import sys
from PyQt6.QtCore import *
from PyQt6.QtWidgets import *
from PyQt6.QtGui import *

class MyApp(QMainWindow):

    def __init__(self):
        super().__init__()

        self.setWindowTitle("Forms")
        self.setProperty("resize", (1000, 800))
        self.setWindowIcon(QIcon("images/rocket.png"))
        self.setStyleSheet("background:#ebebeb")

        QLabel("<h1>Course</h1>", self).setGeometry(10, 10, 100, 30)

        self.cplus = QCheckBox(self)
        self.cplus.setText("C++")
        self.cplus.setGeometry(10,50,300,30)
        self.cplus.setStyleSheet("""background:rgba(142,170,219,150);
                                    border-radius:5px; padding-left:10px""")

        self.javascript = QCheckBox(self)
        self.javascript.setText("JavaScript")
        self.javascript.setGeometry(10,90,300,30)
        self.javascript.setStyleSheet("""background:rgba(142,170,219,150);
                                         border-radius:5px; padding-left:10px""")

        self.python = QCheckBox(self)
        self.python.setText("Python")
        self.python.setGeometry(10,130,300,30)


app = QApplication([])
myapp = MyApp()
myapp.show()
sys.exit(app.exec())
```


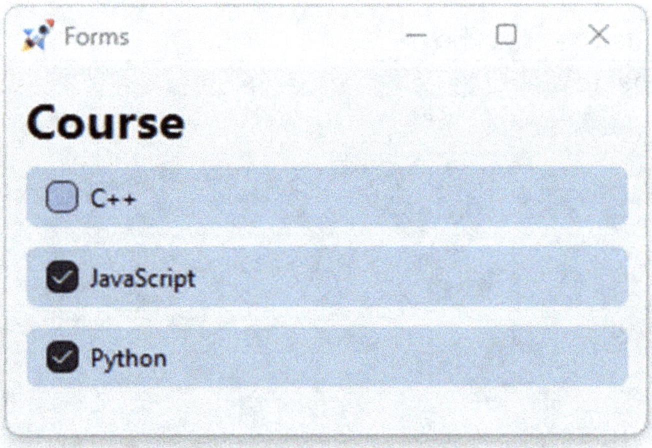

setIcon(QIcon**) and icon( )**

setIcon()	→	Sets an icon (image) to appear alongside the button's text.
icon()	→	Returns the ***QIcon*** currently set for the button.

</> Python

```
cplus = QCheckBox( )
cplus.setIcon("images/cplus.png")
cplus.setIconSize(QSize(35, 35))

python = QCheckBox( )
python.setText("images/cplus.png")
python.setIconSize(QSize(35, 35))
```

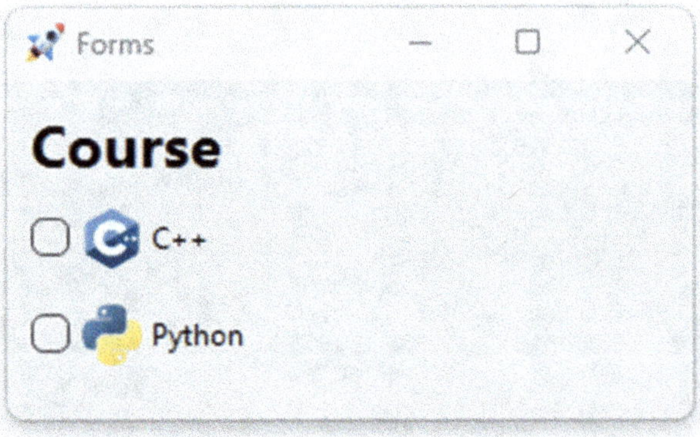

setChecked(bool) and isChecked( )

setChecked()	→	Checks or unchecks the box programmatically.
isChecked()	→	Returns True if the checkbox is currently checked.

```python
python = QCheckBox( )
python.setChecked(True)
```

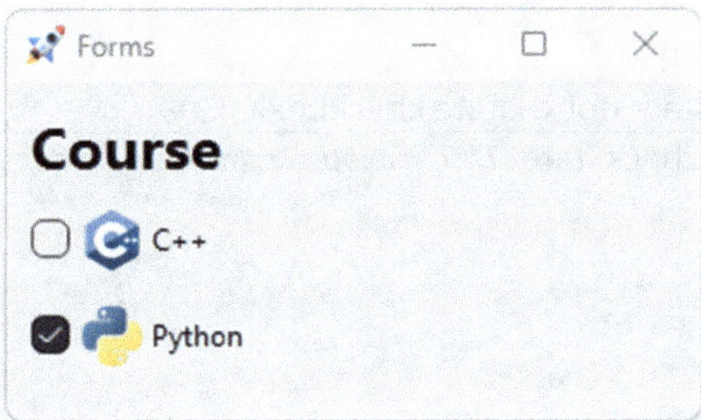

setCheckable(bool) and isCheckable( )

setCheckable()	→	Enables or disables the checkable behavior. Most useful when customizing toggle-like widgets.
isCheckable()	→	Returns True if the checkbox can be checked.

```python
python = QCheckBox( )
python.setCheckable(True)
```

clicked, pressed, released and toggled

clicked	→	Signal emitted when the checkbox is clicked.
pressed	→	Signal emitted when the checkbox is pressed down.
released	→	Signal emitted when the checkbox is released after being pressed.
toggled	→	Signal emitted when the checkbox's checked state changes.

</> Python

```
check = QCheckBox( )
check.clicked.connect(lambda: print("check is clicked"))
check.pressed.connect(lambda: print("check is pressed"))
check.released.connect(lambda: print("check has been released"))
check.toggled.connect(lambda: print("check is toggled"))
```

setCheckState(Qt.CheckState**)** and **checkState()**

setCheckState()	→	Sets the current check state (for tristate checkboxes).
checkState()	→	Returns the current Qt.CheckState (*Unchecked, PartiallyChecked, Checked*).

</> Python

```
check = QCheckBox( )
check.setCheckState(Qt.CheckState.Unckecked)
```

setTristate(bool**)** and **isTristate( )**

setTristate()	→	Enables tristate mode (*Checked, PartiallyChecked, Unchecked*)
isTristate()	→	Returns True if the checkbox supports tristate mode.

</> Python

```
check = QCheckBox( )
check.isTristate(True)
```

stateChanged

Signal emitted when the state changes. Can be connected to custom slots.

</> Python

```
check = QCheckBox( )
check.setText("Check my state")
check.isTristate(True)
check.stateChanged.connect(lambda: print(check.checkState()))
```

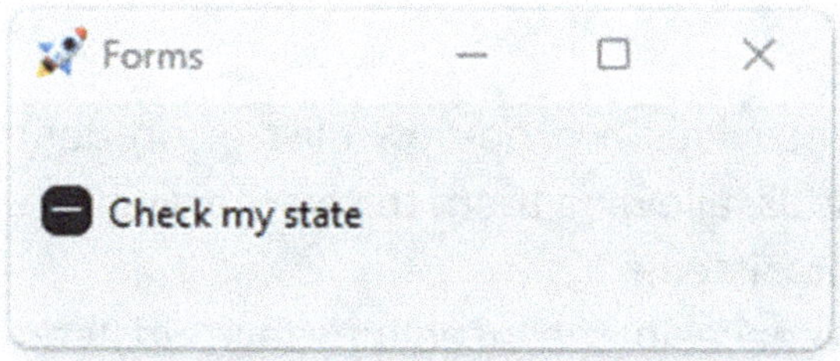

#Output
CheckState.PartiallyChecked

#Output
CheckState.Checked

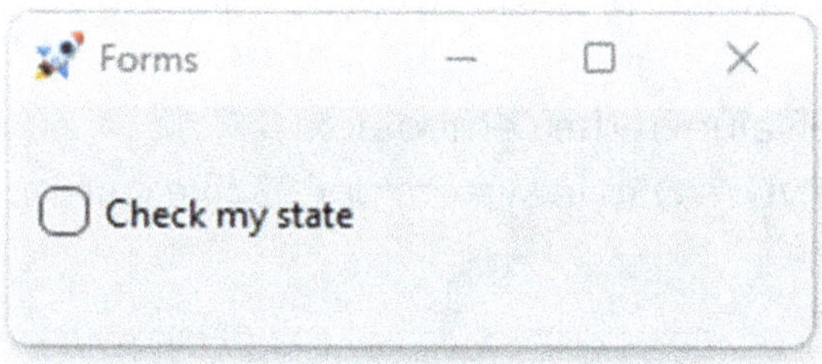

#Output
CheckState.Unchecked

QComboBox

The QComboBox is an input widget in PyQt that provides a drop-down list of predefined options. When the user clicks the box, the list expands, allowing them to select a single item. The selected item is then displayed in the combo box itself.
This widget is particularly useful for conserving space in the user interface. Instead of displaying a long list of choices that may clutter the layout, QComboBox keeps the UI clean and organized by showing only one visible item at a time.

- By default, the **first item** in the list is selected and displayed if the user hasn't made a choice.
- Once an item is selected, it becomes the visible value in the combo box.
- The widget can be **custom-styled** using either PyQt's QStyle system or CSS-like rules with setStyleSheet().

Use Cases

QComboBox is commonly used for form fields like
- country selectors, language or theme selectors
- Form fields like title: (Mr., Mrs., Dr.)
- Choosing fonts or font sizes
- Filtering/search criteria in dashboards

Key Properties and Methods

addItems	textActivated	currentTextChanged	itemDelegate
setItemIcon	itemText	rootModelIndex	itemIcon
setCompleter	insertItems	maxCount	count
__len__	view	duplicatesEnabled	setModelColumn
modelColumn	minimumContentsLength	initStyleOption	findData
currentIndex	addItem	setCurrentIndex	textHighlighted
itemData	setView	completer	insertItem
setItemData	editTextChanged	showPopup	setMinimumContentsLength
setMaxCount	setValidator	isEditable	setFrame
currentIndexChanged	insertPolicy	sizeAdjustPolicy	InsertPolicy
setDuplicatesEnabled	setPlaceholderText	highlighted	hidePopup
insertSeparator	hasFrame	setSizeAdjustPolicy	clear
currentText	setMaxVisibleItems	removeItem	setLineEdit
lineEdit	currentData	setItemDelegate	setItemText

model	SizeAdjustPolicy	clearEditText	setModel
setEditText	setInsertPolicy	placeholderText	setEditable
validator	maxVisibleItems	activated	setRootModelIndex
setCurrentText	findText		

addItem(item, userData **)**

Adds a single item to the combo box. Optionally stores associated data.

</> Python

```
import sys
from PyQt6.QtCore import *
from PyQt6.QtWidgets import *
from PyQt6.QtGui import *

class MyApp(QMainWindow):

    def __init__(self):
        super().__init__()

        self.setWindowTitle("Forms")
        self.setProperty("resize", (1000, 800))
        self.setWindowIcon(QIcon("images/rocket.png"))
        self.setStyleSheet("background:#ebebeb")

        QLabel("<h1>Choose your language</h1>", self).setGeometry(30, 10, 300, 40)
        self.combo = QComboBox(self)
        self.combo.setGeometry(30, 60, 260, 40)

        self.combo.addItem("English")
        self.combo.addItem("French")
        self.combo.addItem("Spanish")
        self.combo.addItem("Dutch")


app = QApplication([])
myapp = MyApp()
myapp.show()
sys.exit(app.exec())
```

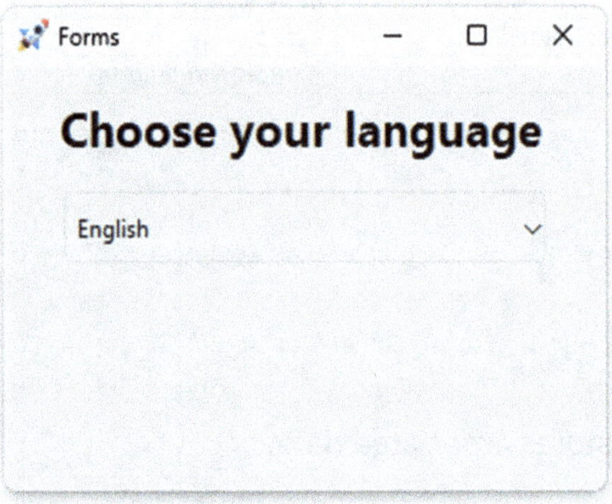

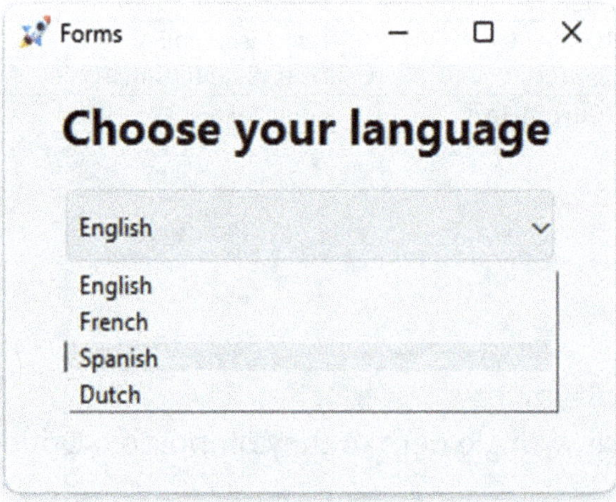

addItems(iterable)

Adds multiple items at once.

```python
items = ["Canada", "Rusia", "Israel"]

combobox = QComboBox( )
combobox.addItems(items)
```

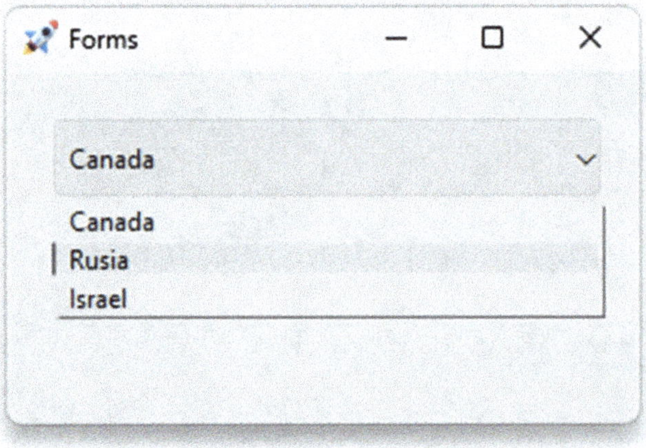

insertItem(index, item**)** and **insertItems(** index, iterable**)**

insertItem()	→	Inserts an item at a specific index.
insertItems()	→	Inserts multiple items at the specified position.

</> Python

```
items = ["Canada", "Rusia", "Israel"]

combobox = QComboBox( )
combobox.addItems(items)
combobox.insertItem(1, "South Africa")
```

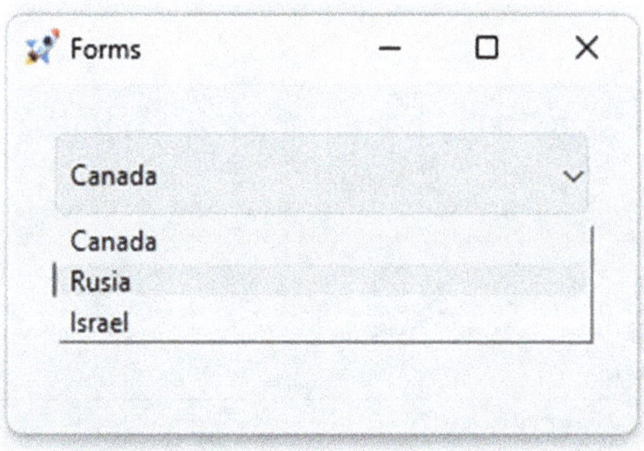

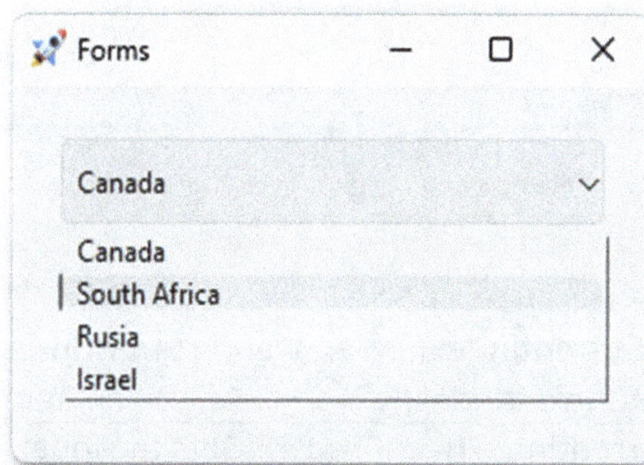

removeItem(index**)**, and **clear( )**

removeItem()	→	Removes the item at the given index.
clear()	→	Removes all items.

</> Python

```
combobox = QComboBox( )
combobox.removeItem( 3 )
combobox.clear()
```

setCurrentText(text) and **currentText(text)**

setCurrentText()	→	Selects an item with matching text.
currentText()	→	Returns the currently displayed text.

</> Python

```
combo = QComboBox( )
combo.setCurrentText("Israel")
```

setCurrentIndex(index) and **currentIndex(text)**

setCurrentIndex()	→	Selects an item by index.
currentIndex()	→	Gets the index of the selected item.

</> Python

```
combo = QComboBox( )
combo.setCurrentIndex( 2 )
```

showPopup( ) and **hidePopup(text)**

showPopup()	→	Programmatically opens the list.
hidePopup()	→	Programmatically closes the list.

</> Python

```
combo = QComboBox( )
combo.showPopup()
combo.hidePopup()
```

count() and __len__()

count()	→	Returns the number of items in the combo box.
__len__()	→	Returns the number of items in the combo box.

```python
combobox = QComboBox( )
temscount = combobox.count()
length = combobox.__len__()
```

insertSeparator(int)

Inserts a visual separator in the list.

```python
items = ["Canada", "Rusia", "Israel", "Norway"]

combo = QComboBox( )
combo.addItems(items)
combo.insertSeparator(3)
combo.insertSeparator(2)
combo.insertSeparator(1)
```

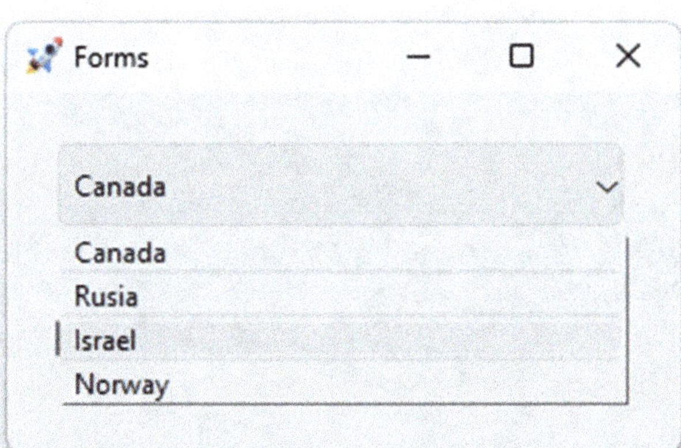

setMaxCount(int) and maxCount()

setMaxCount()	→	Set the maximum number of items allowed.
maxCount()	→	Gets the maximum number of items allowed.

setPlaceholderText(text) and **placeholderText()**

setPlaceholderText()	→	Sets a gray-text hint when no selection is made.
placeholderText()	→	Gets the placeholder text.

</> Python

```
combo = QComboBox( )
combo.setPlaceholderText("Select your country")
```

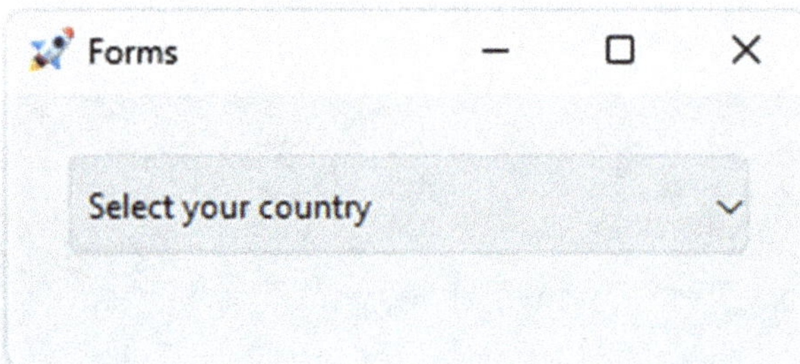

setItemIcon(index, QIcon()) and **itemIcon(index)**

setItemIcon()	→	Sets an icon for a specific item.
itemIcon()	→	Gets the icon of the item.

</> Python

```
items = ["Python", "JavaScript", "Java"]
combo = QComboBox( )
combo.addItems(items)

combo.setItemIcon(0, QIcon("images/python.png"))
```

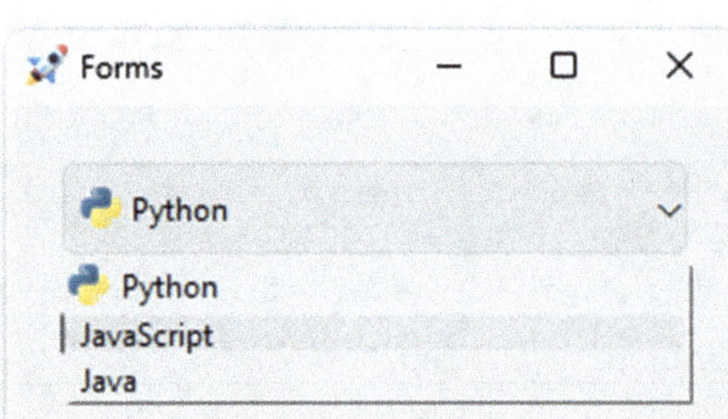

setItemText(index, text **)** and **itemText(** index **)**

setItemText()	→	Sets the text for a specific item.
itemText()	→	Gets the text of the item.

```python
items = ["Python", "JavaScript", "Java"]
combo = QComboBox( )
combo.addItems(items)

combo.setItemText(2 , "C++" )
```

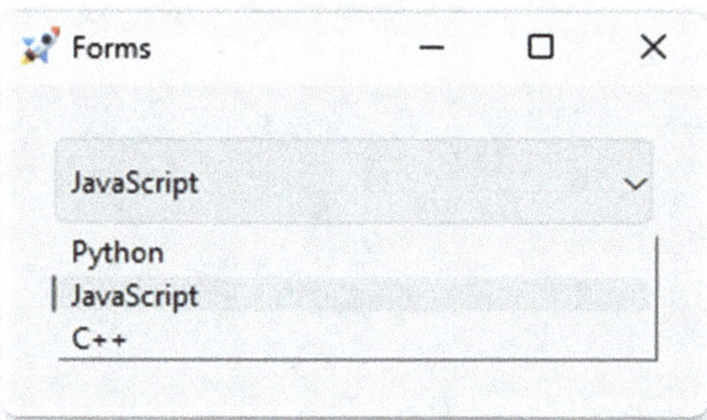

setItemData(index, data **)** and **itemData(** index **)**

setItemData()	→	Sets user data for an item.
itemData()	→	Gets the user data associated with an item.

```python
items = ["America", "Brazil"]
combo = QComboBox( )
combo.addItems(items)

combo.setItemData(0 , "North America" )
combo.setItemData(1 , "South America" )
```

setEditable(bool)

Enables or disables text editing.

```python
combo = QComboBox( )
combo.setEditable( True )
```

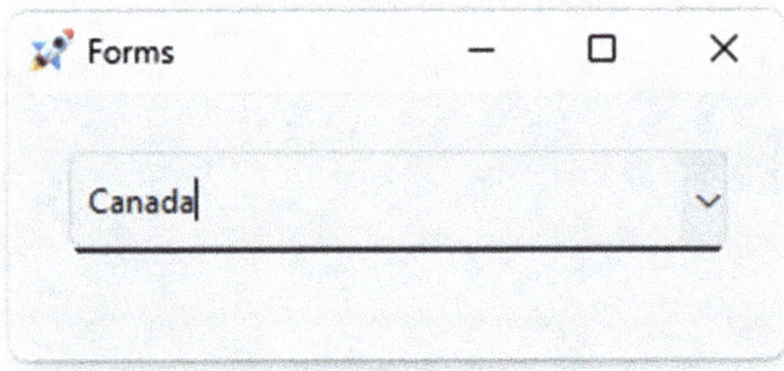

Signals

editTextChanged

Signal emitted when user changes the text.

```python
combo = QComboBox( )
combo.setEditable( True )

combo.editTextChanged.connect(lambda: print(combo.currentText()))
```

activated, currentIndexChanged, currentTextChanged, highlighted, textActivated and textHighlighted

activated	→	Emitted when an item is selected.
currentIndexChanged	→	Emitted when the selection changes.
currentTextChanged	→	Emitted when the current text is updated.

highlighted	→	Emitted when an item is hovered/highlighted.
textActivated	→	Emitted when text is activated (selected or entered).
textHighlighted	→	Emitted when text is highlighted in the list.

</> Python

```python
combo = QComboBox( )

#activated
combo.activated.connect(lambda: print(combo.currentText()))

#currentIndexChanged
combo.currentIndexChanged.connect(lambda: print(combo.currentIndex()))

#currentTextChanged
combo.currentTextChanged.connect(lambda: print(combo.currentText()))

#highlighted
combo.highlighted.connect(lambda: print("highlighted"))

#textActivated
combo.textActivated.connect(lambda: print("activated"))

#textHighlighted
combo.textHighlighted.connect(lambda: print("highlighted"))
```

QCalendarWidget

The **QCalendarWidget** is a PyQt widget used to display a full calendar interface. It shows past, present, and future dates in a monthly grid format. Beyond just displaying dates, it allows users to select dates with ease—making it a powerful alternative to manually typing date values.

Use Cases

- Selecting a date of birth
- Choosing an appointment or meeting date
- Setting travel or booking dates
- Selecting a deadline or due date
- Inputting event dates for calendars or schedulers
- Filtering records by a specific date range

Key Properties and Methods

setFirstDayOfWeek	setMinimumDate	showPreviousYear	firstDayOfWeek
isGridVisible	updateCell	setCalendar	clearMaximumDate
setHeaderTextFormat	setCurrentPage	setWeekdayTextFormat	setNavigationBarVisible
setSelectionMode	weekdayTextFormat	headerTextFormat	setDateTextFormat
clearMinimumDate	maximumDate	horizontalHeaderFormat	currentPageChanged
setDateEditEnabled	clicked	setMaximumDate	verticalHeaderFormat
showSelectedDate	selectionChanged	showToday	isNavigationBarVisible
setHorizontalHeaderFormat	setDateEditAcceptDelay	dateTextFormat	setDateRange
dateEditAcceptDelay	updateCells	setSelectedDate	setGridVisible
SelectionMode	calendar	paintCell	activated
setVerticalHeaderFormat	VerticalHeaderFormat	minimumDate	monthShown
yearShown	selectionMode	showPreviousMonth	HorizontalHeaderFormat
isDateEditEnabled	showNextMonth	selectedDate	showNextYear

showToday( )

Focuses and highlights today's date.

Python

```python
import sys
from PyQt6.QtCore import *
from PyQt6.QtWidgets import *
from PyQt6.QtGui import *

class MyApp(QMainWindow):

    def __init__(self):
        super().__init__()

        self.setWindowTitle("Forms")
        self.setProperty("resize", (1000, 800))
        self.setWindowIcon(QIcon("images/rocket.png"))

        self.calendar = QCalendarWidget(self)
        self.calendar.setGeometry(30, 10, 300, 200)
        self.calendar.showToday()


app = QApplication([])
myapp = MyApp()
myapp.show()
sys.exit(app.exec())
```

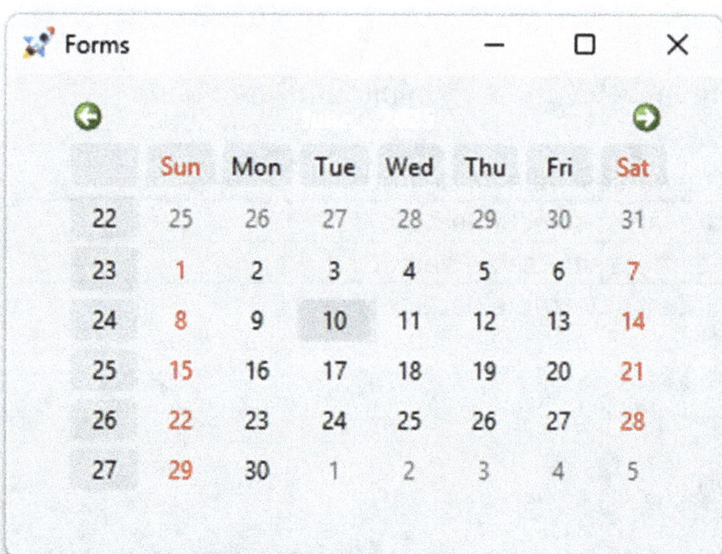

setSelectedDate(QDate) and **selectedDate( )**

setSelectedDate() → Sets the selected date on the calendar.

selectedDate() → Returns the currently selected date.

QDate(year, month, day) → eg. QDate(2025, 10, 3)

</> Python

```
calendar = QCalendarWidget()
calendar.setSelectedDate(QDate(2024, 12, 25))
```

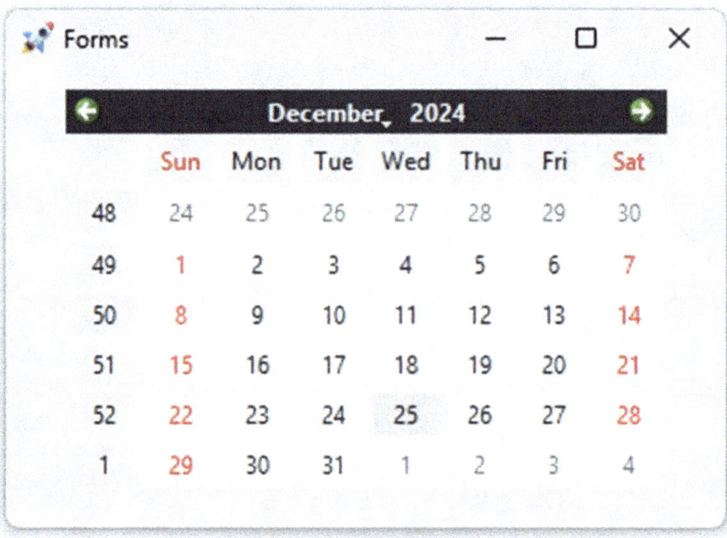

setMinimumDate(QDate), setMaximumDate(QDate), minimumDate() and **maximumDate()**

setMinimumDate() → Defines the earliest selectable date.

setMaximumDate() → Defines the latest selectable date.

minimumDate() → Gets the earliest selectable date.

maximumDate() → Gets the latest selectable date.

</> Python

```
calendar = QCalendarWidget()
calendar.setMinimumDate(QDate(2020, 1, 1))
calendar.setMaximumDate(QDate(2025, 12, 31))
```

setDateRange(min QDate(), max QDate() **)**

Sets both minimum and maximum dates in one call.

```
</> Python
calendar = QCalendarWidget()
calendar.setDateRange(QDate(2020, 1, 1), QDate(2025, 12, 31) )
```

showNextMonth(), showPreviousMonth(), showNextYear(), showPreviousYear monthShown() and **yearShown()**

showNextMonth()	→	Navigates to the next month.
showPreviousMonth()	→	Navigates to the previous month.
showNextYear()	→	Moves forward one year.
showPreviousYear()	→	Moves backward one year.
monthShown()	→	Returns the currently displayed month (1-12).
yearShown()	→	Returns the currently displayed year.

```
</> Python
calendar = QCalendarWidget()
calendar.showNextYear()
```

setGridVisible(bool **)** and **isGridVisible( )**

setGridVisible()	→	Shows or hides grid lines between days.
isGridVisible()	→	Checks if grid is visible.

```
</> Python
calendar = QCalendarWidget()
calendar.setGridVisible(True)
```

setNavigationBarVisible(bool **)** and **isNavigationBarVisible( )**

setNavigationBarVisible()	→	Shows or hides the month or year navigation bar.
isNavigationBarVisible()	→	Checks if the navigation bar is visible.

setFirstDayOfWeek(Qt.DayOfWeek**)** and **firstDayOfWeek( )**

setFirstDayOfWeek()	→	Changes which day starts the week (e.g. Qt.Monday).
firstDayOfWeek()	→	Returns the current first day of the week.

</> Python

```
calendar = QCalendarWidget()
calendar.setFirstDayOfWeek(Qt.DayOfWeek.Friday)
```

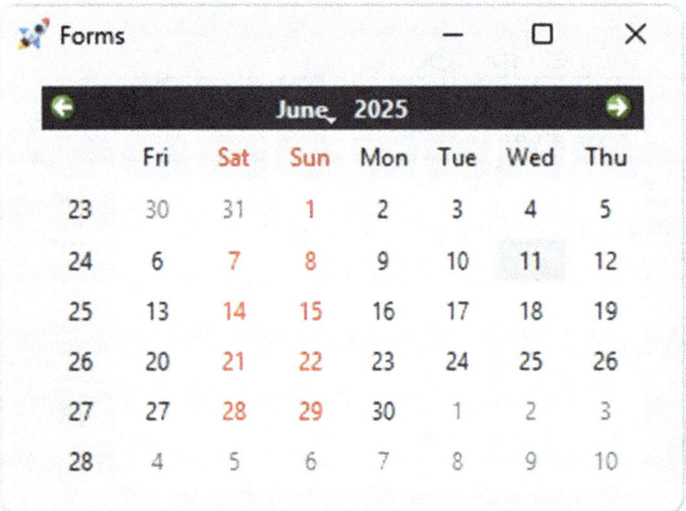

setDateEditEnabled(bool **)** and **isDateEditEnabled( )**

setDateEditEnabled()	→	Enables or disables the editable date spinbox below the calendar.
isDateEditEnabled()	→	Checks if the date edit field is enabled.

setCalendar(QCalendar **)** and **calendar( )**

setDateEditEnabled()	→	Sets a custom QCalendar, e.g., different locale or calendar system.
calendar()	→	Returns the internal ***QCalendar*** object.

Calendars

Gregorian	Julian	Jalali	Milankovic
IslamicCivil			

Table 6.3 : Kinds of calendars

</> Python

```
calendar = QCalendarWidget()
calendar.setCalendar(QCalendar(QCalendar.System.Gregorian))
```

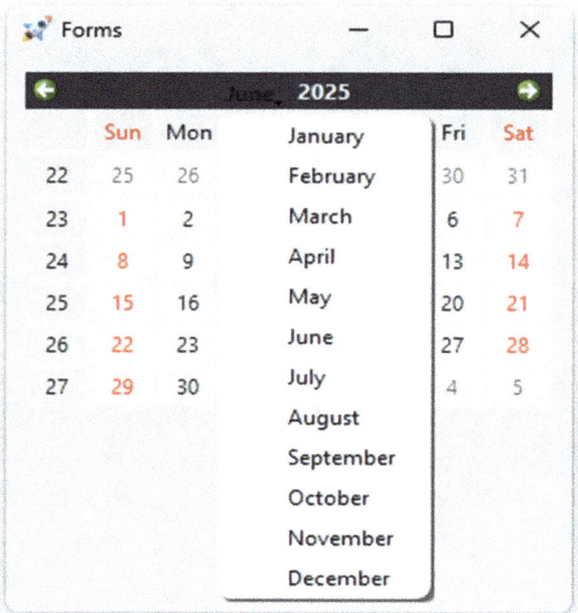

Gregorian

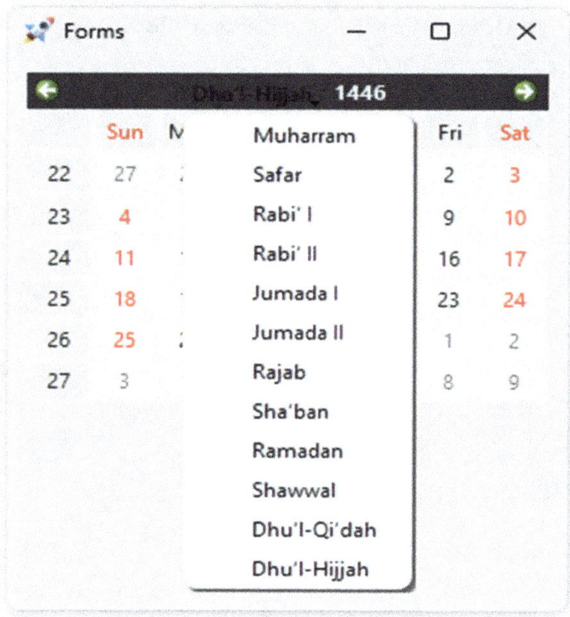

IslamicCivil

Signals

clicked, activated and **selectionChanged**

clicked	→	Emitted when a date is clicked.
activated	→	Emitted when the user double-clicks a date or presses enter.
selectionChanged	→	Emitted when the selected date changes.

```python
calendar = QCalendarWidget()

#clicked
calendar.clicked.connect(lambda: print("Calendar clicked"))

#selectionChanged
calendar.selectionChanged.connect(dateChanged)


def dateChanged():
    date = calendar.selectedDate()
    print(date)
```

QColorDialog

The QColorDialog widget in PyQt provides a convenient, interactive dialog window that allows users to choose colors. Users can pick from a predefined palette, use a color picker, or manually enter hex, RGB, or HSV values. This widget is particularly useful in applications involving color customization, themes, graphic design, or any UI needing color input.
By default, QColorDialog is not visible; it is invoked through another widget, such as a button click.

Use Cases

- Allowing users to pick background or font colors
- Theme and skin configuration tools
- Drawing or painting applications
- Data visualization (setting graph colors)

Key Properties and Methods

setResult	setCustomColor	setModal	setCurrentColor
exec	accepted	DialogCode	open
finished	customColor	customCount	accept
colorSelected	result	selectedColor	ColorDialogOption
setOptions	currentColorChanged	isSizeGripEnabled	rejected
setStandardColor	setOption	done	testOption
setSizeGripEnabled	reject	getColor	standardColor
options	currentColor		

getColor(title)
Static method that opens the dialog and returns the color selected by the user.

</> Python

```
import sys
from PyQt6.QtCore import *
from PyQt6.QtWidgets import *
from PyQt6.QtGui import *
```

```
class MyApp(QMainWindow):

    def __init__(self):
        super().__init__()

        self.setWindowTitle("Forms")
        self.setProperty("resize", (1000, 800))
        self.setWindowIcon(QIcon("images/rocket.png"))

        QLabel("<h1>Change background color</h1>", self).setGeometry(30, 20, 300, 40)
        self.color = QColorDialog(self)

        self.button = QPushButton("Pick color", self)
        self.button.setGeometry(100,100, 150, 40)
        self.button.setIcon(QIcon("images/color-pallete.png"))
        self.button.setIconSize(QSize(25,25))
        self.button.clicked.connect(self.pickColor)


    def pickColor(self):
        selected_color = self.color.getColor()          #Open and get selected color
        self.setStyleSheet(f"background:{selected_color.name()}")
        print(selected_color.name())


app = QApplication([])
myapp = MyApp()
myapp.show()
sys.exit(app.exec())
```

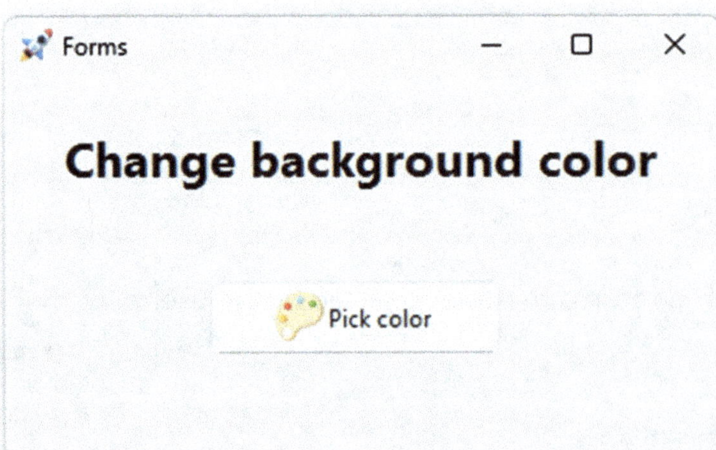

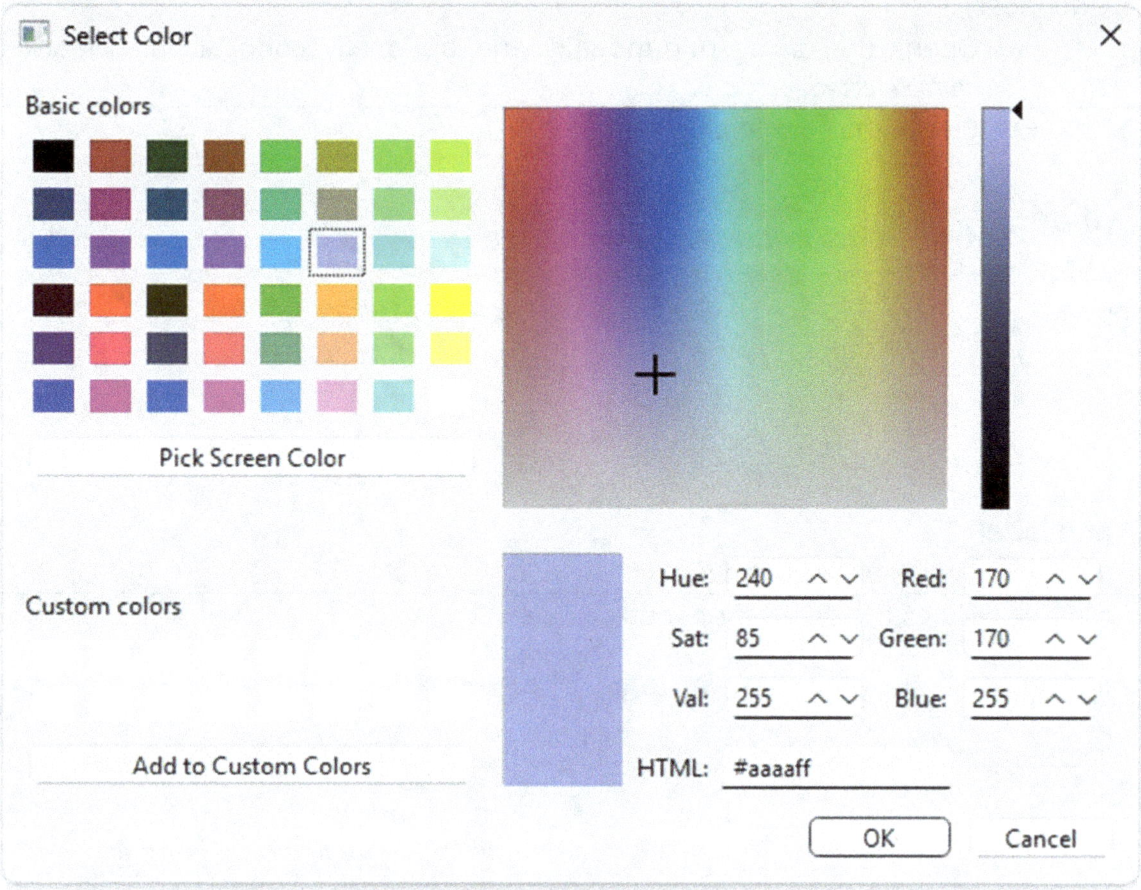

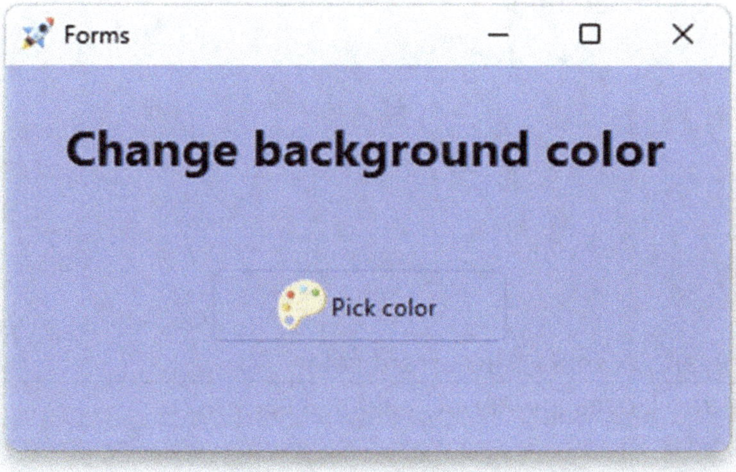

Output

#aaaaff

open( ) and **close( )**

open()	→	Opens the dialog non-modally and optionally connects a callback to *colorSelected*.
close()	→	Closes the color dialog.

</> Python

```
color = QColorDialog()
color.open()
```

show() and **hide()**

show()	→	Shows or open the dialog.
hide()	→	Hides the dialog if opened.

</> Python

```
color = QColorDialog()
color.show()
```

exec()

Executes the dialog modally and waits for user input.

</> Python

```
color = QColorDialog()
color.exec()
```

accept() and **reject()**

accept()	→	Confirms the dialog and accepts the current color.
reject()	→	Cancels the dialog and closes it without making a selection.

</> Python

```
color = QColorDialog()
color.accept()
```

setResult(int) and result()

setResult()	→	Sets the dialog's return result code.
result()	→	Gets the dialog's result code after closing.

currentColor()

Returns the currently selected color (even if not yet accepted).

</> Python

```python
color = QColorDialog()
color.currentColor()
```

setCurrentColor(QColor)

Sets the default selected color when the dialog opens.

</> Python

```python
color = QColorDialog()
color.setCurrentColor(QColor("red"))
```

selectedColor()

Returns the final selected color (after dialog accepted).

Properties

name	black	cyanF	fromHsvF	getCmykF	green	hsvHueF
rgb	blackF	darker	fromRgb	getHsl	greenF	hsvSaturation
rgba	blue	fromCmyk	fromRgbF	getHslF	hslHue	hsvSaturationF
alpha	blueF	fromCmykF	fromRgba	getHsv	hslHueF	hue
alphaF	colorNames	fromHsl	fromRgba64	getHsvF	hslSaturation	hueF
red	convertTo	fromHslF	fromString	getRgb	hslSaturationF	isValid
redF	cyan	fromHsv	getCmyk	getRgbF	hsvHue	isValidColor

Table 6.4 : Properties of the *selectedColor()* object

</> Python

```python
color = QColorDialog()
selected = color.selectedColor()
color_name = selected.name()
```

Tips

Exploring Properties of Selected Color

Use dir() to get the complete list of properties of the selected color.
For example,

```
>>> color = QColorDialog()
>>> selected = color.selectedColor()
>>> print( dir(selected))
.....
```

currentColorChanged

Signal emitted when user picks a different color.

</> Python

```python
color = QColorDialog()
color.currentColorChanged.connect(lambda: getCurrentColor())

def getCurrentColor():
    name = color.color.currentColor().name()
```

colorSelected

Signal emitted when a color is selected and confirmed.

</> Python

```python
color = QColorDialog()
color.currentColorChanged.connect(lambda: getSelectedColor())

def getSelectedColor():
    name = color.color.selectedColor().name()
```

accepted and **rejected**

accepted	→	Signal emitted when dialog is accepted.
rejected	→	Signal emitted when dialog is canceled.

QSlider

The QSlider widget in PyQt is a UI control used to adjust numerical values within a specified range using a sliding handle. It offers a more interactive and visual method for value selection compared to manually entering numbers.
By default, the slider range is from ***0*** to ***99***, but you can customize it to any range using *setMinimum()* and *setMaximum()*.

Use Cases

- Adjusting volume in music or video players
- Changing brightness or opacity in design applications
- Controlling progress in timeline-based animations
- Setting zoom levels, font sizes, or other visual settings
- Providing real-time control in games or simulations

Key Properties and Methods

tickInterval	singleStep	hasTracking	setRepeatAction
setValue	maximum	valueChanged	triggerAction
setPageStep	setSliderDown	sliderPosition	pageStep
SliderAction	orientation	sliderReleased	value
setOrientation	initStyleOption	setMaximum	invertedControls
setRange	setSingleStep	setSliderPosition	setMinimum
repeatAction	tickPosition	setInvertedControls	setTracking
minimum	sliderPressed	isSliderDown	rangeChanged
sliderMoved	SliderChange	setInvertedAppearance	invertedAppearance
TickPosition	sliderChange	setTickPosition	actionTriggered

setMinimum(int value**), minimum( ), setMaximum(** int value**), maximum( )** and **setRange(** int min, int max **)**

setMinimum()	→	Sets the minimum limit of the slider.
minimum()	→	Returns the current min range value.
setMaximum()	→	Sets the maximum limit of the slider.
maximum()	→	Returns the current max range value.

setRange() → Sets both minimum and maximum values in one call.

```python
import sys
from PyQt6.QtCore import *
from PyQt6.QtWidgets import *
from PyQt6.QtGui import *

class MyApp(QMainWindow):

    def __init__(self):
        super().__init__()

        self.setWindowTitle("Forms")
        self.setProperty("resize", (1000, 800))
        self.setWindowIcon(QIcon("images/rocket.png"))
        self.setStyleSheet("background:#ebebeb")

        QLabel("<h1>Set Volume</h1>", self).setGeometry(100, 10, 200, 80)

        self.slider = QSlider(self)
        self.slider.setRange(1, 200)
        self.slider.setOrientation(Qt.Orientation.Horizontal)
        self.slider.setGeometry(50, 80, 250, 40)
        self.slider.valueChanged.connect(lambda: self.getVolume())

        self.volume = QLineEdit(self)
        self.volume.setGeometry(115,120, 100, 40)
        self.volume.setReadOnly(True)
        self.volume.setAlignment(Qt.AlignmentFlag.AlignCenter)
        self.volume.setStyleSheet("background:white")


    def getVolume(self):
        value = str(self.slider.value())
        self.volume.setText(value)



app = QApplication([])
myapp = MyApp()
myapp.show()
sys.exit(app.exec())
```

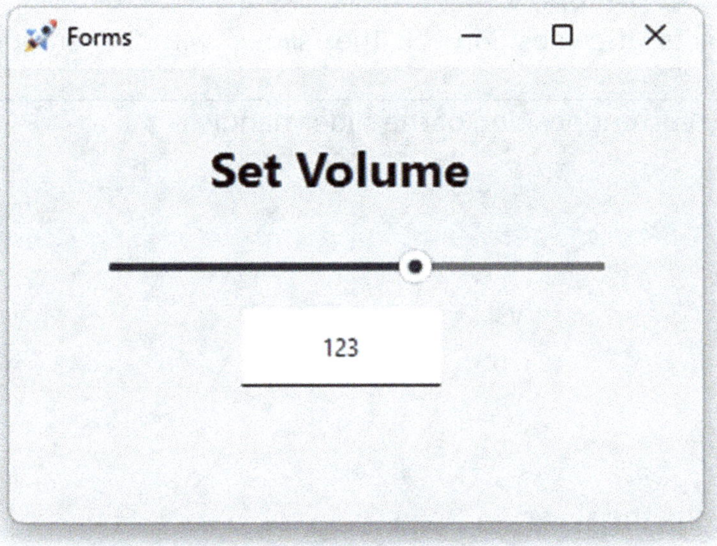

setValue(int value **)** and **value()**

setValue()	→	Sets the slider to a specific value within the range.
value()	→	Returns the current slider value.

```python
slider = QSlider()
slider.setValue( 20 )
```

valueChanged

Signal emitted whenever the slider value changes.

```python
slider = QSlider()
slider.valueChanged.connect(lambda: getSliderValue())

def getSliderValue():
    value = slider.value()
    print(value)
```

setSliderPosition(int value **)** and **sliderPosition()**

setSliderPosition()	→	Manually sets the position of the slider without emitting *valueChanged*.
sliderPosition()	→	Returns the current position of the slider handle.

```python
slider = QSlider()
slider.setSliderPosition( 50 )
```

sliderMoved

Signal emitted while the user is dragging the slider.

```python
slider = QSlider()
slider.sliderMoved.connect(lambda: getSliderValue())

def getSliderValue():
    value = slider.sliderPosition()
    print(value)
```

sliderPressed and **sliderReleased**

sliderPressed	→	Signals emitted when slider is pressed.
sliderReleased	→	Signals emitted when slider is released.

```python
slider = QSlider()
slider.sliderPressed.connect(lambda: print("Thumb has been pressed"))

slider.sliderReleased.connect(lambda: print("Thumb has been released"))
```

setSliderDown(bool **)** and **isSliderDown()**

setSliderDown()	→	Programmatically simulates whether the slider is currently pressed.

isSliderDown() → Checks whether the slider is being dragged.

setOrientation(Qt.Orientation **)** and **orientation()**

setOrientation()	→	Sets the slider to be horizontal or vertical.
orientation()	→	Returns the current orientation.

</> **Python**

```
slider = QSlider()
slider.setOrientation(Qt.Orientation.Vertical)
```

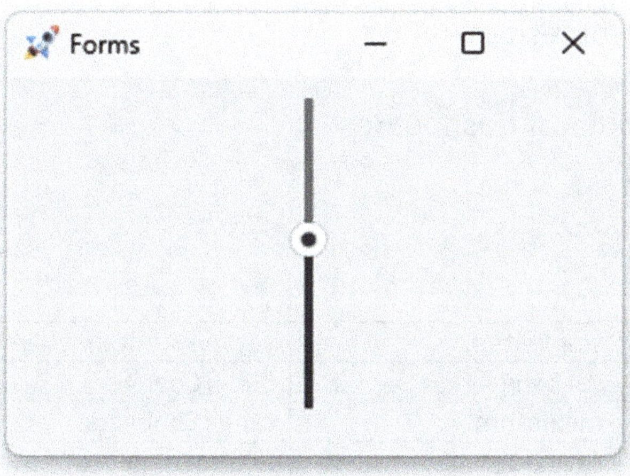

QRadial

The QDial is a rotary widget (a circular dial) in PyQt used to set a value by rotating a knob. It is similar in function to *QSlider*, but it offers a more analog-like, compact, and tactile UI element for setting values within a specified range.

By default, QDial allows values from **0** to **99**, but this can be customized.

Use Cases

- Volume control in audio interfaces
- Rotational controls in scientific or industrial applications
- Dial-based input in virtual instruments or synthesizers
- Gamepad or wheel-like controls in games
- Knob-based setting adjustments in simulations or dashboards

Key Properties and Methods

setPageStep	isSliderDown	singleStep	setInvertedControls
sliderReleased	repeatAction	setRange	SliderChange
notchSize	value	maximum	rangeChanged
setMinimum	minimum	setValue	actionTriggered
sliderPosition	hasTracking	SliderAction	setInvertedAppearance
invertedControls	setNotchTarget	pageStep	setTracking
setSliderPosition	valueChanged	notchesVisible	invertedAppearance
notchTarget	setMaximum	sliderMoved	setSliderDown
orientation	setWrapping	initStyleOption	setSingleStep
setRepeatAction	sliderChange	setNotchesVisible	sliderPressed
wrapping	setOrientation	triggerAction	

setMinimum(int value**), minimum( ), setMaximum(** int value**), maximum( )** and **setRange(** int min, int max **)**

setMinimum()	→	Sets the minimum value of the dial.
minimum()	→	Returns the current min value.
setMaximum()	→	Sets the maximum value of the dial.

maximum()	→	Returns the current max value.
setRange()	→	Sets both minimum and maximum values in one call.

Python

```python
import sys
from PyQt6.QtCore import *
from PyQt6.QtWidgets import *
from PyQt6.QtGui import *

class MyApp(QMainWindow):

    def __init__(self):
        super().__init__()

        self.setWindowTitle("Forms")
        self.setProperty("resize", (1000, 800))
        self.setWindowIcon(QIcon("images/rocket.png"))
        self.setStyleSheet("background:#ebebeb")

        QLabel("<h1>Rotate Image</h1>", self).setGeometry(150, 5, 200, 80)

        self.dial = QDial(self)
        self.dial.setRange(0, 360)
        self.dial.setNotchesVisible(True)
        self.dial.setGeometry(10, 150, 150, 150)
        self.dial.valueChanged.connect(lambda: self.rotateImage())

        self.readings = QLabel(self)
        self.readings.setGeometry(200, 70, 100, 40 )
        self.readings.setStyleSheet("color:tomato; font-size:25px")

        self.label = QLabel(self)
        self.label.setGeometry(210,120, 200, 200)
        self.rotateImage()


    def rotateImage(self):
        value = self.dial.value()
        transform = QTransform().rotate(value)

        image = QPixmap("images/person3.jpg")
        scaled_image = image.scaled(150,150)
        rotated_image = scaled_image.transformed(transform)
        self.label.setPixmap(rotated_image)

        self.readings.setText(f"{value}°")
```

```
app = QApplication([])
myapp = MyApp()
myapp.show()
sys.exit(app.exec())
```

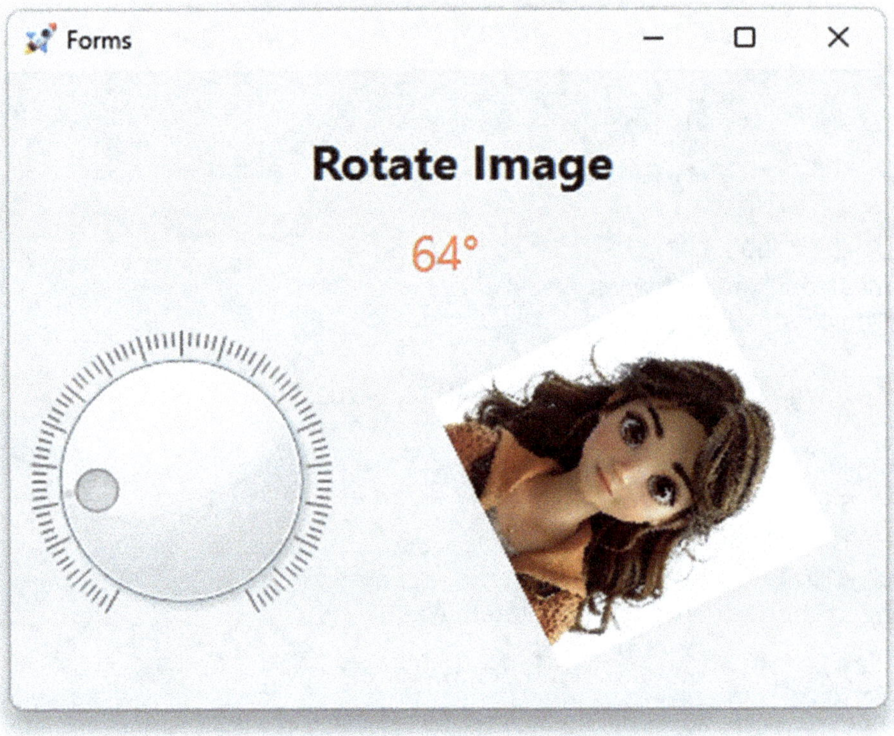

setValue(int value **)** and **value()**

setValue()	→	Sets the current value of the dial.
value()	→	Gets the current value.

</> Python

```
dial = QDial()
dial.setValue( 10 )
```

valueChanged

Signal emitted whenever the value changes.

</> Python

```
dial = QDial()
dial.valueChanged.connect(callbackfun)

def callbackfun():
    value = dial.value()
    print(value)
```

setNotchesVisible(bool value **)** and **notchesVisible()**

setNotchesVisible()	→	Toggles the visibility of notches (ticks).
notchesVisible()	→	Returns whether notches are visible.

</> Python

```
dial = QDial()
dial.setNotchesVisible( False )
```

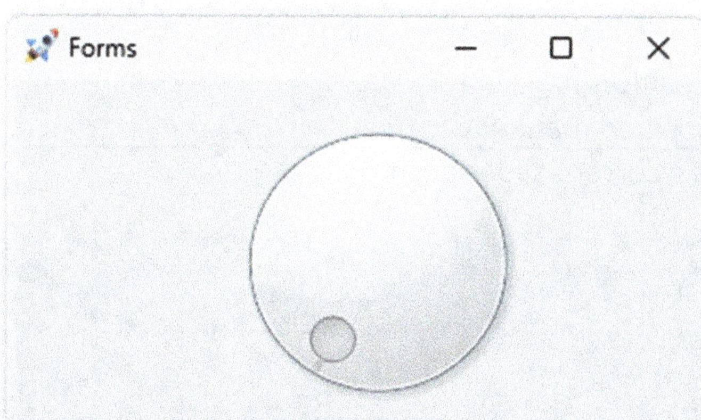

setNotchTarget(float value **)** and **notchTarget()**

setNotchTarget()	→	Sets the target spacing (in pixels) between notches.
notchTarget()	→	Returns the notch target value.

```python
dial = QDial()
dial.setNotchesVisible( True )
dial.setNotchTarget( 5 )
```

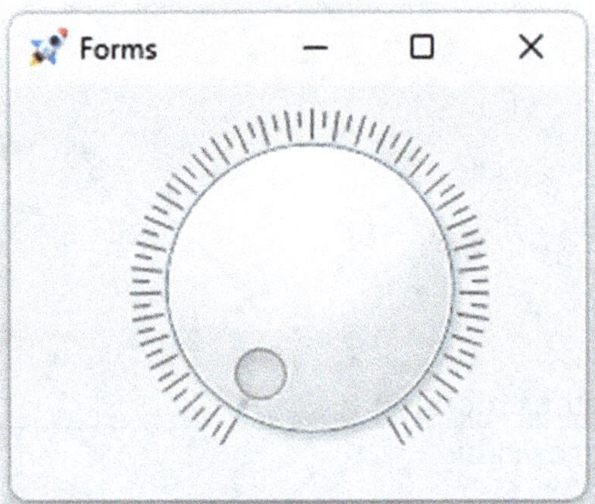

notchTarget = 5

notchTarget = 10

setSliderPosition(int value **)** and **sliderPosition()**

setSliderPosition()	→	Sets the dial's position manually.
sliderPosition()	→	Returns the dial's current slider position.

```python
dial = QDial()
dial.setSliderPosition( 25 )
```

setDown(bool value **)** and **isDown()**

setSliderDown()	→	Programmatically toggles whether the knob is being dragged.
isSliderDown()	→	Checks if the knob is being dragged.

Signals

sliderPressed and **sliderReleased**

sliderPressed	→	Signal emitted when the knob is pressed.
sliderReleased	→	Signal emitted when the user stops dragging the knob.

</> Python

```
dial = QDial()
dial.sliderPressed.connect(lambda: print("Dial has been pressed!"))
dial.sliderReleased.connect(lambda: print("Dial has been released!"))
```

sliderMoved and **rangeChanged**

sliderMoved	→	Signal emitted when the knob starts dragging the knob.
rangeChanged	→	Signal emitted when range is updated.

</> Python

```
dial = QDial()
dial.sliderMoved.connect( callback)

def callback():
    pos = dial.sliderPosition()
    print(pos)
```

Finalizing Project - Building a Login Page

</> Python

```
import sys
from PyQt6.QtCore import *
from PyQt6.QtWidgets import *
from PyQt6.QtGui import *

class MyApp(QMainWindow):

    def __init__(self):
        super().__init__()

        self.setWindowTitle("Forms")
        self.setWindowIcon(QIcon("images/rocket.png"))
        self.setStyleSheet("background:#ebebeb")
        self.setMinimumSize(500,500)

        self.main = QWidget()
        self.setCentralWidget(self.main)

        self.lay = QHBoxLayout()
        self.main.setLayout(self.lay)

        self.frame1 = QFrame()
        self.frame2 = QFrame()
        self.frame2.setStyleSheet("border-radius:10px")

        self.lay.addWidget(self.frame1)
        self.lay.addWidget(self.frame2)

        self.backPicture = QLabel(self.frame1)
        self.backPicture.setPixmap(QPixmap("images/music.jpg"))

        self.musicStore = QLabel("<h1 style='margin:20px;text-align:center'><b>PyQt      Music
                                 Store</b></h1>", self.frame1)

        self.musicStore.setGeometry(100,100,300,80)
        self.musicStore.setStyleSheet("background:rgba(234,239,243,100);font-family:'Georgia';
                                 border-radius:35px;")

        self.power = QLabel("<h1 style='color:white;margin:30px;'><b>Music Heals the Soul</b></h1>",
                             self.frame1)

        self.power.setGeometry(100,self.height()-20,300,80)
        self.power.setStyleSheet("border:2px solid tomato;border-radius:20px; background:none;")
```

```
self.createAccount = QLabel("<b style='font-size:37px'>Create an Account</b>", self.frame2)

self.createAccount.setGeometry(10,10,350,50)
self.createAccount.setStyleSheet("background:none; font-weight:bold")

QLabel("""<b>Already have an account?<a href='https://www.google.com/' style='color:blue'>
              Login</b>""", self.frame2).move(10,60)

QLabel("<b>First Name</b>", self.frame2).move(10,100)
QLabel("<b>Last Name</b>", self.frame2).move(250,100)

self.firstname = QTextEdit(self.frame2)
self.firstname.setGeometry(10,120, 200, 30),
self.firstname.setStyleSheet("border:1px solid; border-radius:3px")

self.lastname = QTextEdit(self.frame2)
self.lastname.setGeometry(250,120, 200, 30),
self.lastname.setStyleSheet("border:1px solid; border-radius:3px")

self.maleRadio = QRadioButton(self.frame2)
self.maleRadio.setText("Male")
self.maleRadio.move(10,180)
self.maleRadio.setChecked(self.isMale)

self.femaleRadio = QRadioButton(self.frame2)
self.femaleRadio.setText("Female")
self.femaleRadio.move(250,180)
self.femaleRadio.setChecked(not self.isMale)

QLabel("<b>Email</b>", self.frame2).move(10,220)
self.email = QTextEdit(self.frame2)
self.email.setGeometry(10,240, 440, 30),
self.email.setStyleSheet("border:1px solid; border-radius:3px")

QLabel("<b>Password</b>", self.frame2).move(10,290)
self.password = QTextEdit(self.frame2)
self.password.setGeometry(10,310, 440, 30),
self.password.setStyleSheet("border:1px solid; border-radius:3px")

self.termsCheck = QCheckBox(self.frame2)
self.termsCheck.move(10,360)
self.termsCheck.setText("I agree to Terms and Conditions")
self.termsCheck.setChecked(self.acceptTerms)

self.createAccountButton = QPushButton("Create Account", self.frame2)
self.createAccountButton.setGeometry(10,410, 440, 40)
self.createAccountButton.setStyleSheet('background:#5c8BD6; color:white;font-size:30;
                                        border-radius:4px')

QLabel("<center><b>Or register with</b></center>", self.frame2).setGeometry(10,470, 440, 40)

self.googleButton = QPushButton("Google", self.frame2)
```

```
        self.googleButton.setGeometry(10,530, 145, 40)
        self.googleButton.setIcon(QIcon("images/google.png"))
        self.googleButton.setStyleSheet('border:2px solid; border-radius:20px')

        self.appleButton = QPushButton("Apple", self.frame2)
        self.appleButton.setGeometry(160,530, 145, 40)
        self.appleButton.setIcon(QIcon("images/apple.png"))
        self.appleButton.setStyleSheet('border:2px solid; border-radius:20px')

        self.facebookButton = QPushButton("Facebook", self.frame2)
        self.facebookButton.setGeometry(310,530, 145, 40)
        self.facebookButton.setIcon(QIcon("images/facebook.png"))
        self.facebookButton.setStyleSheet('border:2px solid; border-radius:20px')


app = QApplication([])
myapp = MyApp()
myapp.show()
sys.exit(app.exec())
```

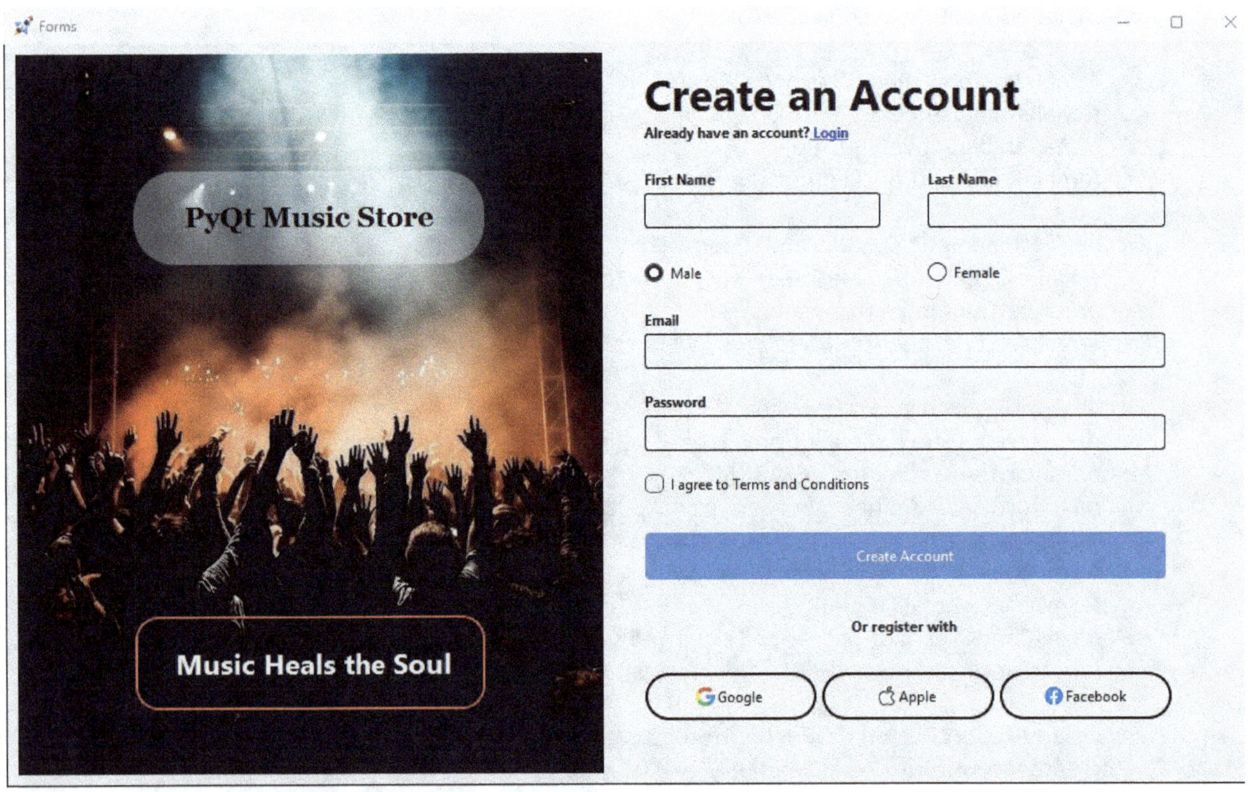

Chapter 7

PyQt Widgets - Set C (Pages and Menu)

Chapter Objectives

- Use QMessageBox
- Implement QTabWidget
- Work with QTabBar
- Use QListWidget
- Create items with QListWidgetItem
- Apply QFont for text styling
- Create menus with QMenu
- Add menus to QMenuBar
- Define actions with QAction

Project C– Developing an English App

In this project, we will explore how to integrate various PyQt widgets to create a functional English language application. The app combines GUI development with natural language processing (NLP) to offer interactive language tools.

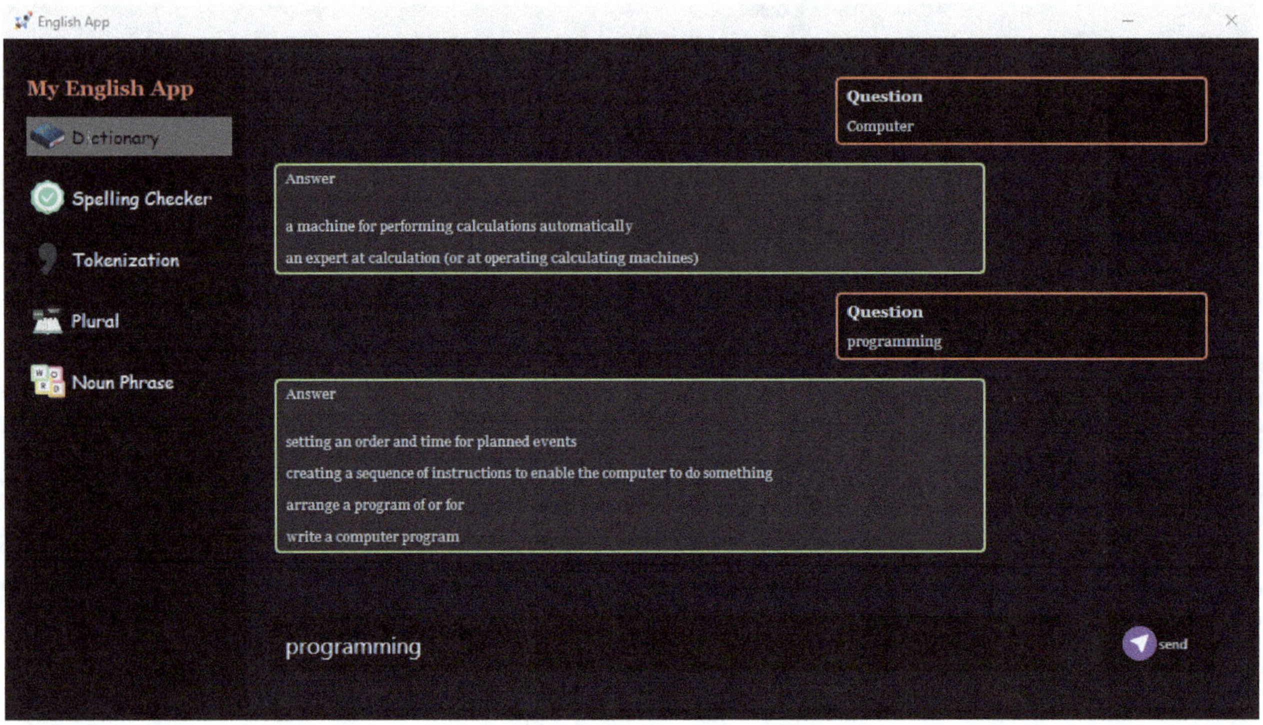

Key Features of the App

1. **Dictionary Lookup** – Get definitions of English words.
2. **Spelling Checker** – Suggest corrections for misspelled words.
3. **Tokenization** – Break a sentence into individual words (tokens).
4. **Pluralization** – Convert singular nouns to their plural form.
5. **Noun Phrase Extraction** – Identify noun phrases in a sentence.

How It Works

1. The user selects a functionality (e.g., Dictionary or Spelling Checker) from the available options.
2. A **QLineEdit** widget is used for the user to enter an input sentence or word.
3. Upon pressing a button (e.g., "Send"), the app processes the input using **TextBlob**.
4. The response is displayed in a scrollable chat area, allowing users to review past interactions.

Library Requirement

The app makes use of the **TextBlob** library for language processing. To install and prepare the required corpora:

① install textblob using pip

```
pip install textblob
```

② download necessary data

```
python -m textblob.download_corpora
```

Tips

Python Textblob

TextBlob is a simple Python library for natural language processing (NLP). It supports common text operations such as:

- Word definitions
- Pluralization and singularization
- Spelling correction
- Translation
- Tokenization
- Noun phrase extraction

Dialogs

Dialogs are essential components of software applications, serving as a means of communication between the application and the user. These are typically popup windows that display important messages or request user input or actions.

Dialogs can be used to:

- ❖ Display application reports
- ❖ Show alerts or notifications
- ❖ Trigger warnings or errors
- ❖ Provide informational messages
- ❖ Request confirmations (e.g., "Do you want to save changes?")
- ❖ Gather input from the user
- ❖ Facilitate file selections, color pickers, date pickers, and more

Types of Dialogs in PyQt

PyQt provides two primary tools for working with dialog boxes:

1. QMessageBox

The QMessageBox is a ready-made dialog box for displaying simple messages. It is commonly used for:

- Alerts
- Warnings
- Confirmation messages (Yes/No, OK/Cancel)
- Critical error messages

You can customize the icon, title, message, and available buttons, and even capture the user's response.

2. QDialog

QDialog offers a customizable framework to design and build your own dialog boxes from scratch. It allows you to:

- Add any combination of widgets (e.g., labels, input fields, buttons)
- Control layout and styling
- Handle user actions explicitly (e.g., accept/reject)

This makes QDialog perfect for complex forms, input forms, or dialogs that serve a specific function within your application.

QMessageBox

The QMessageBox is a built-in PyQt dialog widget used for displaying message prompts to the user, typically accompanied by standard buttons such as OK, Cancel, Yes, No, etc. It is a simple and effective way to communicate feedback or ask questions in GUI applications.

Common Use Cases

- Displaying informational messages (e.g., “Settings saved successfully”)
- Showing warnings (e.g., “This action cannot be undone”)
- Displaying critical errors (e.g., “File could not be opened”)
- Asking for confirmation (e.g., “Are you sure you want to exit?”)
- Showing about dialogs (e.g., "About this app")
- Reporting results or feedback after a task
- Providing detailed messages or interactive texts

Key Properties and Methods

warning	escapeButton	options	isSizeGripEnabled
informativeText	removeButton	checkBox	clickedButton
setInformativeText	StandardButton	setDetailedText	Icon
information	setResult	setOption	button
finished	setTextInteractionFlags	testOption	icon
iconPixmap	setSizeGripEnabled	text	question
exec	Option	about	rejected
setCheckBox	defaultButton	done	setDefaultButton
textInteractionFlags	open	standardButtons	addButton
detailedText	critical	setIconPixmap	standardButton
setStandardButtons	setIcon	setOptions	buttonClicked
DialogCode	reject	result	buttons
textFormat	setEscapeButton	buttonRole	ButtonRole
aboutQt	accept	setText	accepted
setTextFormat	setModal	standardIcon	

warning(parent, title, text, buttons **)**

Displays a warning message dialog.

</> Python

```
import sys
from PyQt6.QtCore import *
from PyQt6.QtWidgets import *
from PyQt6.QtGui import *

class PracticalApp:

    def __init__(self):

        app = QApplication(sys.argv)

        self.win = QMainWindow()
        self.win.setWindowTitle("English App")
        self.win.setFixedSize(400,200)
        self.win.setWindowIcon(QIcon("images/rocket.png"))
        self.win.setStyleSheet("background:#ebebeb")

        self.but = QPushButton("Reset App", self.win)
        self.but.move(150, 80)
        self.but.clicked.connect(lambda: self.resetApp())

        self.win.show()
        sys.exit(app.exec())

    def resetApp(self):

        self.message = QMessageBox(self.win)
        self.message.warning( self.win, "Resetting Application",
         "This action will wipe your entire database.\nDo you want to continue?")


if __name__ == "__main__":
    PracticalApp()
```


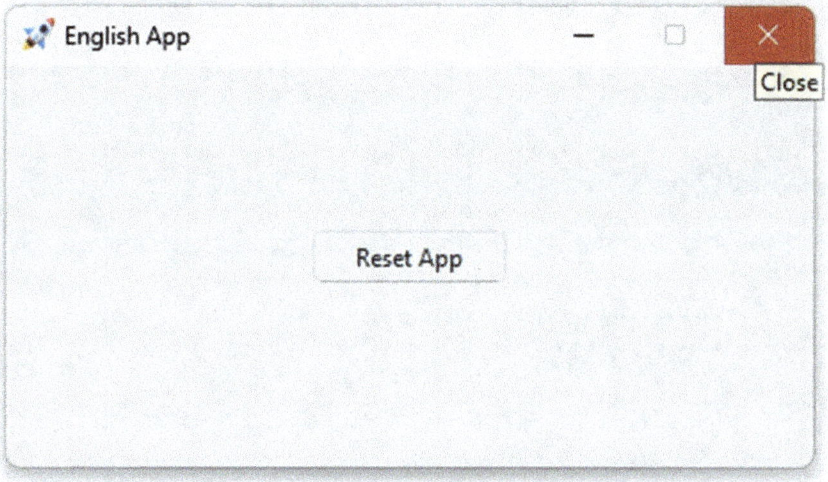

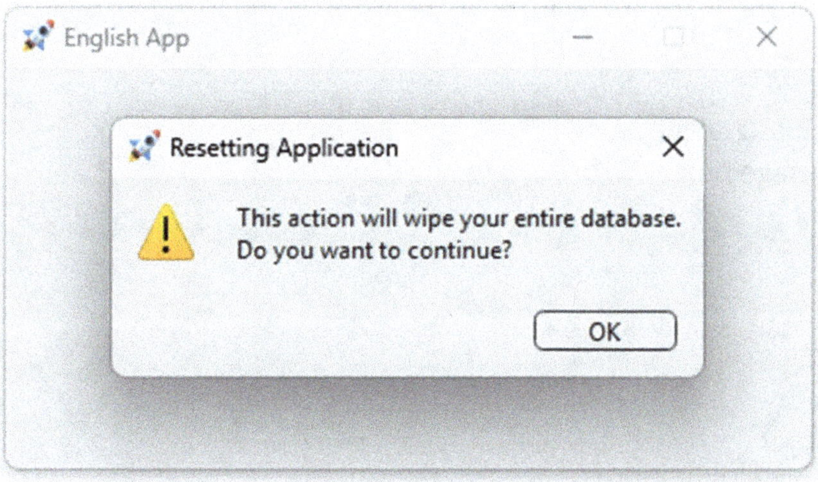

critical(parent, title, text, buttons **)**
Displays a critical error message dialog.

</> Python

```python
message = QMessageBox( parent )
message.critical(
        parent,
        "Low Battery",
        "Battery is too low.\nYou need to charge your device"
)
```

information(parent, title, text, buttons **)**
Displays an informational message box.

</> Python

```
message = QMessageBox( parent )
message.information(
        parent,
        "Do more with English App",
        "Just enter a word and get a definition for it."
)
```

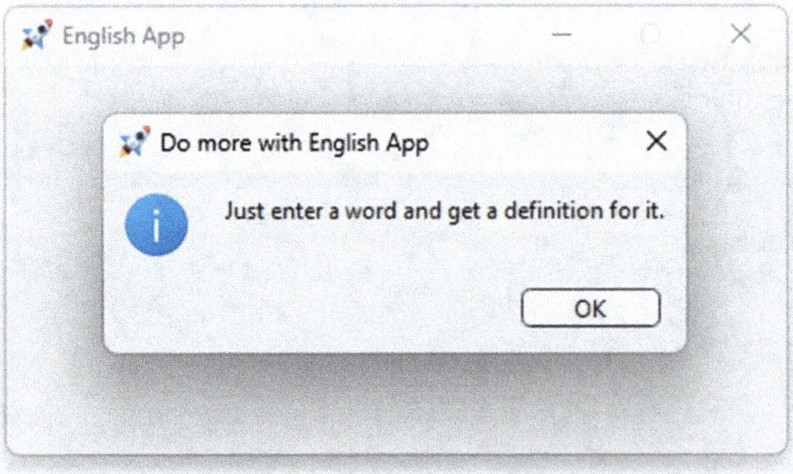

question(parent, title, text, buttons **)**
Displays a question dialog with options like Yes/No.

</> Python

```
message = QMessageBox( parent )
message.question(
        parent,
        "Close Application",
        "Are you sure you want to quit?"
)
```

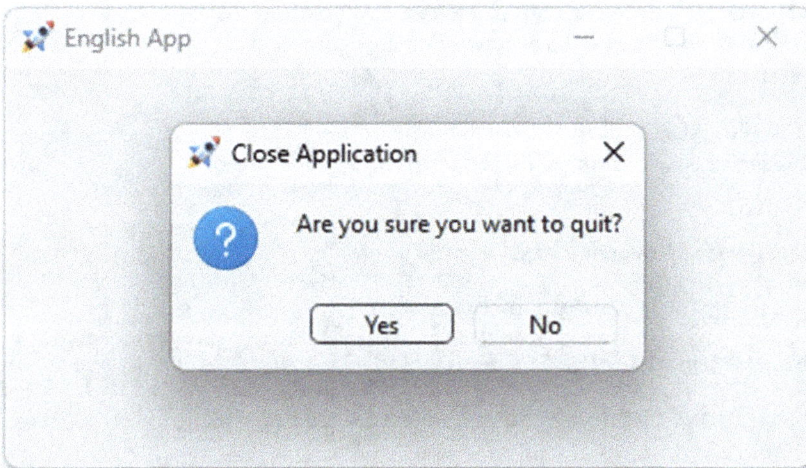

about(parent, title, text, buttons **)**
Displays a simple "About" message box.

aboutQt(parent, title**)**
Displays information about the Qt framework.

</> Python

```
message = QMessageBox( parent )
message.aboutQt( parent, "PyQt Information")
```

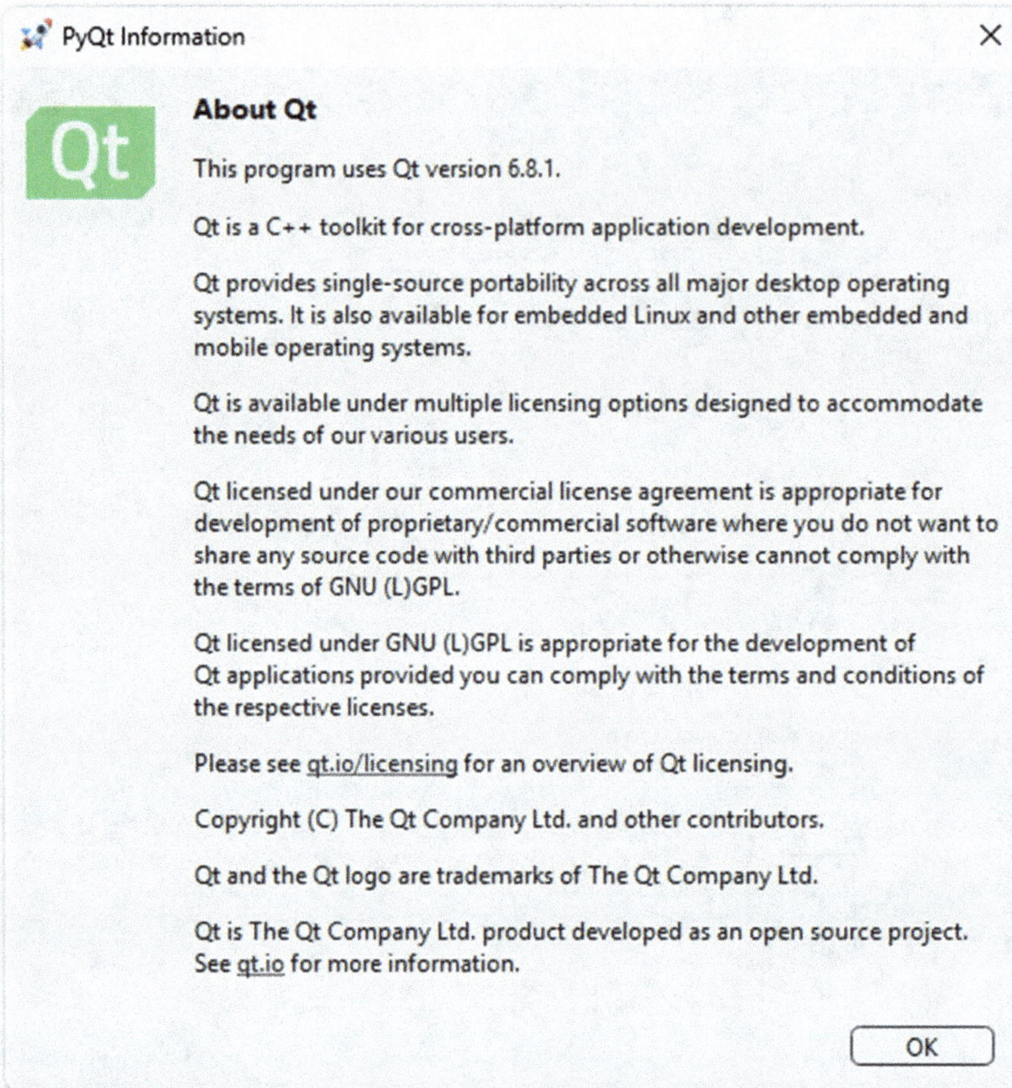

setInformativeText(text **)** and **informationText()**

setInformativeText()	→	Adds extra information below the main message.
informationText()	→	Returns the additional info text.

</> Python

```
message = QMessageBox( parent )
message.critical(
        parent,
```

```
        "Low Battery",
        "Battery is too low.\nYou need to charge your device"
)
message.setInformativeText("You can still run app in safe mode")
message.exec()
```

setIcon(QMessage.Icon **)** and **icon()**

setIcon()	→	Sets the icon (e.g., Information, Warning, Critical, Question).
icon()	→	Returns the icon type.

</> **Python**

```python
message = QMessageBox( parent )
message.setIcon(QMessage.Icon.Question)
```

QMessageBox Icons

Question	Critical	Information	NoIcon
Warning			

Table 7.0 : The available QMessageBox icons

setIconPixmap(QPixmap **)** and **iconPixmap()**

setIconPixmap()	→	Sets a custom image as the icon.
iconPixmap()	→	Retrieves the pixmap used.

</> **Python**

```python
pixmap = QPixmap("images/chatbot.png").scaled(50,50)

message = QMessageBox( parent )
message.setIconPixmap(pixmap)
message.setText("Open a chatbot")
message.exec()
```

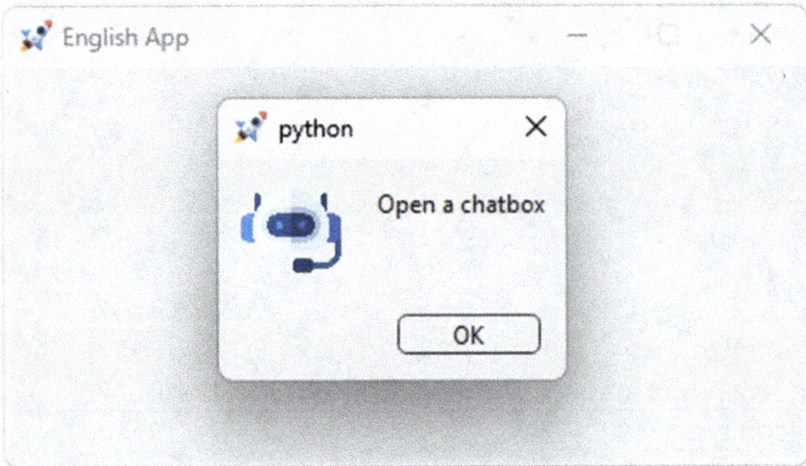

open()

Shows the message box without blocking.

setStandardButtons(QMessage.StandardButton) and **standardButton()**

setStandardButtons()	→	Adds standard buttons (e.g., Ok, Cancel, Yes).
standardButtons()	→	Returns the list of standard buttons in use.

Example 1

</> Python

```
message = QMessageBox( parent )
message.setStandardButtons(
        QMessageBox.StandardButton.Open | QMessageBox.StandardButton.Close)

pixmap = QPixmap("images/chatbot.png").scaled(50,50)

message.setIconPixmap(pixmap)
message.setText("Open a chatbot")
message.setInformativeText("For questions and inquiries,\nChat with chatbot ")
message.exec()
```

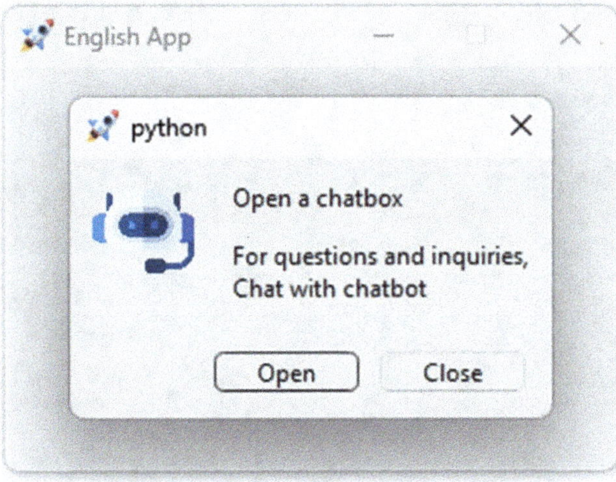

QMessageBox Standard buttons

Open	Discard	NoAll	Yes
Close	Escape	NoButton	YesAll
Ok	FirstButton	NoToAll	YesToAll
Abort	FlagMask	Reset	Save
Apply	Help	RestoreDefaults	SaveAll
ButtomMask	Ignore	Retry	LastButton
Cancel	Default	No	

Table 7.1 : Standard buttons of the QMessageBox

Example 2

</> Python

```
message = QMessageBox( parent )
        message.question(
        parent,
        "Save Document",
        "Do you want to save the document?",
        QMessageBox.StandardButton.Save |
        QMessageBox.StandardButton.SaveAll |
        QMessageBox.StandardButton.Abort
    )
```

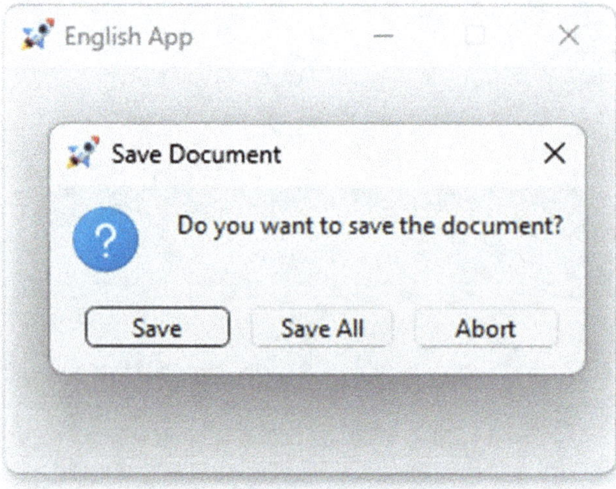

Signals

exec()
Executes the message box and blocks the code until a button is clicked.

```python
message = QMessageBox(parent)
message.setIcon(QMessageBox.Icon.Information)
message.setText("Subscribe to our newsletter?",)
message.setInformativeText("Receive our daily newsletter on the best recipes")
message.setStandardButtons(QMessageBox.StandardButton.Yes | QMessageBox.StandardButton.No)
result = message.exec()

if result == message.StandardButton.Yes:
    print("Thank you for subscription")
```

```
if result == self.message.StandardButton.No:
    print("Oh nooo")
```

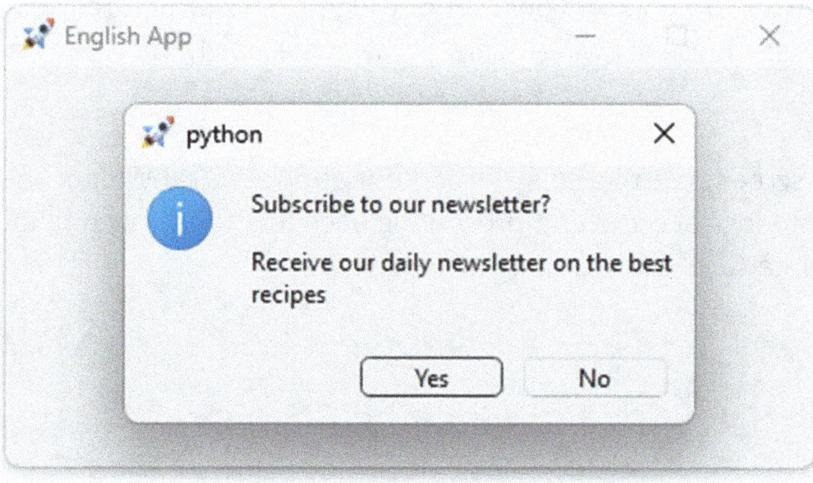

accepted and **rejected**

accepted	→	Signal emitted when the dialog is accepted.
rejected	→	Signal emitted when the dialog is rejected.

</> **Python**

```
message = QMessageBox( parent )
message.accepted.connect(callback)
message.rejected.connect(callback)
```

QTabWidget

The QTabWidget is a container widget in PyQt that allows you to organize content into multiple tabs or pages, where each tab holds its own set of widgets. This structure is useful for applications with multiple sections, allowing users to navigate easily between them without cluttering the interface.

Devices, especially on smaller screens, can't display all content at once. QTabWidget solves this by breaking the content into logical parts and presenting each in a tab. Only one tab is shown at a time, making your interface clean and user-friendly.

Common Use Cases

- Settings or Preferences pages
- Form-based applications with sections (e.g., Personal Info, Education, Contact)
- Tabbed browsers or editors
- Multi-section dashboards
- Multi-language forms or views
- Help centers with categorized FAQs

Key Properties and Methods

setTabVisible	initStyleOption	elideMode	cornerWidget
tabCloseRequested	setTabToolTip	isTabVisible	setTabIcon
setTabBarAutoHide	TabShape	tabBarClicked	setTabEnabled
setCurrentWidget	insertTab	setUsesScrollButtons	setTabBar
addTab	currentIndex	removeTab	tabsClosable
tabWhatsThis	tabBarDoubleClicked	tabText	currentChanged
tabBarAutoHide	clear	__len__	usesScrollButtons
isMovable	TabPosition	tabBar	widget
setMovable	setTabText	count	setTabWhatsThis
currentWidget	indexOf	tabRemoved	isTabEnabled
tabIcon	setCornerWidget	setTabsClosable	setElideMode
tabInserted	setCurrentIndex	tabToolTip	

addTab(widget, icon, title)

Adds a new tab with a widget and label text

Python

```
import sys
from PyQt6.QtCore import *
from PyQt6.QtWidgets import *
from PyQt6.QtGui import *

class PracticalApp:
    def __init__(self):

        app = QApplication(sys.argv)

        self.win = QMainWindow()
        self.win.setWindowTitle("English App")
        self.win.setFixedSize(400,200)
        self.win.setWindowIcon(QIcon("images/rocket.png"))
        self.win.setStyleSheet("background:#ebebeb")

        self.page1 = QWidget()
        self.label1 = QLabel("<h1>Page1</h1>", self.page1).setGeometry(220, 100, 100, 50)

        self.page2 = QWidget()
        self.page2.setStyleSheet("background-image:url('images/bg3.jpg')")
        self.label2 = QLabel("<h1>Page2</h1>", self.page2)
        self.label2.setGeometry(220, 100, 100, 50)
        self.label2.setStyleSheet("background:none;")

        self.page3 = QWidget()
        self.label3 = QLabel("<h1>Page3</h1>", self.page3).setGeometry(220, 100, 100, 50)

        self.tab = QTabWidget(self.win)
        self.tab.resize(self.win.width(), self.win.height())
        self.tab.addTab(self.page1, QIcon("images/home.png"), "page1")
        self.tab.addTab(self.page2, QIcon("images/user.png"), "page2")
        self.tab.addTab(self.page3, QIcon("images/like.png"), "page3")

        self.win.show()
        sys.exit(app.exec())

if __name__ == "__main__":
    PracticalApp()
```

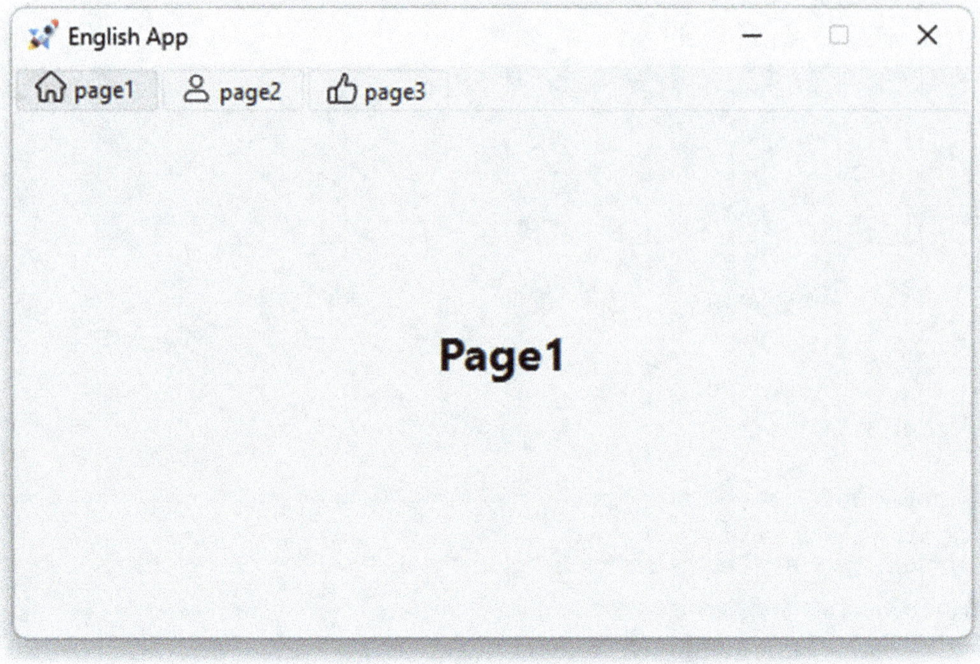
English App
page1
page2
page3
Page1

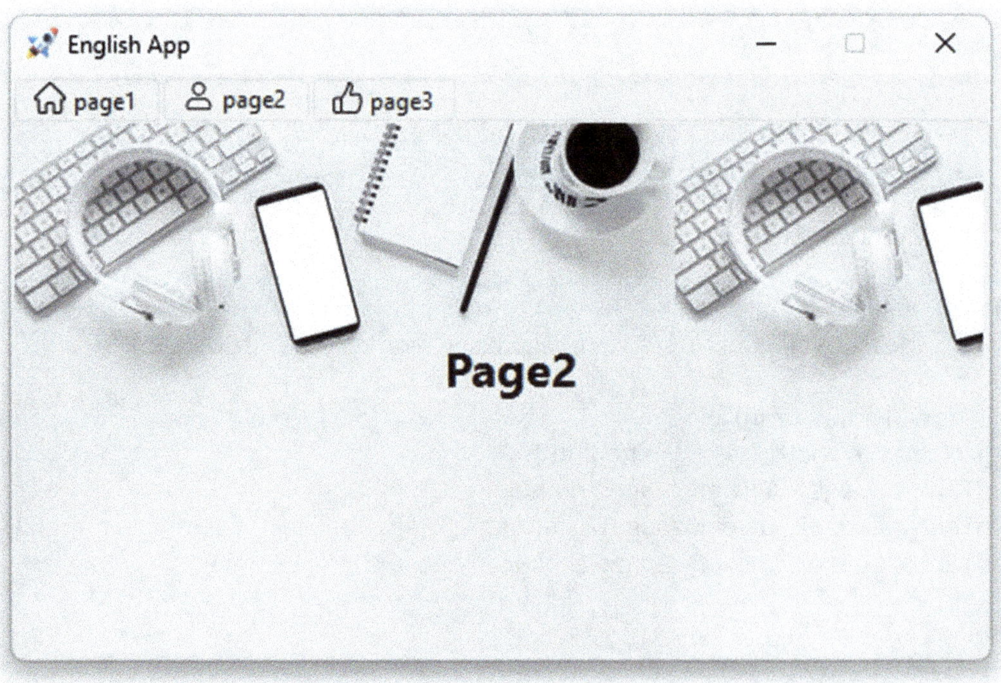
English App
page1
page2
page3
Page2

insertTab(index, widget, icon, title**)**

Inserts a new tab at a specific index.

```python
page4 = QWidget()

tab = QTabWidget()
tab.insertTab(1, page4, QIcon("python.png"), "page4")
```

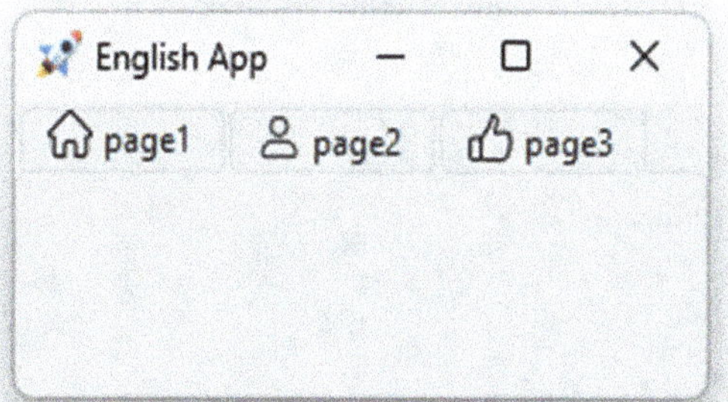

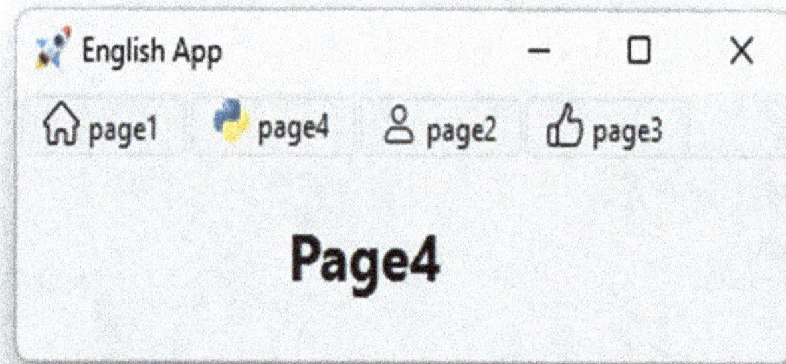

removeTab(index**)**

Removes the tab at the given index

```python
tab = QTabWidget()
tab.removeTab( 0 )
```

setCurrentIndex(index**)** and **currentIndex()**

setCurrentIndex()	→	Sets which tab is currently visible
currentIndex()	→	Returns the index of the currently visible tab

```python
tab = QTabWidget()
page2 = QWidget()

button = QPushButton("next page", page2)
button.clicked.connect(lambda: tab.setCurrentIndex(2))  #change tab to page3
```

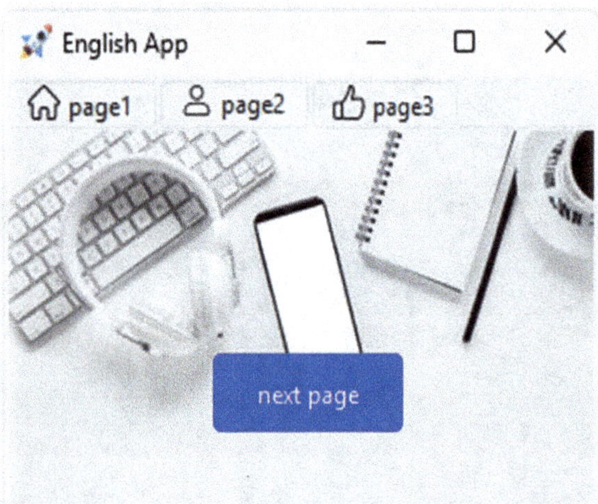

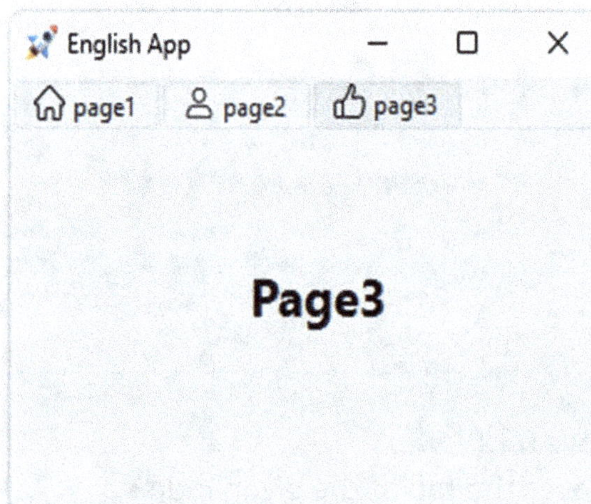

count() and **clear()**

count()	→	Returns the total number of tabs
clear()	→	Removes all tabs

```python
tab = QTabWidget()
total = tab.count()
```

setTabPosition(QTabWidget.TabPosition **)** and **tabPosition()**

setTabPosition()	→	Sets the positions of the tab bar as ***North***, ***South***, ***East*** or ***West***
tabPosition()	→	Returns the tab positions (North, South, East, West)

</> Python

```
tab = QTabWidget()
total = tab.setTabPosition(QTabWidget.TabPosition.South)
```

setTabText(index, text **), tabText(** index **)** and **setTabIcon(** index, icon **), tabIcon(** index **)**

setTabText()	→	Sets the label of a tab
tabText()	→	Gets the label text of a tab
setTabIcon()	→	Sets an icon for the tab
tabIcon()	→	Gets the icon of the tab

</> Python

```
tab = QTabWidget()
tab.setTabText(3, "books")
tab.setTabIcon(3, QIcon("books.png"))
```

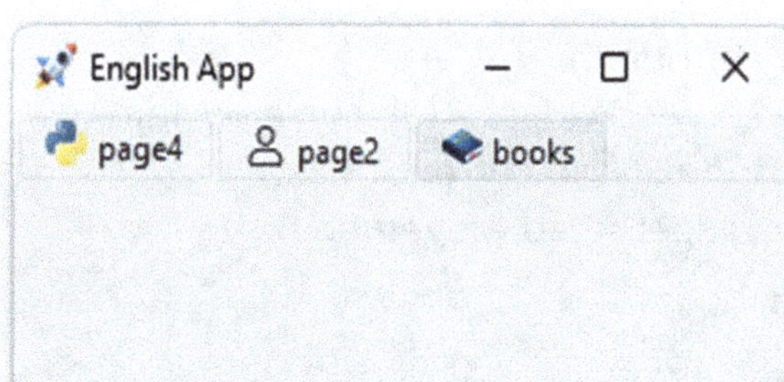

Signals

currentChanged , **tabBarClicked** and **tabBarDoubleClicked**

currentChanged	→	Signal emitted when the current tab changes
tabBarClicked	→	Signal emitted when a tab is clicked
tabBarDoubleClicked	→	Signal emitted when a tab is double-clicked

```
</> Python
tab = QTabWidget()
tab.currentChanged.connect(getIndex)

def getIndex():
    index = tab.currentIndex()
    print(index)
```

setCurrentWidget(widget **), currentWidget()** and **widget(** index **)**

setCurrentWidget()	→	Sets the current visible tab by widget
currentWidget()	→	Returns the widget of the current tab
widget()	→	Gets the widget at a given tab index

```
</> Python
tab = QTabWidget()

label = QLabel("Current Page")
tab.setCurrentWidget( label )

tab.currentChanged.connect(getIndex)

def getIndex():
    currentWidget = tab.currentWidget()
    index = tab.currentIndex()
    widget = tab.widget(index)
```

QTabBar

The QTabBar is the internal component that manages and displays the tabs themselves in a QTabWidget. While QTabWidget provides a complete tabbed interface with a content area, QTabBar focuses only on the tabs—making it ideal for developers who need complete customization over the tab presentation without being tied to the page management.

Use Cases

Although *QTabWidget* uses *QTabBar* under the hood, you can replace or subclass *QTabBar* to:

- ❖ Customize how tabs appear (icons, tooltips, alignment, size)
- ❖ Implement dynamic tab behaviors
- ❖ Handle tabs independently of the content area

When to Use QTabBar

- When you want to build a tabbed interface from scratch
- To create non-traditional tab arrangements (e.g., scrollable horizontal tabs, stylized labels)
- When only tab selection is needed, not tabbed content

Key Properties and Methods

tabData	setTabWhatsThis	drawBase	setCurrentIndex
selectionBehaviorOnRemove	expanding	setTabEnabled	ButtonPosition
setAccessibleTabName	tabToolTip	isTabVisible	tabAt
tabMoved	autoHide	Shape	count
initStyleOption	setTabVisible	setTabData	shape
setDrawBase	SelectionBehavior	accessibleTabName	tabButton
isTabEnabled	tabCloseRequested	tabRect	tabBarDoubleClicked
setExpanding	removeTab	setUsesScrollButtons	insertTab
moveTab	setTabButton	tabText	setTabsClosable
setTabIcon	setMovable	currentChanged	setTabText
setElideMode	changeCurrentOnDrag	elideMode	tabSizeHint
tabBarClicked	setTabTextColor	tabWhatsThis	currentIndex
tabRemoved	tabLayoutChange	setChangeCurrentOnDrag	addTab
tabIcon	tabInserted	tabsClosable	setShape
setTabToolTip	tabTextColor	setSelectionBehaviorOnRemove	usesScrollButtons
setAutoHide	minimumTabSizeHint	isMovable	__len__

addTab(icon, title)
Adds a new tab with a label and optional icon

```python
import sys
from PyQt6.QtCore import *
from PyQt6.QtWidgets import *
from PyQt6.QtGui import *

class PracticalApp:

    def __init__(self):

        app = QApplication(sys.argv)

        self.win = QMainWindow()
        self.win.setWindowTitle("English App")
        self.win.setFixedSize(400,200)
        self.win.setWindowIcon(QIcon("images/rocket.png"))
        self.win.setStyleSheet("background:#ebebeb")

        self.tabbar = QTabBar()
        self.tabbar.resize(self.win.width(), self.win.height())
        self.tabbar.addTab(QIcon("images/book.png"), "page1")
        self.tabbar.addTab("page2")
        self.tabbar.addTab("page3")

        self.tabbar.setTabIcon(2, QIcon("images/python.png"))
        self.tabbar.currentChanged.connect(self.changePage)

        self.tabwidget = QTabWidget(self.win)
        self.tabwidget.resize(self.win.width(), self.win.height())
        self.tabwidget.setTabBar(self.tabbar)

        self.win.show()
        sys.exit(app.exec())

    def changePage(self):
        index = self.tabbar.currentIndex()
        print(index)


if __name__ == "__main__":
    PracticalApp()
```

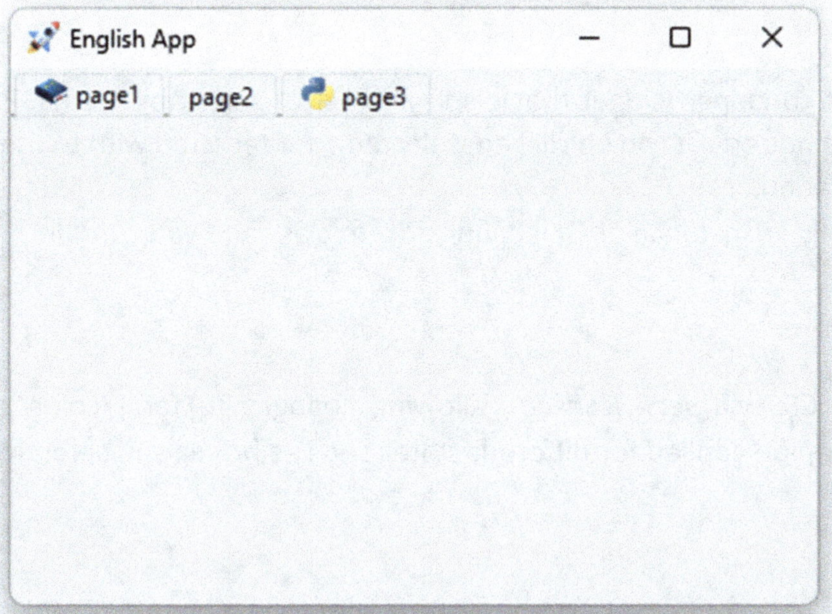

Note

Most of QTabBar methods and properties are shared or used indirectly in QTabWidget.

Key Difference from QTabWidget

- QTabBar only manages tabs.
- QTabWidget manages both tabs and their content.

QListWidget

QListWidget is a convenient container widget that displays a list of selectable items. Each item in the list behaves like a button—it can be clicked, selected, or interacted with to trigger specific actions in the application.

Each item in the list is typically an instance of **QListWidgetItem** class and can contain:

- Plain text
- Text with icons

Items can be styled using CSS via *setStyleSheet()*, allowing changes to font, color, and background. Visual effects can be applied for different states such as **hover** and **selection**.

Primary Use Cases

- Creating a menu-style interface for navigating app sections
- Allowing users to select from a list of items
- Building email clients (like inbox message list)
- Showing file or contact lists
- Grouping options for actions (e.g. selecting filters or templates)

Key Properties and Methods

verticalScrollBarPolicy	EditTrigger	horizontalScrollMode	verticalScrollbarAction
setItemDelegate	clearPropertyFlags	updateEditorGeometries	itemFromIndex
count	commitData	setViewport	setCurrentRow
currentTextChanged	setLineWidth	movement	setMovement
setSpacing	ScrollMode	removeItemWidget	batchSize
viewportMargins	currentItem	itemDoubleClicked	scrollBarWidgets
setFlow	setIndexWidget	cornerWidget	setItemDelegateForRow
addItem	setLayoutMode	updateEditorData	setupViewport
entered	itemDelegateForColumn	selectionChanged	setAlternatingRowColors
selectionMode	initViewItemOption	currentIndex	__len__
State	addScrollBarWidget	editItem	setSelection
rowsInserted	selectionBehavior	setAutoScrollMargin	midLineWidth
currentItemChanged	itemWidget	itemDelegateForRow	currentRow
flow	viewMode	uniformItemSizes	findItems
isPersistentEditorOpen	indexAt	resetHorizontalScrollMode	state
setAutoHide	currentItemChanged	setAutoScroll	setDefaultDropAction
selectedItems	dataChanged	updateGeometries	verticalScrollbarAction
setTextElideMode	scrollContentsBy	setDragDropMode	items
currentRowChanged	hasAutoScroll	clicked	state

scrollDirtyRegion	showDropIndicator	setModel	setDefaultDropAction
modelColumn	setFrameShape	indexFromItem	sizeHintForIndex
SizeAdjustPolicy	sizeHintForColumn	horizontalScrollbarValueChanged	verticalScrollMode
setDirtyRegion	resetVerticalScrollMode	itemDelegateForIndex	setVerticalScrollBar
addItems	Movement	setSelectionRectVisible	setSelectionModel
rectForIndex	sizeHintForRow	reset	LayoutMode
frameRect	rootIndex	executeDelayedItemsLayout	drawFrame
layoutMode	pressed	verticalScrollBar	frameShape
horizontalScrollBar	setSizeAdjustPolicy	insertItems	selectionModel
lineWidth	itemChanged	setCurrentIndex	viewport

Tips

Exploring Methods and Properties of the QListWidget

QListWidget offers over 200 methods and properties that can be used to control its behavior, appearance, and interaction with items. To explore these available attributes, you can use Python's built-in dir() function:

```
>>> from PyQt5.QtWidgets import QListWidget
>>> widget = QListWidget()
>>> print( dir(widget))
.....
```

addItem(text)

Adds a single item to the list

</> Python

```
import sys
from PyQt6.QtCore import *
from PyQt6.QtWidgets import *
from PyQt6.QtGui import *

class PracticalApp:

    def __init__(self):
        app = QApplication(sys.argv)

        self.win = QMainWindow()
        self.win.setWindowTitle("English App")
```

```
        self.win.setFixedSize(400,200)
        self.win.setWindowIcon(QIcon("images/rocket.png"))
        self.win.setStyleSheet("background:#ebebeb")

        self.panel = QListWidget(self.win)
        self.panel.resize(100, self.win.height())
        self.panel.addItem("Dashboard")
        self.panel.addItem("Recipe")
        self.panel.addItem("Classroom")
        self.panel.addItem("Edit Profile")
        self.panel.addItem("Calendar")
        self.panel.currentItemChanged.connect(self.changePage)

        #Dashboard Page
        self.dashboard = QWidget(self.win)
        self.dashboard.setGeometry(105, 0, self.win.width() - 105, self.win.height())

        QLabel("<h2>Dashboard</h2>", self.dashboard).move(10,10)
        courseButton = QPushButton(self.dashboard)
        courseButton.setGeometry(10, 50, 150,150)
        courseButton.setStyleSheet("background:#424349;border-radius:15px")

        courseLayout = QVBoxLayout(courseButton)
        courseImage = QLabel()
        courseImage.setPixmap(QPixmap("images/education.png").scaled(100,100))
        courseLayout.addWidget(courseImage)
        courseLayout.addWidget(QLabel("<h3><center style='color:white'>Course</center></h3>"))

        projectButton = QPushButton(self.dashboard)
        projectButton.setGeometry(180, 50, 150,150)
        projectButton.setStyleSheet("background:#424349;border-radius:15px")

        projectLayout = QVBoxLayout(projectButton)
        projectImage = QLabel()
        projectImage.setPixmap(QPixmap("images/dashboard.png").scaled(100,100))
        projectLayout.addWidget(projectImage)
        projectLayout.addWidget(QLabel("<h3><center style='color:white'>Project</center></h3>"))

        #Recipe Page
        self.recipe = QWidget(self.win)
        self.recipe.setGeometry(105, 0, self.win.width() - 105, self.win.height())

        QLabel("<h2>Recipe</h2>", self.recipe).move(10,10)
        recipeImage = QLabel(self.recipe)
        recipeImage.setGeometry(10,50, self.recipe.width(), 200)
        recipeImage.setPixmap(QPixmap("images/burg.jpg").scaled(300,200))
        QLabel("<h1><center style='color:tomato'>Try this new recipe</center></h1>", self.recipe).move(10,250)


        self.win.show()
        sys.exit(app.exec())

    def changePage(self):
        panel = self.panel.currentItem().text().lower()

        if panel == "dashboard":
          self.dashboard.show()
          self.recipe.hide()
```

```
        if panel == "recipe":
            self.recipe.show()
            self.dashboard.hide()


if __name__ == "__main__":
    PracticalApp()
```

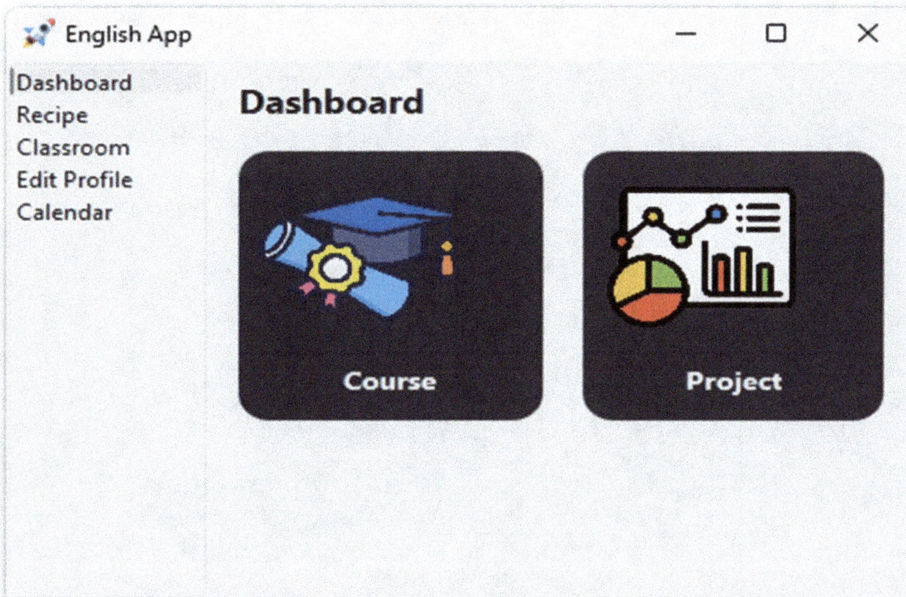

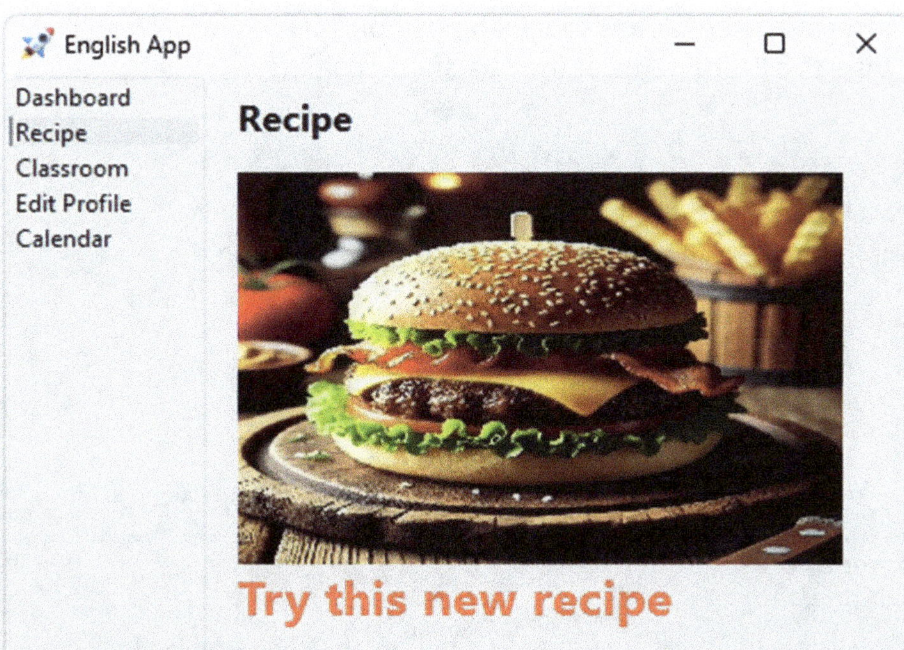

addItems(list **)**

Adds multiple items at once

```python
items = ["Home", "About us", "Contact us", "Settings" ]
panel = QListWidget( parent )
panel.addItems( items )
```

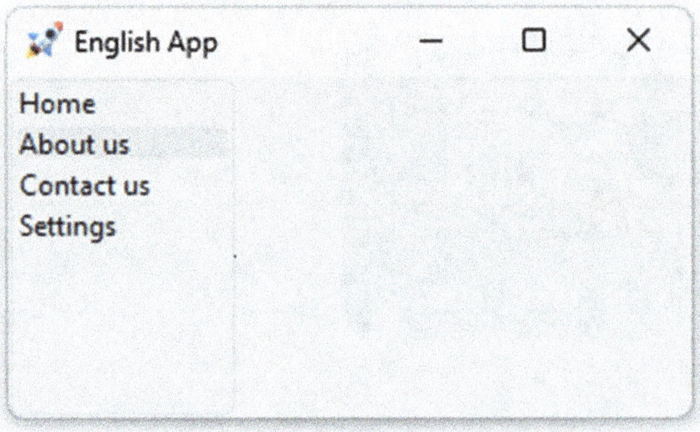

insertItem(index, item **)** and **insertItems(** index, list**)**

insertItem() → Inserts an item at the specified position
insertItems() → Inserts a list of items at the specified position

```python
panel = QListWidget( parent )
panel.insertItem( 2, "Help")
```

clear()

Removes all items

```python
panel = QListWidget( parent )
panel.clear()
```

setFont(QFont(family, size, weight, italic) **) and font()**

setFont() → Changes the text font (bold, italic, etc).
font() → Returns the current font.

```python
panel = QListWidget( parent )
self.panel.setFont(QFont("Comic Sans MS", 15, 20, True))
```

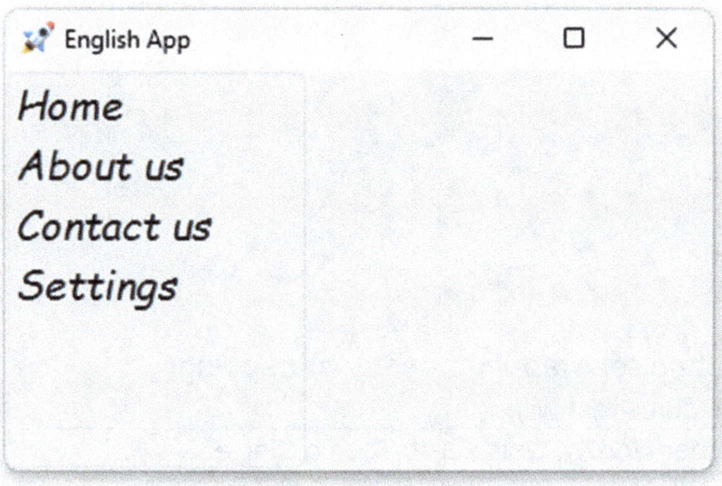

Available Font-Family

Georgia	Cursive	Trebuchet MS	Comic Sans MS
Times New Roman	fantasy	Courier New	Brush Script MT
Arial	Garamond	Consolas	Tahoma
Serif	Helvetica	Lucida Console	Mono-space
Sans-serif	Verdana	Monaco	

Table 7.2 : Accepted font names

setSpacing(int **) and spacing()**

setSpacing()	→	Spacing between items.
spacing()	→	Returns the spaces between items.

```python
panel = QListWidget( parent )
panel.setSpacing(10 )
```

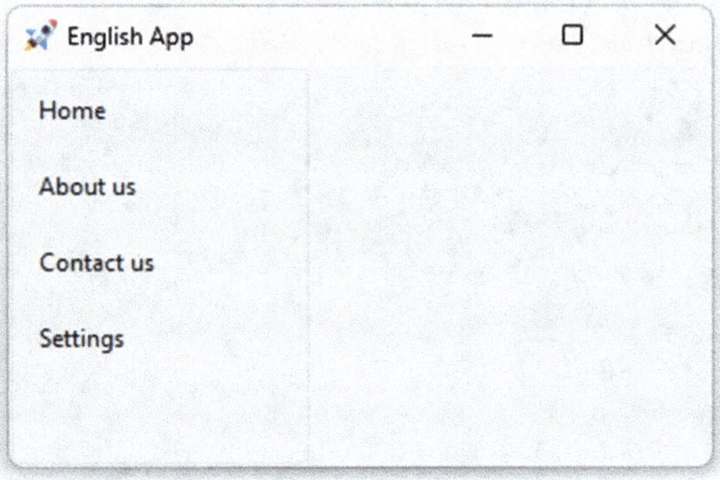

setWordWrap(bool **), wordWrap( ),** and **setWrapping(** bool **), isWrapping( )**

setWordWrap()	→	Enables or disables text wrapping
wordWrap()	→	Returns whether *wordWrap* is set to True or False
setWrapping()	→	Allows wrapping of items when space is constrained
isWrapping()	→	Returns the value (True or False) of *setWrapping()*

</> Python

```python
panel = QListWidget( parent )
panel.setWordWrap(True)
```

setGridSize(QSize() **)**

Sets custom item size in grid

</> Python

```python
panel = QListWidget( parent )
panel.setGridSize(QSize(2, 50))
```

QListWidgetItem

The QListWidgetItem is a versatile object used to represent individual entries (items) in a QListWidget. Each item can display a label (text), an icon, and can be customized with various properties like font, color, alignment, selection, and data storage.

You can create a QListWidgetItem in two main ways:

① Directly attach to list:

```
list_widget = QListWidget()
item = QListWidgetItem(list_widget, QIcon("icon.png"), "my_label")
```

② Create then add:

```
list_widget = QListWidget()
item = QListWidgetItem(QIcon("icon.png"), "my_label")
list_widget.addItem(item)
```

Constructor Parameters

- parent: The target *QListWidget* to attach the item to.
- icon: Optional *QIcon* to show beside the label.
- title: The text or label shown to the user.

Key Properties and Methods

setBackground	setIcon	toolTip	setForeground
setStatusTip	setFlags	setCheckState	read
write	ItemType	background	font
setFont	setTextAlignment	setHidden	setToolTip
setData	text	setText	whatsThis
listWidget	statusTip	isSelected	checkState
icon	foreground	sizeHint	clone
flags	isHidden	textAlignment	setSizeHint
setWhatsThis	data	type	setSelected

addItem(QListWidgetItem(parent, icon, title) **)**

Adds a single QListWidgetItem

```python
panel = QListWidget( parent )

dashboard = QListWidgetItem(QIcon("images/home.png"), "Dashboard")
course = QListWidgetItem(QIcon("images/course.png"), "Course")
tutorial = QListWidgetItem(QIcon("images/video.png"), "Tutorial")
profile = QListWidgetItem(QIcon("images/profile.png"), "Profile")

panel.addItem(dashboard)
panel.addItem(course)
panel.addItem(tutorial)
panel.addItem(profile)
```

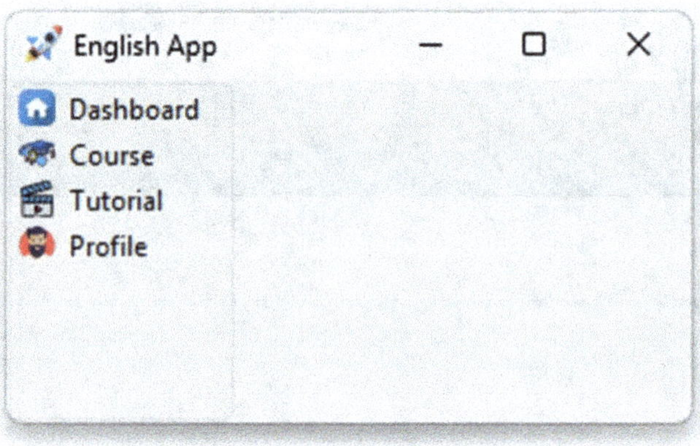

setText(text **), text()** and **setIcon(** QIcon **) , icon()**

setText()	→	Sets the label (text) of the item.
text()	→	Returns the current text.
setIcon()	→	Sets the icon for the item.
icon()	→	Gets the item's icon.

```python
panel = QListWidget( parent )

dashboard = QListWidgetItem(panel)
```

```
dashboard.setText("Dashboard")
dashboard.setIcon(QIcon("images/dashboard.png"))

course = QListWidgetItem(panel)
course.setText("Course")
course.setIcon(QIcon("images/course.png"))
```

setBackground(color **), background()** and **setForeground(** color **), foreground()**

setBackground()	→	Sets the background color or brush.
background()	→	Returns background brush.
setForeground()	→	Sets the text color.
foreground()	→	Returns text color brush.

</> Python

```
panel = QListWidget( parent )
course = QListWidgetItem(QIcon("images/course.png"), "Course")
corse.setBackground(QColor("#0E121A"))
corse.setForeground(QColor("#8AE98D"))
```

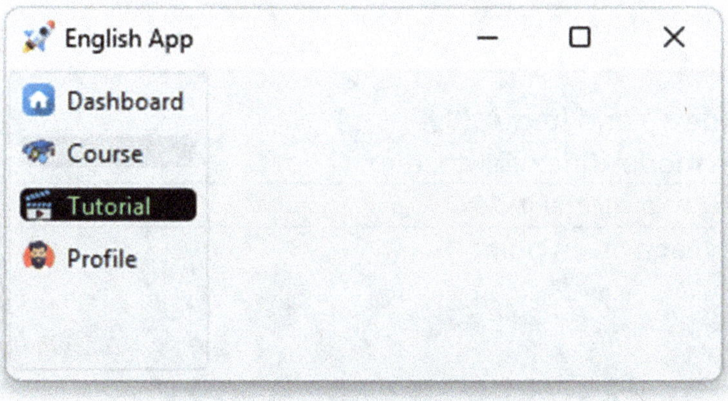

setFlow(QListWidget.Flow **)**

Set Horizontal (LeftToRight) or vertical (TopToDown) arrangement of list.

</> Python

```
panel = QListWidget( parent )
panel.setFlow(QListWidget.Flow.LeftToRight)
```

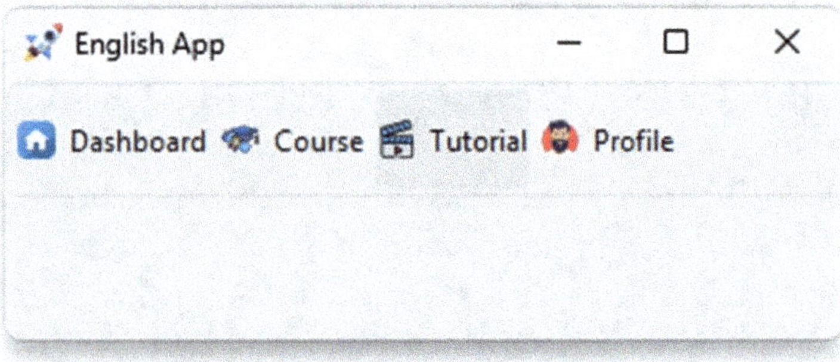

currentItem( ) , selectedItems( ) and **item(** row**)**

currentItem()	→	Returns the currently selected item.
selectedItems()	→	Returns a list of all selected items.
item()	→	Returns the item at a given row.

</> Python

```
panel = QListWidget( parent )
item = panel.currentItem()
```

indexFromItem(item **) , itemFromIndex( )** and **itemAt(** QPoint **)**

indexFromItem()	→	Returns the model index for an item
itemFromIndex()	→	Gets item from a model index
itemAt()	→	Returns item at a given point

</> Python

```
panel = QListWidget( parent )

home = QListWidgetItem(panel, QIcon("home.png"), "Home")
settings = QListWidgetItem(panel, QIcon("settings.png"), "Settings")

index = panel.indexFromItem(home)
item = panel.itemAt(QPoint(1, 3))
```

Signals

currentItemChanged

Fires when a new item is selected.

```python
panel = QListWidget( parent )
panel.currentItemChanged.connect( myFunction )

def myFunction():
    item = panel.currentItem().text()
    index = panel.currentIndex()
```

itemClicked, itemDoubleClicked, itemActivated, and **itemSelectionChanged**

itemClicked	→	Emitted when an item is clicked.
itemDoubleClicked	→	Emitted on double click.
itemActivated	→	Triggered by click or key-activation.
itemSelectionChanged	→	Triggered on any change in selected items.

```python
panel = QListWidget( parent )

panel.itemClicked.connect(callback )

panel.itemActivated.connect(callback )

panel.itemSelectionChanged.connect(callback )
```

QScrollArea

A QScrollArea is a container widget in PyQt that provides scrollbars around another widget. It is used to make sure large content (bigger than the visible area) can be scrolled and fully viewed. It is perfect for adding scroll ability to forms, images, documents, or layouts that don't fit on screen.

Use Cases

- Showing large images that don't fit in the window
- Displaying long forms or settings panels
- Scrolling text, documents, or HTML content
- Viewing long lists or tables in limited space
- Building custom viewers (maps, blueprints, diagrams)

Key Properties and Methods

scrollContentsBy	setHorizontalScrollBar	setLineWidth	setMidLineWidth
setFrameStyle	SizeAdjustPolicy	setFrameShape	frameShape
horizontalScrollBarPolicy	initStyleOption	cornerWidget	frameStyle
setSizeAdjustPolicy	setWidgetResizable	viewport	setFrameRect
takeWidget	setAlignment	maximumViewportSize	alignment
StyleMask	scrollBarWidgets	sizeAdjustPolicy	ensureVisible
setupViewport	viewportMargins	setCornerWidget	horizontalScrollBar
setFrameShadow	setVerticalScrollBar	drawFrame	widget
ensureWidgetVisible	setViewport	addScrollBarWidget	lineWidth
frameWidth	setViewportMargins	setHorizontalScrollBarPolicy	midLineWidth
viewportSizeHint	setVerticalScrollBarPolicy	widgetResizable	frameRect
setWidget	verticalScrollBar	frameShadow	viewportEvent
Shape	Shadow	verticalScrollBarPolicy	addTab

setWidget(widget **)** and **widget()**

setWidget()	→	Sets the widget to be displayed inside the scroll area.
widget()	→	Returns the currently set child widget.

</> Python

```
import sys
from PyQt6.QtCore import *
from PyQt6.QtWidgets import *
from PyQt6.QtGui import *

class PracticalApp:

    def __init__(self):
        app = QApplication(sys.argv)

        self.win = QMainWindow()
        self.win.setWindowTitle("English App")
        self.win.setFixedSize(400,200)
        self.win.setWindowIcon(QIcon("images/rocket.png"))
        self.win.setStyleSheet("background:#ebebeb")


        scroll = QScrollArea(self.win)
        scroll.setWidgetResizable(True)
        self.win.setCentralWidget(scroll)

        page = QWidget()
        scroll.setWidget(page)

        layout = QVBoxLayout(page)

        article = QLabel(
          """<h3>Business Finance</h3><p>Managing business finances means planning, budgeting,
          and controlling cash flow to keep operations smooth. Good financial management helps businesses pay
          bills on time, track expenses, and make smart investment decisions. Regularly reviewing financial reports
          ensures stability and supports long-term growth.</p>
          """)

        article.resize(350, 150)
        article.setWordWrap(True)
        article.setStyleSheet("border-radius:5px; border:2px solid green; padding:10px")

        financeBackground = QLabel()
        financeBackground.setPixmap(QPixmap("images/finan.jpg").scaled(350, 200))

        layout.addWidget(article)
        layout.addWidget(financeBackground)


if __name__ == "__main__":
    PracticalApp()
```

takeWidget(widget)

Removes and returns the contained widget.

```python
scroll = QScrollArea( parent )
scroll.takeWidget( widget )
```

setResizableWidget(bool **)** and **resizableWidget()**

setResizableWidget()	→	Sets whether the content should resize to match the scroll area.
resizableWidget()	→	Returns **True** if the content resizes to fit the scroll area size.

setVerticalScrollBar(Qt.ScrollBar **), verticalScrollBar()** and **setHorizontalScrollBar(** QScrollBar **), horizontalScrollBar()**

setVerticalScrollBar()	→	Sets a new vertical scrollbar.
setHorizontalScrollBar()	→	Sets a new horizontal scrollbar.
verticalScrollBar()	→	Returns the vertical scrollbar.
horizontalScrollBar()	→	Returns the horizontal scrollbar.

</> Python

```
scroll = QScrollArea( parent )
scroll.setHorizontalScrollBar( QScrollBar(parent) )
```

setVerticalScrollBarPolicy(Qt.ScrollBarPolicy **), verticalScrollBarPolicy()** and **setHorizontalScrollBarPolicy(** Qt.ScrollBarPolicy **), horizontalScrollBarPolicy()**

setVerticalScrollBarPolicy()	→	Sets the policy for vertical scrollbar.
setHorizontalScrollBarPolicy()	→	Sets the policy for horizontal scrollbar.
verticalScrollBarPolicy()	→	Gets the vertical scrollbar visibility policy.
horizontalScrollBarPolicy()	→	Gets the scrollbar visibility policy

</> Python

```
scroll = QScrollArea( parent )
scroll.setVerticalScrollBarPolicy( Qt.ScrollBarPolicy.AsNeeded )
```

ScrollBar Policies

ScrollBarPolicyAsNeeded	ScrollBarPolicyAlwaysOn	ScrollBarPolicyAlwaysOff

Table 7.3 : QScrollArea scrollbar policies

setCornerWidget(widget **)** and **cornerWidget()**

setCornerWidget()	→	Sets a widget for the scrollbar corner.
cornerWidget()	→	Gets the widget shown in the corner where scrollbars meet.

</> Python

```
scroll = QScrollArea( parent )
scroll.setCornerWidget(QLabel("scroll up"))
```

QMenu

Menus are a fundamental part of application design, as they help organize related functions into a clean and accessible structure. They break down a complex user interface into manageable sections, making it easier for users to navigate and interact with the application. Menus are typically placed on a menu bar and can contain multiple submenus, which are revealed when the user clicks on a parent menu item. Menu entries can be represented by text labels, icons, or both, providing both clarity and visual cues.

In PyQt, **QMenu** is used to create individual menus and submenus. Menus are added to a **QMenuBar**, which is usually placed at the top of the main window.

Use Cases

- Organizing complex user interfaces into manageable sections.
- Providing access to commands like Save, Open, Exit, etc.
- Building context menus (right-click menus) with relevant actions.
- Creating submenu hierarchies for categorized options.
- Triggering tool dialogs, settings, or application modes.
- Adding icons and keyboard shortcuts to commands.

Key Properties and Methods

actionAt	setIcon	isTearOffEnabled	insertMenu
addMenu	aboutToShow	hideTearOffMenu	setSeparatorsCollapsible
insertSeparator	popup	hovered	exec
setToolTipsVisible	setDefaultAction	menuInAction	icon
addSeparator	actionGeometry	showTearOffMenu	setTitle
aboutToHide	columnCount	activeAction	title
setNoReplayFor	clear	toolTipsVisible	initStyleOption
triggered	isEmpty	addSection	setTearOffEnabled
menuAction	setActiveAction	separatorsCollapsible	

QMenuBar

The **QMenuBar** is a horizontal bar placed typically at the top of the application window. It is designed to host menus (QMenu) which further contain actions or submenus. This creates a structured and user-friendly interface for navigating features and commands in your application.

Key Properties and Methods

setDefaultUp	actionGeometry	setNativeMenuBar	insertMenu
triggered	addSeparator	setCornerWidget	cornerWidget
insertSeparator	isNativeMenuBar	activeAction	actionAt
hovered	setActiveAction	isDefaultUp	addMenu
clear	initStyleOption		

addMenu(QMenu or label **)**
Adds a new menu (with label or QMenu object) to the menubar.

Example 1

</> Python

```
import sys
from PyQt6.QtCore import *
from PyQt6.QtWidgets import *
from PyQt6.QtGui import *

class PracticalApp:

    def __init__(self):
        app = QApplication(sys.argv)

        self.win = QMainWindow()
        self.win.setWindowTitle("English App")
        self.win.setFixedSize(400,200)
        self.win.setWindowIcon(QIcon("images/rocket.png"))
        self.win.setStyleSheet("background:#ebebeb")

        self.menubar = QMenuBar(self.win)
        self.menubar.setGeometry(10,10, self.win.width()-20, 35)
```

```
        self.menubar.setStyleSheet("background:#424349; color:white")

        self.menubar.addMenu("File")
        self.menubar.addMenu("Edit")
        self.menubar.addMenu("View")
        self.menubar.addMenu("Tools")
        self.menubar.addMenu("Windows")


if __name__ == "__main__":
    PracticalApp()
```

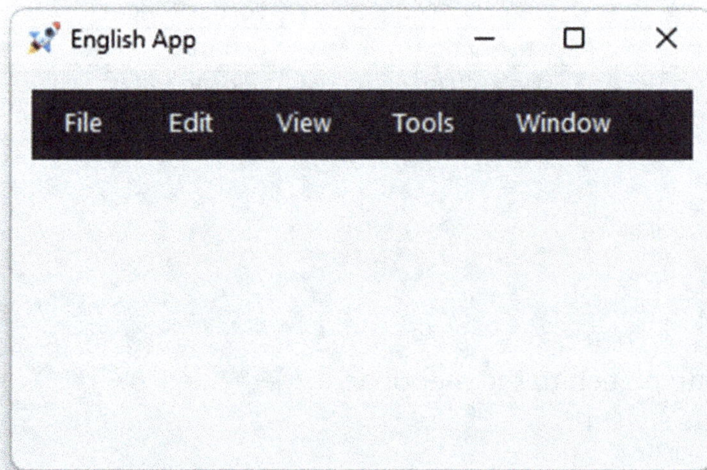

Example 2

</> Python

```
menubar = QMenuBar( parent )
menubar.setGeometry(10,10, parent.width()-20, 35)
menubar.setStyleSheet("background:#424349; color:white")

fileMenu = QMenu("File")
editMenu = QMenu("Edit")
viewMenu = QMenu("View")
toolMenu = QMenu("Tools")
windowMenu = QMenu("Window")
```

```
menubar.addMenu(fileMenu)
menubar.addMenu(editMenu)
menubar.addMenu(viewMenu)
menubar.addMenu(toolMenu)
menubar.addMenu(windowMenu)
```

insertMenu(before, QMenu)

Inserts a menu before a specified one.

</> Python

```python
menubar = QMenuBar(parent)

newMenu = QMenu("Help")
menubar.insert(QAction(editMenu), newMenu)
```

setCornerWidget(widget) and cornerWidget()

setCornerWidget()	→	Places a custom widget in the corner (e.g. search bar, logo).
cornerWidget()	→	Retrieves the corner widget.

</> Python

```python
menubar = QMenuBar(parent)

button = QPushButton("Tips")
button.setIcon(QIcon("images/lightbulb.png"))
menubar.setCornerWidget(button)
```

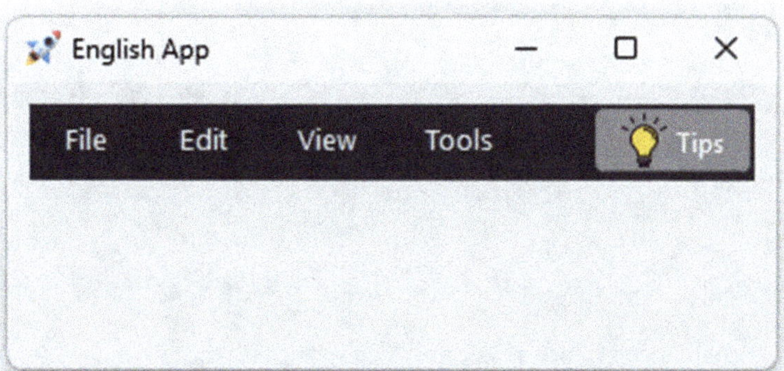

addSeparator( ) and **insertSeparator(** before QAction **)**

addSeparator()	→	Adds a visual separator between menus.
insertSeparator()	→	Inserts a separator before a given action.

</> Python

```python
menubar = QMenuBar(parent)

menubar.addMenu("File")
menubar.addSeparator()          #Add separator
menubar.addMenu("Edit")
menubar.addSeparator()          #Add separator
menubar.addMenu("View")
```

hovered and **triggered**

hovered	→	Signal emitted when a menu action is hovered.
triggered	→	Signal emitted when any menu action is triggered.

</> Python

```python
menubar = QMenuBar(parent)

menubar.hovered.connect(lambda: print("MenuBar is focused"))
```

setActiveAction() and **activeAction()**

setActiveAction()	→	Sets the active (highlighted) action.
activeAction()	→	Returns the currently active menu action.

</> Python

```python
menubar = QMenuBar(parent)

menubar.setActiveAction( QAction("File"))
```

setTitle(text) and title()

setTitle()	→	Sets the title text of the menu.
title()	→	Gets the title of the menu.

</> Python

```
menubar = QMenuBar(parent)

open = QMenu()
open.setTitle("Open")

save = QMenu()
save.setTitle("Save")

copy = QMenu()
copy.setTitle("Copy")

menubar.addMenu(open)
menubar.addMenu(save)
menubar.addMenu(copy)
```

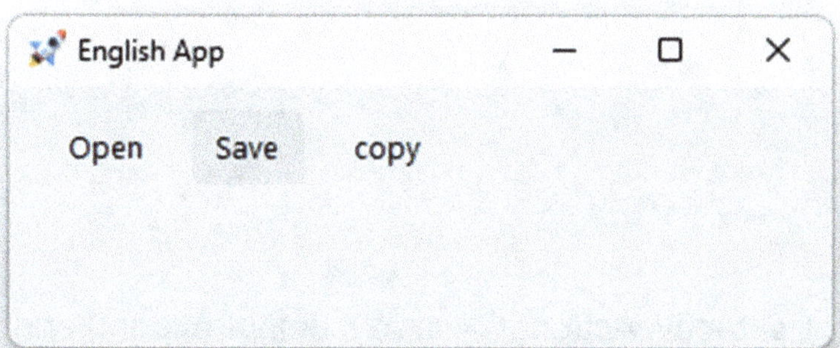

setIcon(QIcon) and icon()

setIcon()	→	Sets an icon for the menu title.
icon()	→	Returns the menu's icon.

</> Python

```
menubar = QMenuBar(parent)

open.setIcon(QIcon("open.png"))
save.setIcon(QIcon("save.png"))
```

```
copy.setIcon(QIcon("copy.png"))
cut.setIcon(QIcon("cut.png"))
undo.setIcon(QIcon("undo.png"))
redo.setIcon(QIcon("redo.png"))

menubar.addMenu(open)
menubar.addMenu(save)
menubar.addMenu(copy)
menubar.addMenu(cut)
menubar.addMenu(undo)
menubar.addMenu(redo)
```

addAction(QAction), activeAction( ), setActiveAction(QAction), defaultAction() and **isEmpty()**

addAction()	→	Adds an action to the menu.
activeAction()	→	Returns the currently active action.
setActiveAction()	→	Sets a specific action as actively highlighted.
defaultAction()	→	Gets the default action of the menu.
isEmpty()	→	Returns True if the menu has no actions.

SubMenu and Menu Structure in PyQt

In PyQt, menus are typically situated on a ***QMenuBar***. These menus help group related functionalities, reduce UI clutter, and create a clear navigation structure.

Menu Types

Every **menu item**, whether on the menu bar or nested as a submenu, serves one of two purposes:

1. Action Menu
   Executes a specific function when clicked. These do not contain further submenus. *(Connected using **QAction**)*
2. Parent Menu
   Does not execute a function directly but instead **exposes submenus** when hovered or clicked.

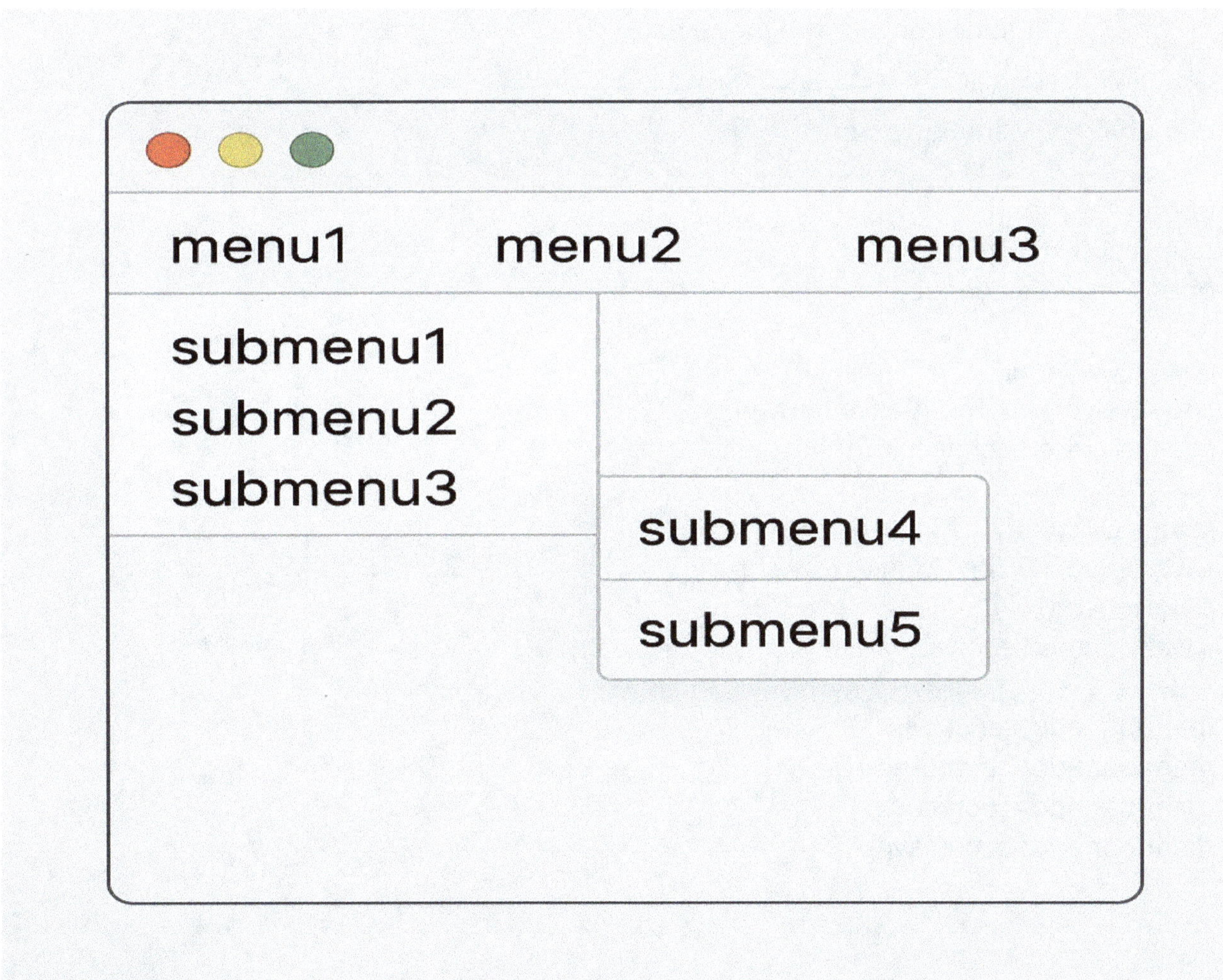

Figure 7.0 : Structure of a complex menu

Menu Behavior (Based on Diagram)

- **Menu1**: A parent menu — contains submenus (submenu1, submenu2, submenu3).
- **Menu2 and Menu3**: Action menus — no child menus; clicking them triggers direct actions.
- **Submenu1 and Submenu2**: Action submenus that trigger specific functions when clicked.
- **Submenu3**: A parent submenu that opens to reveal more nested menus (submenu4, submenu5).

QAction

This widget is used for adding clickable (actionable) items.

Example 1 – Adding items to the menu bar

</> Python

```
menubar = QMenuBar(parent)

open = QAction()
open.setText("Open")
open.triggered.connect(lambda: print("helloo"))

copy = QAction()
copy.setIcon(QIcon("images/copy.png"))
copy.triggered.connect(lambda: print("Copy Text"))

save = QAction()
save.setIcon(QIcon("images/save.png"))
save.setIconText("Save As")
save.triggered.connect(lambda: print("Save Text"))

menubar.addMenu("File")
menubar.addAction(open)
menubar.addAction(copy)
menubar.addAction(save)
```

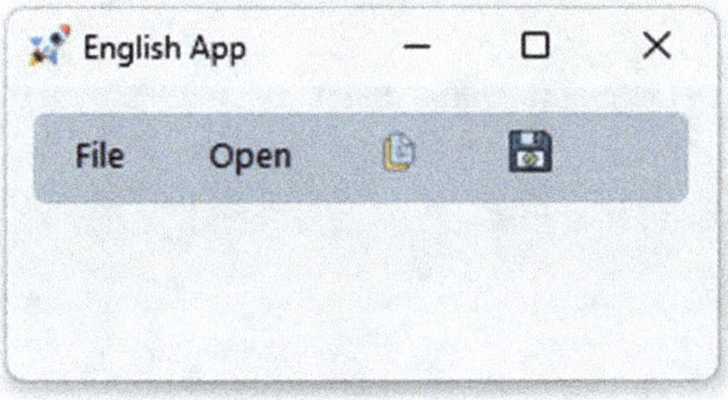

Example 2 – Adding items to the menu bar by using arguments directly in *addAction()*

</> Python

```
menubar = QMenuBar(parent)

menubar.addMenu("File")
menubar.addAction("Edit", callFunction)
menubar.addAction(QIcon("images/undo.png"), "Undo", callFunction)
menubar.addAction(QIcon("images/forward.png"), "Redo", callFunction)

def callFunction():
    pass
```

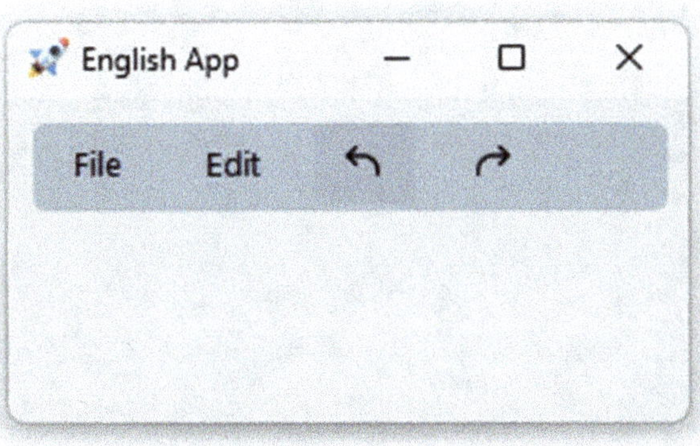

Example 3 - Creating submenus

</> Python

```
menubar = QMenuBar(parent)
menubar.setStyleSheet("background:#b1bed2; border-radius:5px")

file = QMenu("File")

newSubmenu = QMenu("New")
file.addMenu(newSubmenu)
file.addAction(QIcon("images/saveas.png"), "Save As", callFunction)
file.addAction(QIcon("images/printer.png"), "Print", callFunction)
file.addAction(QIcon("images/share.png"), "Share", callFunction)
file.addAction(QIcon("images/settings.png"), "Settings", callFunction)

newSubmenu.addAction("Document", callFunction)
newSubmenu.addAction("Book", callFunction)
newSubmenu.addAction("PDF", callFunction)

menubar.addMenu(file)
menubar.addAction("Edit", callFunction)
menubar.addAction("View", callFunction)
menubar.addAction("Tools", callFunction)
menubar.addAction("Windows", callFunction)


def callFunction():
    pass
```

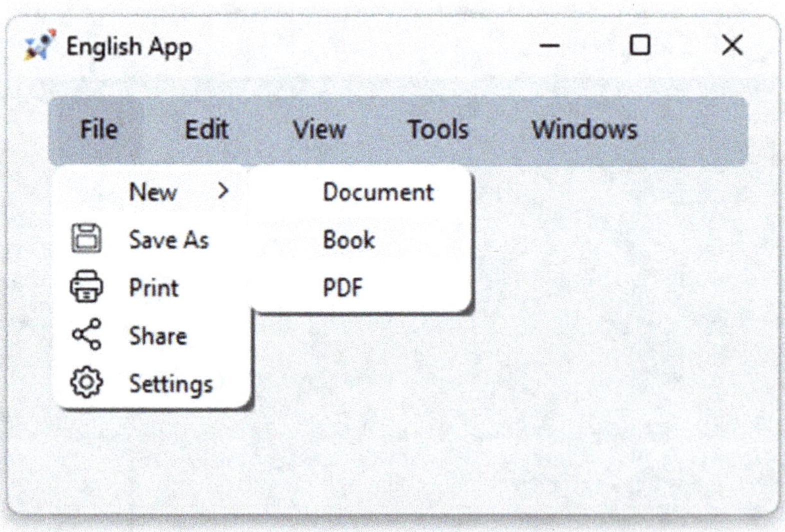

addSeparator( ) and **insertSeparator(** before QAction **)**

addSeparator()	→ Adds a visual separator between menus
insertSeparator()	→ Inserts a separator before a given action.

</> Python

```
menubar = QMenuBar(parent)

file = QMenu("File")

newSubmenu = QMenu("New")
file.addMenu(newSubmenu)
file.addSeparator()        #Add separator
file.addAction(QIcon("Save As"), callFunction)
file.addSeparator()        #Add separator
file.addAction(QIcon( "Print"), callFunction)
file.addSeparator()        #Add separator
file.addAction(QIcon( "Share"), callFunction)
file.addSeparator()        #Add separator
file.addAction(QIcon("Settings"), callFunction)

menubar.addMenu(file)

file.setStyleSheet("""
  QMenu{background:#0A0E15;color:white;}
  QMenu::separator{background: white; height: 1px;}
  """)

def callFunction():
    pass
```

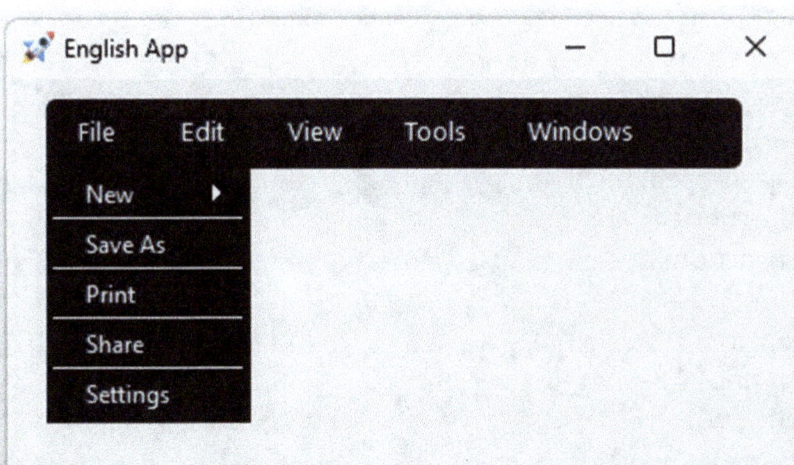

Integrating MenuBar in the QMainWindow

The **QMainWindow** widget in PyQt provides a built-in and seamless way to integrate a **QMenuBar**.

While it's technically possible to create a QMenuBar as a normal widget and add it manually to layouts, this is not the recommended or idiomatic approach in PyQt.

Instead, QMainWindow has the ***setMenuBar()*** method that is specifically designed for this purpose.

This method accepts a QMenuBar instance (with all its menus and actions already added) and integrates it automatically at the top of the window in the standard OS-consistent style.

Example

</> Python

```
from PyQt5.QtWidgets import QMainWindow, QApplication, QMenuBar, QMenu, QAction
import sys

class MyApp(QMainWindow):
    def __init__(self):
        super().__init__()

        self.setWindowTitle("QMainWindow with MenuBar")

        # Create the QMenuBar
        menu_bar = QMenuBar()

        # Create Menus
        file_menu = QMenu("File", self)
        edit_menu = QMenu("Edit", self)

        # Add Actions
        new_action = QAction("New", self)
        open_action = QAction("Open", self)
        file_menu.addAction(new_action)
        file_menu.addAction(open_action)

        # Add Menus to the MenuBar
        menu_bar.addMenu(file_menu)
        menu_bar.addMenu(edit_menu)

        # Integrate with QMainWindow
```

```
        self.setMenuBar(menu_bar)


if __name__ == "__main__":
    app = QApplication(sys.argv)
    myapp = MyApp()
    window.show()
    sys.exit(app.exec_())
```


QToolButton

In the previous tutorial, we studied **QMenu** and **QMenuBar**, where QMenus are usually text labels on the menubar that expand to show submenus or actions.

QToolButton works very similarly to QMenu but is meant to be used on a **QToolBar**. It is typically represented by an **icon** (or text) button rather than a label.

It is designed for quick-access buttons in a toolbar. You can think of QToolButton as a compact, icon-friendly button perfect for toolbars.

Use Cases

- Adding quick-access tools (Save, Open, Print) to a toolbar.
- Providing icon-based shortcuts for frequent actions (Cut, Copy, Paste).
- Adding toggles (Bold, Italic) in a text editor toolbar.
- Creating compact action bars in drawing or design apps (Brush, Eraser).
- Adding dropdown menus for grouped actions (e.g., "New File" with subtypes).
- Navigation buttons (Back, Forward).
- Settings or options buttons in toolbars.

Key Properties and Methods

defaultAction	setAutoRaise	shortcut	toggled
triggered	autoRepeat	autoRaise	setDefaultAction
text	setAutoRepeat	isCheckable	isDown
showMenu	setAutoExclusive	setMenu	initStyleOption
setArrowType	released	isChecked	setText
hitButton	setIcon	autoRepeatInterval	checkStateSet
arrowType	clicked	autoExclusive	menu
setAutoRepeatDelay	group	pressed	setAutoRepeatInterval
nextCheckState	setShortcut	animateClick	toggle
setDown	ToolButtonPopupMode	setChecked	autoRepeatDelay
click	icon	setCheckable	popupMode
setPopupMode			

QToolBar

The **QToolBar** is a container widget in PyQt that holds **QToolButton** and other widgets.

It acts as a static or floating bar in your application's main window, providing easy access to frequently used actions.

A toolbar can be docked to the sides of a main window or floated in its own window.

It's typically used to organize tools, actions, or shortcuts in a compact, accessible way.

Key Properties and Methods

isFloating	isFloatable	widgetForAction	isAreaAllowed
setOrientation	initStyleOption	visibilityChanged	addWidget
allowedAreasChanged	orientationChanged	insertSeparator	insertWidget
orientation	actionGeometry	setMovable	actionTriggered
movableChanged	topLevelChanged	clear	setAllowedAreas
isMovable	addSeparator	toggleViewAction	allowedAreas
setFloatable	actionAt		

addAction(icon, text, function **)**
Add an action (which becomes a button) to the toolbar.

</> Python

```
import sys
from PyQt6.QtCore import *
from PyQt6.QtWidgets import *
from PyQt6.QtGui import *

class PracticalApp:

    def __init__(self):
        app = QApplication(sys.argv)

        self.win = QMainWindow()
        self.win.setWindowTitle("English App")
        self.win.setFixedSize(400,200)
        self.win.setWindowIcon(QIcon("images/rocket.png"))
        self.win.setStyleSheet("background:#ebebeb")
```

```
        toolbar = QToolBar(self.win)
        toolbar.setGeometry(50, 10, 200, 40)
        toolbar.setStyleSheet("background:white")

        toolbar.addAction(QIcon("images/home.png"),"home", self.callback)
        toolbar.addAction(QIcon("images/saveas.png"),"save", self.callback)
        toolbar.addAction(QIcon("images/undo.png"),"undo", self.callback)
        toolbar.addAction(QIcon("images/redo.png"),"redo", self.callback)
        toolbar.addAction(QIcon("images/settings.png"),"settings", self.callback)
        toolbar.addAction(QIcon("images/printer.png"),"printer", self.callback)


    def callback(self):
        print("signal received")


if __name__ == "__main__":
    PracticalApp()
```

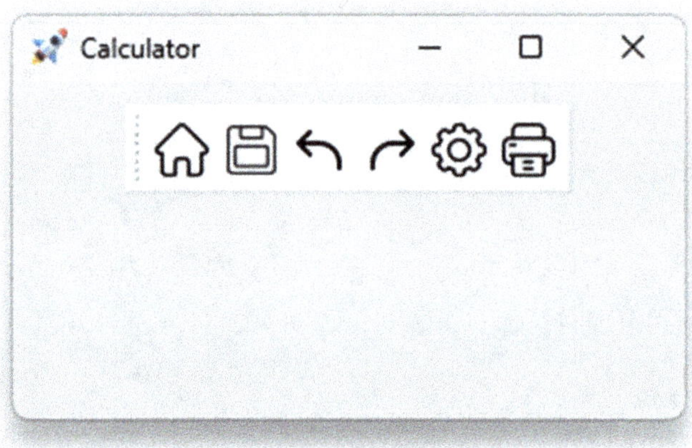

addWidget(widget)

Adds any QWidget to the toolbar (e.g. QToolButton, combo box, line edit).

</> Python

```
toolbar = QToolBar(self)
toolbar.setGeometry(10, 10, 250, 40)
toolbar.setStyleSheet("background:white")
```

```
openfolder = QToolButton()
openfolder.setIcon(QIcon("images/open-folder.png"))
openfolder.clicked.connect(self.callback)
toolbar.addWidget(openfolder)

save = QToolButton()
save.setIcon(QIcon("images/save.png"))
save.clicked.connect(self.callback)
toolbar.addWidget(save)

video = QToolButton()
video.setIcon(QIcon("images/video.png"))
video.clicked.connect(self.callback)
toolbar.addWidget(video)

download = QToolButton()
download.setIcon(QIcon("images/paint.png"))
download.clicked.connect(self.callback)
toolbar.addWidget(download)


def callback(self):
    print("signal received")
```

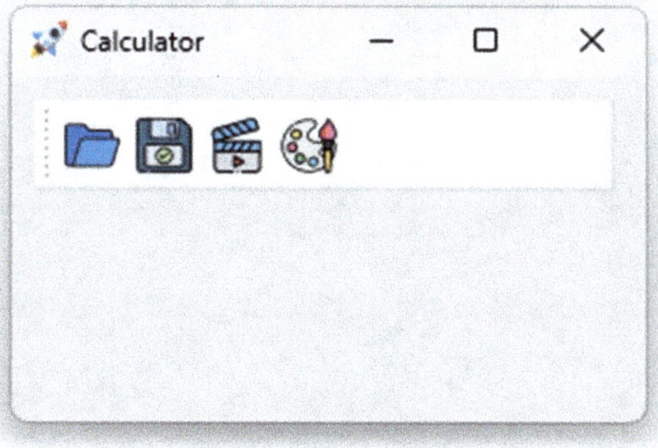

Integrating ToolBar in the QMainWindow

Just as **QMainWindow** has a special slot for the **QMenuBar**, it also provides a better way to add **QToolBar** objects.

Rather than adding a QToolBar directly as a child widget (which would break layout and look unnatural), QMainWindow provides the ***addToolBar()*** method.

This method automatically docks the toolbar in a standard position (top, bottom, left, or right) and allows for standard docking behavior.

Example

</> Python

```python
from PyQt5.QtWidgets import QMainWindow, QApplication, QMenuBar, QMenu, QAction
import sys

class MyApp(QMainWindow):
  def __init__(self):
    super().__init__()

    self.setWindowTitle("QMainWindow with MenuBar")

    # Create a ToolBar
    tool_bar = QToolBar("Main Toolbar", self)

    # Add Actions
    save_action = QAction("Save", self)
    open_action = QAction("Open", self)

    tool_bar.addAction(save_action)
    tool_bar.addAction(open_action)

    # Integrate with QMainWindow
    self.addToolBar(tool_bar)

if __name__ == "__main__":
  app = QApplication(sys.argv)
  myapp = MyApp()
  window.show()
  sys.exit(app.exec_())
```


Finalizing Project - Developing an English App

</> Python

```
import sys
from PyQt6.QtCore import *
from PyQt6.QtWidgets import *
from PyQt6.QtGui import *
from PyQt6.QtGui import QIcon
import textblob

class PracticalApp(QMainWindow):

    def __init__(self):
        super().__init__()

        self.setWindowTitle("English App")
        self.setFixedSize(1100,600)
        self.setWindowIcon(QIcon("images/rocket.png"))
        self.setStyleSheet("background:#17191f")

        self.main_widget = QWidget()
        self.setCentralWidget(self.main_widget)
        self.lay = QHBoxLayout(self.main_widget)

        self.leftPanel = QWidget()
        self.lay.addWidget(self.leftPanel, stretch=2)
        self.appName = QLabel("<h2>My English App</h2>", self.leftPanel)
        self.appName.setGeometry(10,10,200, 50)
        self.appName.setStyleSheet("color:tomato; font-family:'Georgia'")

        self.listwidget = QListWidget(self.leftPanel)
        self.listwidget.setGeometry(0,50, 200, self.width()-50)
        self.listwidget.setFont(QFont("comic sans ms", 12, 10))
        self.listwidget.setStyleSheet("color:white;background:#17191f; border-radius:10px")
        self.listwidget.setIconSize(QSize(30,30))
        self.listwidget.setSpacing(10)

        itemDictionary = QListWidgetItem(QIcon("dictionary.png"),"Dictionary", self.listwidget)
        itemSpellCheck = QListWidgetItem(QIcon("approve.png"),"Spelling Checker", self.listwidget)
        itemTokenization = QListWidgetItem(QIcon("comma.png"),"Tokenization", self.listwidget)
        itemPlural = QListWidgetItem(QIcon("sentences.png"),"Plural", self.listwidget)
        itemNounPhrase = QListWidgetItem(QIcon("word.png"),"Noun Phrase", self.listwidget)

        self.rightPanel = QWidget()
```

```
        self.rightPanel.setStyleSheet("background:#21232b")
        self.lay.addWidget(self.rightPanel, stretch=9)

        self.chatArea = QWidget()
        self.chatlayout = QVBoxLayout(self.chatArea)

        self.chatScroll = QScrollArea(self.rightPanel)
        self.chatScroll.setWidgetResizable(True)
        self.chatScroll.setWidget(self.chatArea)
        self.chatScroll.setGeometry(10,10,self.width()-250, self.height()-150)
        self.chatScroll.setVerticalScrollBarPolicy(Qt.ScrollBarPolicy.ScrollBarAlwaysOff)

        self.texteditor = QLineEdit(self.rightPanel)
        self.texteditor.setGeometry(20, self.height()-100, self.width()- 400, 50)
        self.texteditor.setStyleSheet("""color:white;background:#17191f; border:2px solid #17191f;
                                        border-radius:5px;padding-left:10px; font-size:20px""")

        self.sendbutton = QPushButton("send", self.rightPanel)
        self.sendbutton.setGeometry(self.width()-350, self.height()-100, 100, 50)
        self.sendbutton.setIcon(QIcon("images/send.png"))
        self.sendbutton.setIconSize(QSize(30,30))
        self.sendbutton.setStyleSheet("color:white;background:#17191f; border:2px solid
                                        #17191f;border-radius:5px ")
        self.sendbutton.clicked.connect(lambda: self.sendMessage())


    def sendMessage(self):
        getMessage = self.texteditor.text()

        if getMessage != "":
          question = QLabel(f"<h3>Question</h3><p>{getMessage}</p>")
          question.setStyleSheet("""color:#ebebeb;background:#17191f;border:2px solid
                        tomato;border-radius:5px; padding:5px; margin:5px 5px 5px 500px""")

          question.setWordWrap(True)
          self.chatlayout.addWidget(question)

          answer = QLabel()
          answer.setStyleSheet("""color:#ebebeb;background:#424349;border:2px
                        solid#8AF98D;border-radius:5px; padding:5px;margin:5px 200px 5px 5px""")

          answer.setMaximumWidth(self.chatScroll.width()-20)
          answer.setWordWrap(True)

          selItem = self.listwidget.currentItem().text().replace(" ", "").lower()
```

```
        definitions = ""
        if selItem == "dictionary":
          define = textblob.Word(getMessage).definitions
          for item in define:
              definitions = definitions + "\n\n" + item

          answer.setText(f"Answer\n{definitions}")
          self.chatlayout.addWidget(answer)

        if selItem == "spellingchecker":
          corrected = textblob.Sentence(getMessage).correct()
          answer.setText(f"Answer\n{corrected}")
          self.chatlayout.addWidget(answer)

        if selItem == "nounphrase":
          nouns = textblob.Sentence(getMessage).noun_phrases
          answer.setText(f"Answer\n{nouns}")
          self.chatlayout.addWidget(answer)

        if selItem == "tokenization":
          token = textblob.Sentence(getMessage).tokenize()
          answer.setText(f"Answer\n{token}")
          self.chatlayout.addWidget(answer)

        if selItem == "plural":
          plural = textblob.Word(getMessage).pluralize()
          answer.setText(f"Answer\n{plural}")
          self.chatlayout.addWidget(answer)



style  = """
      QLabel{font-family:'Georgia'}
      QListWidget::item:hover{ background:rgba(255,255,255,50);}

      QListWidget::item:selected{background:'grey';color:'#131821';}
      """


app = QApplication([])
app.setStyleSheet(style)
myapp = PracticalApp()
myapp.show()
sys.exit(app.exec())
```

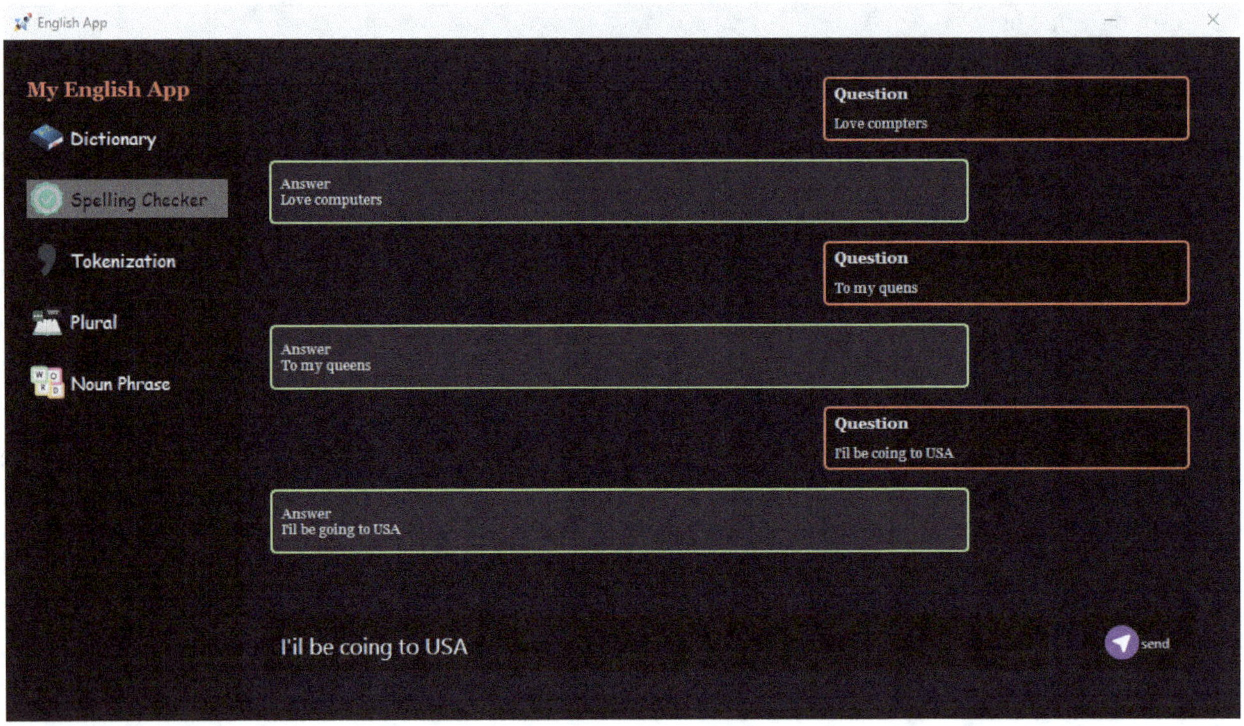
English App
My English App
Dictionary
Spelling Checker
Tokenization
Plural
Noun Phrase
Question
Love compters
Answer
Love computers
Question
To my quens
Answer
To my queens
Question
I'il be coing to USA
Answer
I'il be going to USA
I'il be coing to USA
send

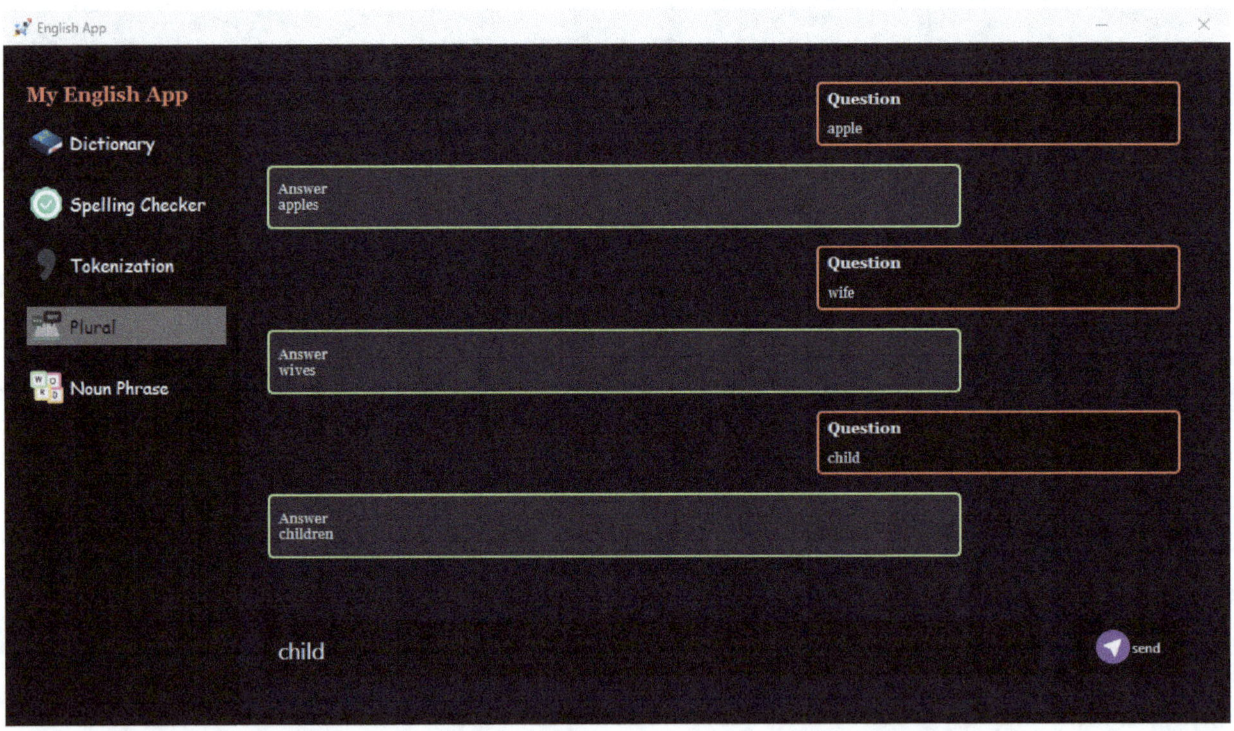
English App
My English App
Dictionary
Spelling Checker
Tokenization
Plural
Noun Phrase
Question
apple
Answer
apples
Question
wife
Answer
wives
Question
child
Answer
children
child
send

Chapter 8

PyQt Widgets - Set D (Files and Media)

Chapter Objectives

- Use QProgressBar
- Open files with QFileDialog
- Play media with QMediaPlayer
- Display video with QVideoWidget
- Output audio with QAudioOutput

Project D – Developing a Music Player

In this project, we will explore how to build a basic music player using PyQt. This project introduces essential PyQt widgets and tools for working with media files and user interaction.

Project Features

1. **Open and Load Audio Files**
   The player allows users to browse and select audio files from their device using a file dialog.

2. **Play Audio Files**
   Once an audio file is selected, the player initiates playback and outputs sound through the system's default audio device.

3. **Control Playback**
   Users can:
   - **Pause** and **resume** audio playback
   - **Seek forward** and **seek backward** to navigate through the track
   - **Monitor progress** via a progress bar or slider showing the current playback position

QProgressBar

In software applications, it's important to provide real-time feedback about internal operations. Users should be able to monitor the progress of ongoing tasks such as loading, downloading, rendering, converting, and saving. This helps set expectations for wait time and offers a more interactive experience. In PyQt, the QProgressBar widget is designed specifically to show the progress of long-running or continuous tasks.

Use Cases

1. Media players - To show the current position in audio or video playback
2. File download/upload managers - To display progress of data transfer
3. Installers or setup wizards - To indicate installation progress
4. Rendering engines - To display rendering time or status
5. Data processing applications - To show status of tasks like compression, conversion, or analysis
6. Simulations or scientific computing - To track iteration progress or model completion
7. Batch operations - Such as uploading multiple images or running loops with visible progress

Key Properties and Methods

format	minimum	setOrientation	reset
text	valueChanged	setValue	setRange
resetFormat	setAlignment	isTextVisible	setInvertedAppearance
setFormat	setMinimum	setTextDirection	alignment
setMaximum	Direction	value	maximum
orientation	initStyleOption	setTextVisible	

setValue(int **)** and **value( )**

setValue()	→	Sets the current value of the progress bar (between min and max).
value()	→	Returns the current progress value.

</> Python

```
import sys
from PyQt6.QtCore import *
from PyQt6.QtWidgets import *
import time
import threading

class PracticalApp(QMainWindow):

    def __init__(self):
        super().__init__()

        self.setWindowTitle("Music Player")
        self.resize(300,150)
        self.setWindowIcon(QIcon("images/rocket.png"))
        self.setStyleSheet("background:#ebebeb")

        self.progress = QProgressBar(self)
        self.progress.setValue(0)              #Set initial value
        self.progress.setGeometry(20, 50, 300, 50)

        self.button = QPushButton("Run", self)
        self.button.move(100,100)
        self.button.pressed.connect(self.runOnThread)

    def runOnThread(self):
        thread = threading.Thread(target=self.getValue )
        thread.start()

    def getValue(self):
        i = 0
        while i<100:
            i = i + 5
            time.sleep(2)
            self.progress.setValue(i)


app = QApplication([])
myapp = PracticalApp()
myapp.show()
sys.exit(app.exec())
```

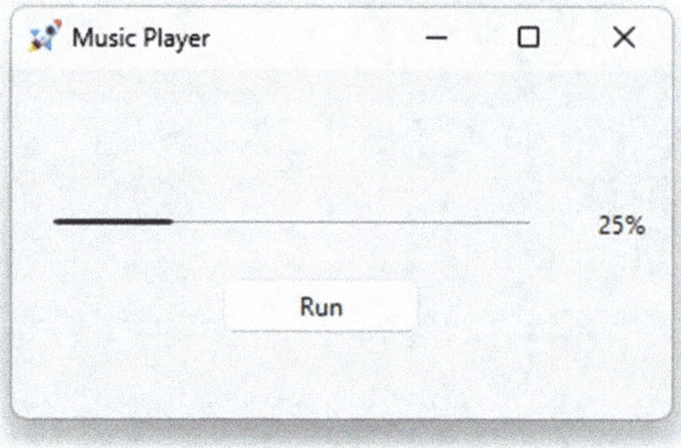

Tips

More about Python Threads

Python's threading module allows functions to run in a separate thread, apart from the main application thread. This is especially useful for handling time-consuming or blocking tasks, such as downloading files, processing data, or waiting for external responses.

By moving such tasks to a different thread, you help keep the main application responsive, preventing it from freezing or becoming unresponsive during heavy operations.
This concept also applies in PyQt, where **QThread** is used to achieve similar multitasking behavior within GUI applications.

setRange(int min, int max**), setMinimum(** int min**)** and **setMaximum(** int max **)**

setRange()	→	Sets both the minimum and maximum range of the progress bar.
setMinimum()	→	Sets the minimum value of the range.
setMaximum()	→	Sets the maximum value of the range.

</> Python

```
progressbar = QProgressBar(parent)
progressbar.setRange(0, 100)
```

setFormat(str format **)** and **format( )**

setFormat()	→	Defines the text format shown (e.g. %p% for percentage).
format()	→	Returns the current format string.

</> Python

```
progressbar = QProgressBar(parent)
progressbar.setFormat("%ps")        #for seconds
progressbar.setRange(0, 100)
```

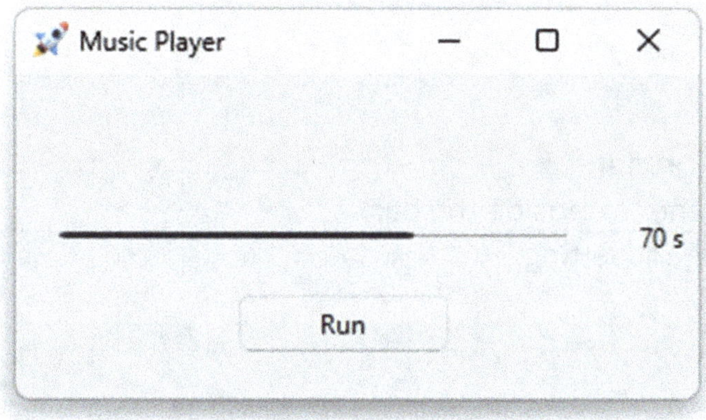

reset()

Resets the progress bar to its initial state.

</> Python

```
progressbar = QProgressBar(parent)
progressbar.reset()
```

setOrientation(Qt.Orientation **)** and **orientation( )**

setOrientation()	→	Determines the direction of the progress bar (horizontal is default).
orientation()	→	Returns the current orientation.

</> Python

```
progressbar = QProgressBar(parent)
progressbar.setOrientation(Qt.Orientation.Vertical)
```

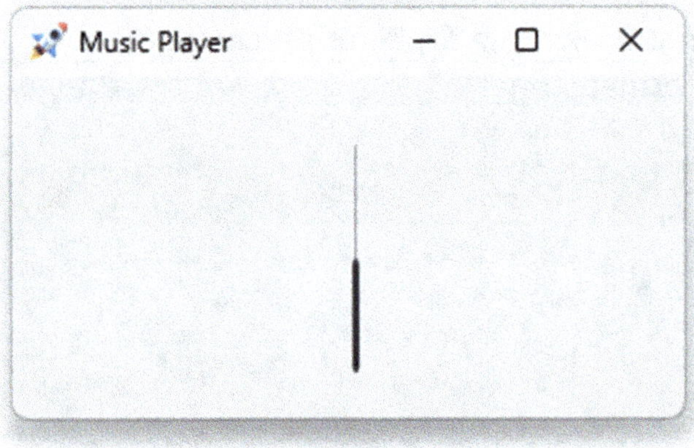

setAlignment(Qt.AlignmentFlag **)** and **alignment( )**

setAlignment()	→	Sets alignment of the text inside the bar.
alignment()	→	Returns the alignment setting.

```python
progressbar = QProgressBar(parent)
progressbar.setOrientation(Qt.AlignmentFlag.AlignCenter)
```

Common Alignment Flags

AlignCenter	AlignJustify	AlignHCenter	AlignBottom	AlignBaseline
AlignLeft	AlignLeading	AlignHorizontal_Mask	AlignTop	AlignAbsolute
AlignRight	AlignTrailing	AlignVCenter	AlignVertical_Mask	

Table 8.0 : The Alignment Flags

setDirection(QProgress.Direction **)** and **direction( )**

setDirection()	→	Specifies text direction (for vertical orientation). ***BottomToTop*** or ***TopToBottom***.
direction()	→	Returns the progress bar text direction.

```python
progressbar = QProgressBar(parent)
progressbar.setDirection(QProgressBar.BottomToTop)
```

setInvertedAppearance(bool **)**

Reverses the direction of the progress fill.

```python
progressbar = QProgressBar(parent)
progressbar.setInvertedAppearance(True)
```

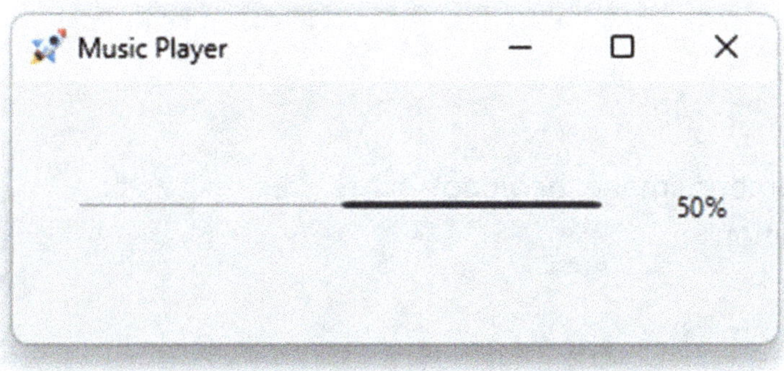

setTextVisible(bool **)** and **isTextVisible( )**

setTextVisible()	→	Controls whether the progress text is shown.
isTextVisible()	→	Returns True if text is visible.

```python
progressbar = QProgressBar(parent)
progressbar.setTextVisible(True)
```


QFileDialog

QFileDialog is a dialog widget in PyQt that provides a native file explorer interface. It allows users to **open files**, **save files** and **browse folders**. This dialog box integrates directly with the operating system's file explorer, offering a familiar interface to the user. Although the dialog looks like part of the OS, it can be customized to restrict or guide file selection based on filters and modes.

Use Cases

- Opening files (e.g. selecting a document, image, or video)
- Saving files to a user-specified location
- Choosing a directory/folder
- Filtering files by type (e.g. .txt, .png, .mp3)
- Selecting multiple files
- Getting file path input from the user

Key Properties and Methods

setDirectory	result	setProxyModel	getExistingDirectory
selectedUrls	labelText	selectedMimeTypeFilter	selectUrl
getSaveFileName	setModal	saveFileContent	Option
getOpenFileNames	selectedFiles	getOpenFileName	sidebarUrls
setDirectoryUrl	done	finished	setResult
history	setOption	itemDelegate	currentChanged
nameFilters	directoryUrl	accept	mimeTypeFilters
getOpenFileUrls	setAcceptMode	filter	supportedSchemes
exec	directoryEntered	selectNameFilter	setDefaultSuffix
options	setFileMode	viewMode	accepted
directoryUrlEntered	filterSelected	urlsSelected	fileMode
selectFile	FileMode	setHistory	urlSelected
setNameFilters	acceptMode	setIconProvider	defaultSuffix
setSizeGripEnabled	setItemDelegate	getExistingDirectoryUrl	ViewMode
getSaveFileUrl	proxyModel	setSidebarUrls	iconProvider
setLabelText	setFilter	selectedNameFilter	AcceptMode
setNameFilter	currentUrlChanged	testOption	setSupportedSchemes
rejected	isSizeGripEnabled	open	DialogCode
setMimeTypeFilters	fileSelected	getOpenFileUrl	Reject
filesSelected	setOptions	DialogLabel	setViewMode
directory	selectMimeTypeFilter		

getOpenFileName(parent, caption, directory, filter) and
getOpenFileNames(parent, caption, directory, filter)

getOpenFileName()	→	Opens a dialog to select a single file to open. Returns the file path as a string.
getOpenFileNames()	→	Lets the user select multiple files. Returns a list of file paths.

Arguments:

parent → The parent widget that owns the file dialog. Usually, the main window or self.

caption → The **title** of the dialog window. It indicates the purpose of the file selection (e.g., "Open Image", "Select Audio File").

directory → The **initial folder** path that opens when the dialog appears. You can set it to "" or a specific path like "C:/Users".

filter → The types of files the dialog should display. It controls the selectable file types using wildcards and optional filter labels.

- "*"
Shows all file types.

- "*.png *.jpg *.mp3"
Shows only PNG, JPG, and MP3 files.

- "Text Files (*.txt);; Documents (*.docx *.xlsx *.pptx);; Audio (*.mp3 *.wav)"
A well-structured multi-option filter, each with a descriptive label.

</> Python

```
import sys
from PyQt6.QtCore import *
from PyQt6.QtWidgets import *

class PracticalApp(QMainWindow):

    def __init__(self):
        super().__init__()

        self.setWindowTitle("Music Player")
        self.resize(300,150)
```

```
        self.setWindowIcon(QIcon("images/rocket.png"))
        self.setStyleSheet("background:#ebebeb")

        self.importFile = QPushButton("Import file", self)
        self.importFile.move(100, 70)
        self.importFile.setIcon(QIcon("images/upload.png"))
        self.importFile.setIconSize(QSize(20,20))
        self.importFile.pressed.connect(lambda: self.chooseFile())


    def chooseFile(self):
        fileName, _ = QFileDialog().getOpenFileName(
         self,              #parent
         "Choose a File",   #caption
         "",                #directory
        " All (*);; Text Files (*.txt);; Documents (*.docx *.xlsx *.pptx);; Audio (*.mp3 *.wav)"  #filter
         )
        print(fileName)


app = QApplication([])
myapp = PracticalApp()
myapp.show()
sys.exit(app.exec())
```

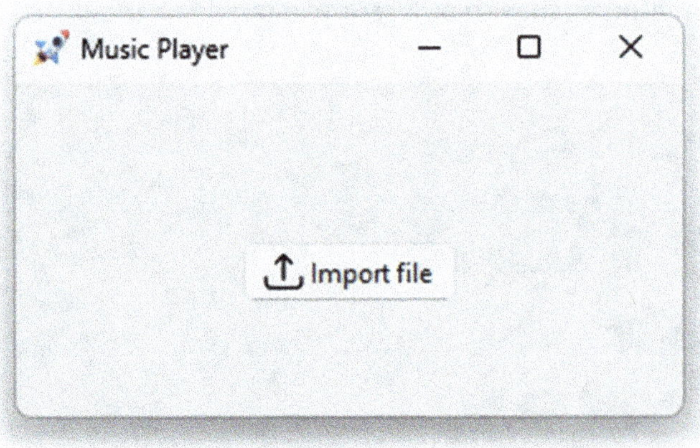

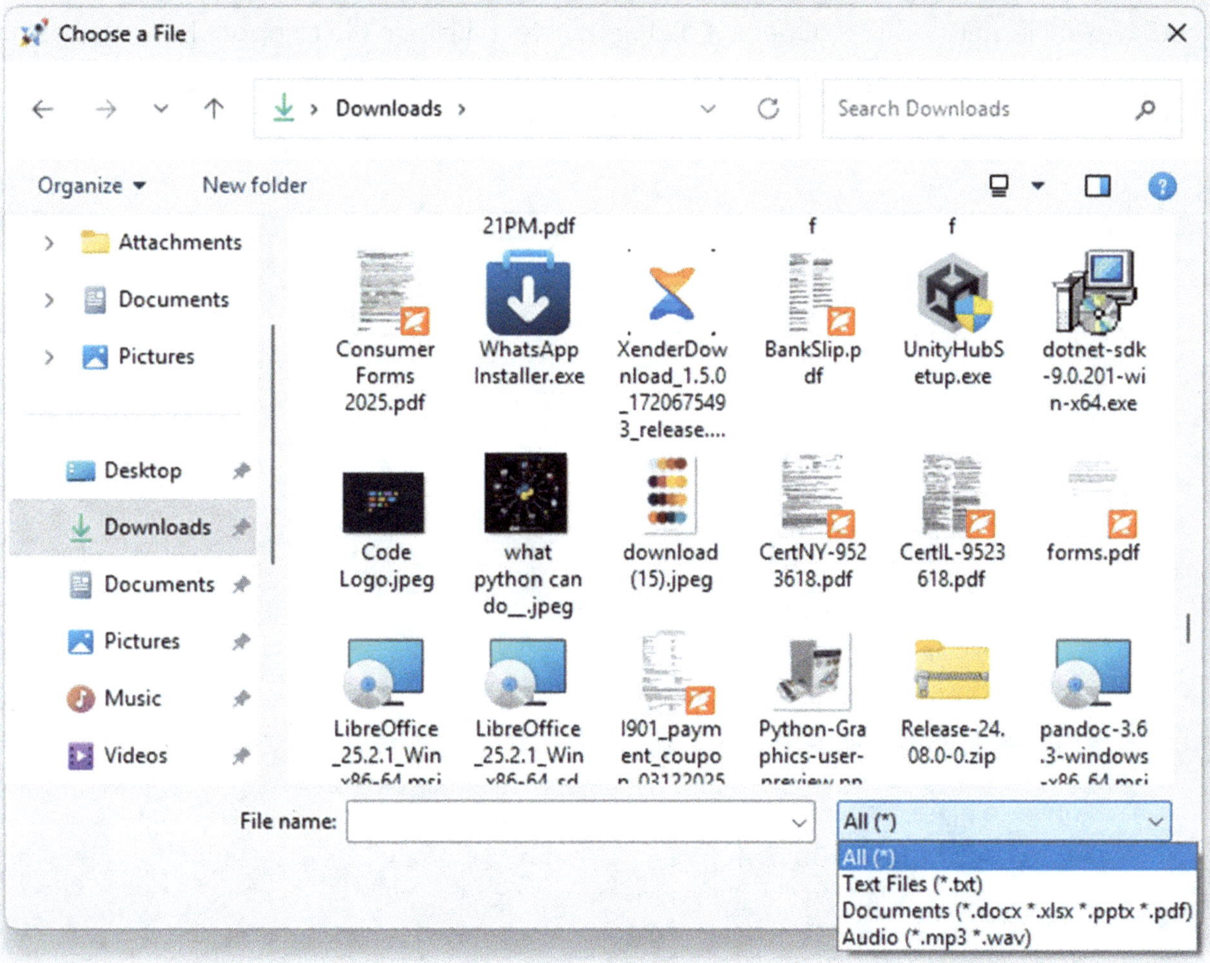

getOpenFileUrl(parent, caption, directory, filter**)** and
getOpenFileUrls(parent, caption, directory, filter **)**

getOpenFileUrl()	→	Same as above but returns QUrls instead of paths
getOpenFileUrls()	→	Returns multiple Urls

getSaveFileName(parent, caption, directory, filter)

getSaveFileName()	→	Opens a dialog to select a single file to open. Returns the file path as a string.
getSaveFileNames()	→	Lets the user select multiple files. Returns a list of file paths.

</> Python

```
import sys
from PyQt6.QtCore import *
from PyQt6.QtWidgets import *

class PracticalApp(QMainWindow):

    def __init__(self):
        super().__init__()

        self.setWindowTitle("Music Player")
        self.resize(300,150)
        self.setWindowIcon(QIcon("images/rocket.png"))
        self.setStyleSheet("background:#ebebeb")

        self.savefile = QPushButton("Save file", self)
        self.savefile.move(100, 70)
        self.savefile.setIcon(QIcon("images/save.png"))
        self.savefile.setIconSize(QSize(20,20))
        self.savefile.pressed.connect(lambda: self.saveFile())


    def saveFile(self):
        fileName, _ = QFileDialog().getSaveFileName(
         self,                #parent
         "Choose a File",     #caption
         "",                  #directory
        " All (*);; Text Files (*.txt);; Documents (*.docx *.xlsx *.pptx);; Audio (*.mp3 *.wav)")  #filter

        print(fileName)


app = QApplication([])
myapp = PracticalApp()
myapp.show()
sys.exit(app.exec())
```

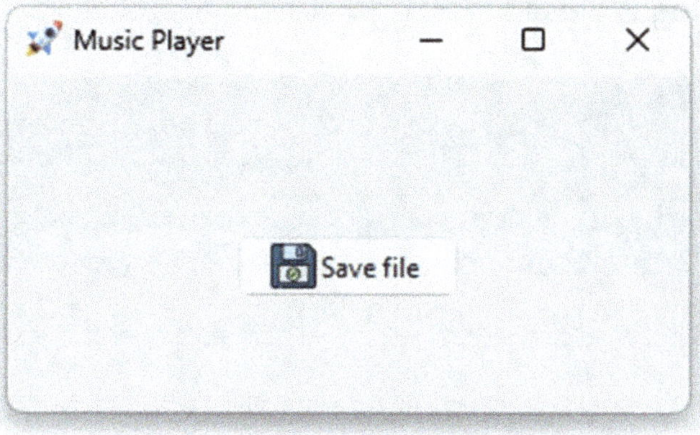
Music Player
Save file

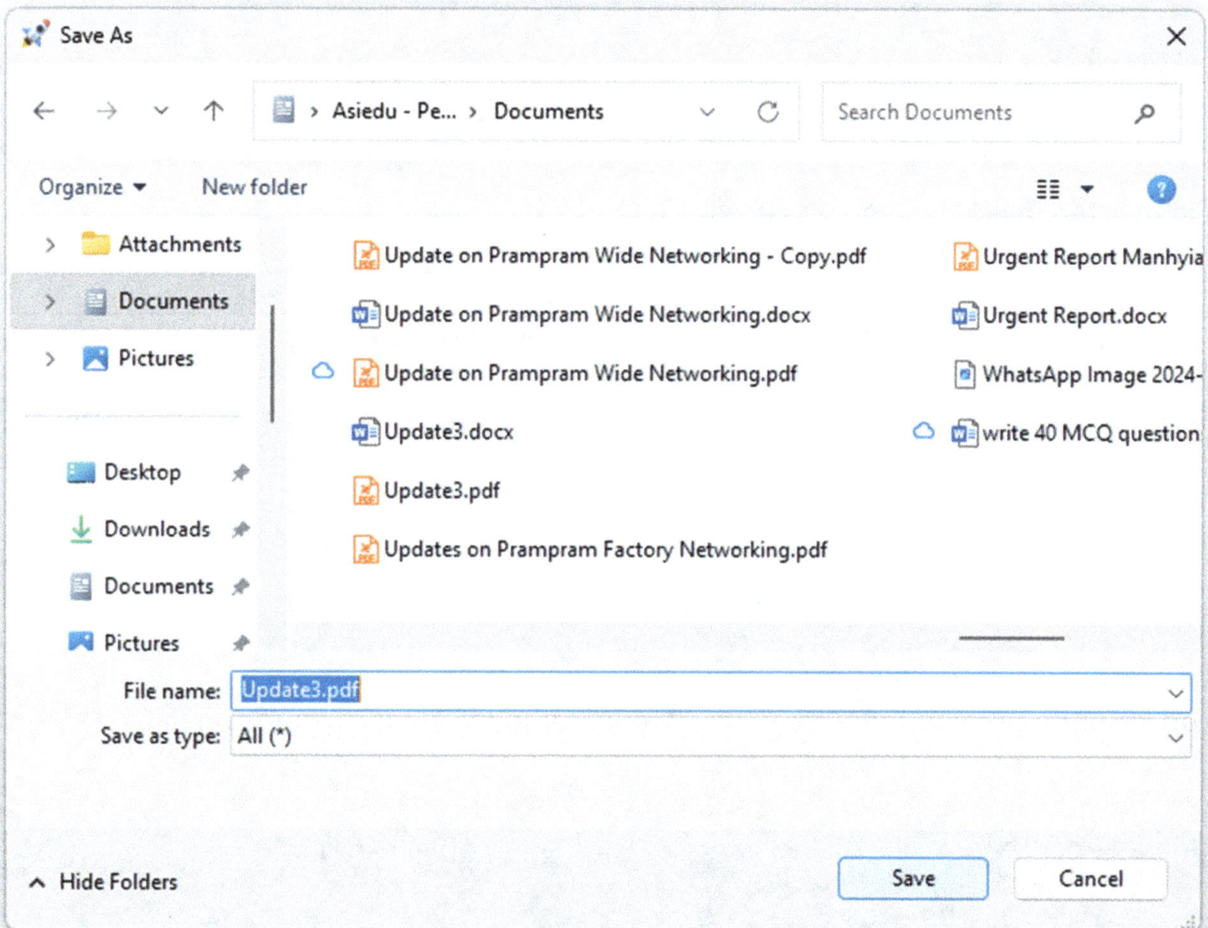
Save As
Asiedu - Pe... › Documents
Search Documents
Organize
New folder
Attachments
Documents
Pictures
Desktop
Downloads
Documents
Pictures
Update on Prampram Wide Networking - Copy.pdf
Update on Prampram Wide Networking.docx
Update on Prampram Wide Networking.pdf
Update3.docx
Update3.pdf
Updates on Prampram Factory Networking.pdf
Urgent Report Manhyia
Urgent Report.docx
WhatsApp Image 2024-
write 40 MCQ question
File name:
Update3.pdf
Save as type:
All (*)
Hide Folders
Save
Cancel

selectedFiles()

Returns a list of selected files after the dialog is closed.

</> **Python**

```
filedialog = QFileDialog(parent)
files = filedialog.selectedFiles()
```

Signals

fileSelected, filesSelected and **currentChanged**

fileSelected	→	Signal emitted when a single file is selected.
filesSelected	→	Signal emitted when multiple files are selected.
currentChanged	→	Signals emitted when a new file is selected.

</> **Python**

```
filedialog = QFileDialog(parent)
filedialog.fileSelected.connect(getSelected)

filedialog.currentChanged.connect(lambda: print("new file has been selected"))

openButton = QPushButton("Select File", parent )
openButton.pressed.connect(lambda: filedialog.open() )  #open the file dialog


def getSelected():
    files = filedialog.selectedFiles()
    firstFile = files[0]

    print(firstFile)
```

selectFile(filename)

Preselects a specific file in the dialog.

</> Python

```
filedialog = QFileDialog(parent)
filedialog.selectFile("Document/personal.pdf")
```

setDirectory(str or QDir **)** and **directory()**

setDirectory()	→	Sets the starting directory shown in the dialog.
directory()	→	Returns the current directory being shown.

</> Python

```
filedialog = QFileDialog(parent)
filedialog.setDirectory( QDir("C:/Users/John/Downloads/") )
```

setNameFilter(str filter **), setNameFilters(** str filter **)** and **selectedNameFilter()**

setNameFilter()	→	Sets a file filter like "Images (*.png *.jpg)".
setNameFilters()	→	Allows setting multiple file filters.
selectedNameFilter()	→	Returns the filter that was used to select the file.

</> Python

```
filedialog = QFileDialog(parent)
filedialog.setNameFilter( "Audio (*.mp3*.wav)")
```

setAcceptMode(QFileDialog.AcceptMode **)** and **acceptMode()**

setAcceptMode()	→	Defines if the dialog is for opening or saving files- (***AcceptSave*** or ***AcceptOpen***)
acceptMode()	→	Returns the current acceptMode.

</> Python

```
filedialog = QFileDialog(parent)
filedialog.setAcceptMode(QFileDialog.AcceptMode.AcceptSave)
filedialog.open()
```

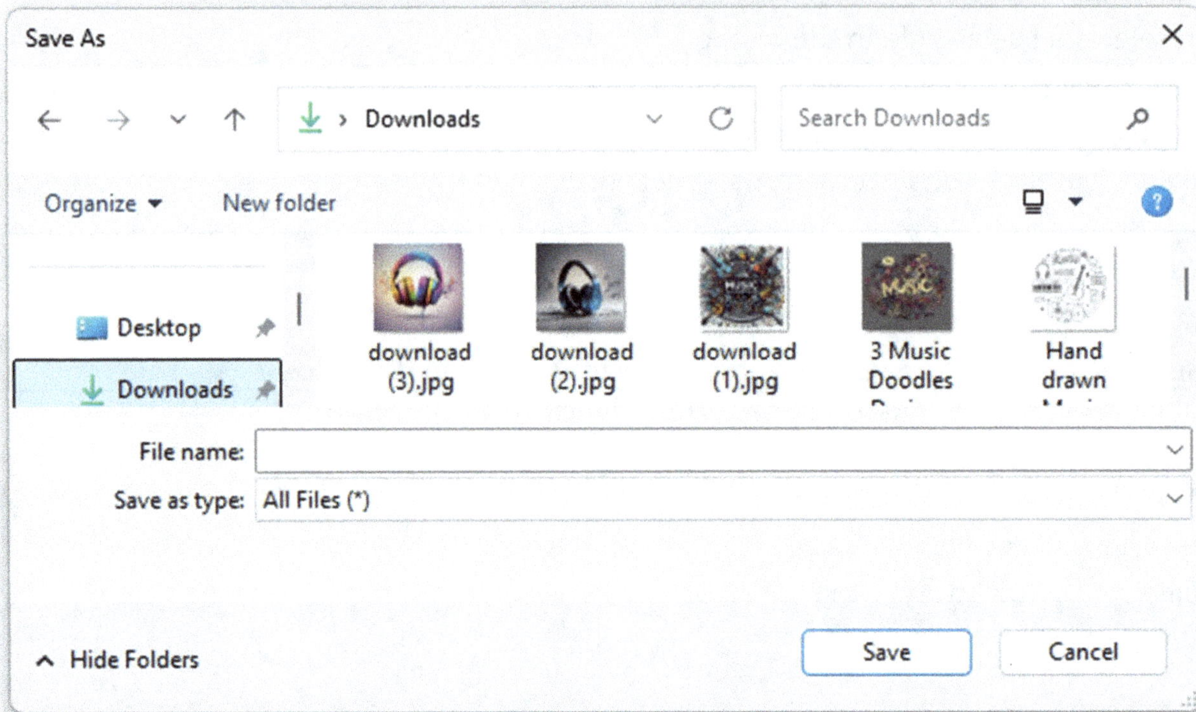

accept(), reject() and **result()**

accept()	→	Programmatically accept the dialog.
reject()	→	Programmatically reject the dialog.
result()	→	Returns QDialog.Accepted or QDialog.Rejected based on the user action.

</> **Python**

```
filedialog = QFileDialog(parent)

filedialog.accept()     #Accept
filedialog.reject()     #Reject
```

exec( )

Shows the dialog and waits for user action.

</> **Python**

```
filedialog = QFileDialog(parent)
filedialog.exec()
```

setViewMode(QFileDialog.ViewMode **)** and **viewMode()**

setViewMode()	→	Controls the view type (***Detail*** or ***List***).
viewMode()	→	Gets the current view mode.

</> **Python**

```
filedialog = QFileDialog(parent)
filedialog.setAcceptMode(QFileDialog.ViewMode.Detail)
filedialog.open()
```

setFileMode(QFileDialog.FileMode **)** and **fileMode()**

setFileMode()	→	Specifies what kind of file selection is allowed.
fileMode()	→	Returns the current file mode.

</> **Python**

```
filedialog = QFileDialog(parent)
filedialog.setFileMode(QFileDialog.FileMode.Directory)
filedialog.open()
```

File Modes

Directory	AnyFile	ExistingFile
ExistingFiles		

Table 8.1 – QFileDialog file modes

QMediaPlayer

QMediaPlayer is a powerful widget in PyQt that allows you to **play audio and video files**. It handles **media resources** and supports a wide range of media formats, devices and sources. This widget forms the **backend engine** for media playback and can be paired with visual components like **QVideoWidget** or **QAudioOutput**.

Use Cases

- Building music players and video players
- Embedding audio/video playback in multimedia apps
- Implementing podcasts, voice note features, or video tutorials
- Previewing media files in file managers
- Audio-visual teaching apps
- Apps requiring voice narration or sound effects

Key Properties and Methods

setVideoOutput	audioBufferOutputChanged	videoSink	hasVideo
setSource	setPosition	audioBufferOutput	hasVideoChanged
setSourceDevice	tracksChanged	metaData	activeSubtitleTrack
playbackRate	setAudioOutput	error	sourceDevice
setActiveSubtitleTrack	play	videoOutputChanged	isSeekable
sourceChanged	videoTracks	errorOccurred	playingChanged
playbackState	videoOutput	setAudioBufferOutput	stop
bufferProgressChanged	mediaStatus	setActiveAudioTrack	metaDataChanged
setActiveVideoTrack	audioOutputChanged	activeAudioTrack	setPlaybackRate
errorString	isAvailable	activeVideoTrack	hasAudio
duration	subtitleTracks	isPlaying	hasAudioChanged
activeTracksChanged	PlaybackState	pause	Loops
MediaStatus	bufferedTimeRange	playbackStateChanged	setVideoSink
loopsChanged	positionChanged	position	audioOutput
mediaStatusChanged	source	durationChanged	bufferProgress
Error	playbackRateChanged	errorChanged	setLoops
audioTracks	seekableChanged	loops	

setSource(QUrl)
Sets the media file source (e.g. audio/video file).

```python
from PyQt6.QtMultimedia import *
from PyQt6.QtMultimediaWidgets import *

player = QMediaPlayer(parent)
player.setSource(QUrl.fromLocalFile("my_music.mp3"))
```

setAudioOutput(audio)
Sets the media file source (e.g. audio file).

```python
import sys
from PyQt6.QtCore import *
from PyQt6.QtGui import *
from PyQt6.QtWidgets import *
from PyQt6.QtMultimedia import *
from PyQt6.QtMultimediaWidgets import *

class PracticalApp(QMainWindow):

    def __init__(self):
        super().__init__()

        self.setWindowTitle("Music Player")
        self.resize(300,150)
        self.setWindowIcon(QIcon("images/rocket.png"))
        self.setStyleSheet("background:#ebebeb")

        self.player = QMediaPlayer(self)
        self.audio = QAudioOutput()
        self.player.setAudioOutput(self.audio)
        self.player.setSource(QUrl.fromLocalFile("D:/Music/Dean Lewis - Be Alright.mp3"))

        self.label = QLabel(self)
        self.label.setGeometry(50,20, 200, 50)
        self.label.setText(self.player.source().fileName())

        self.playAuido = QPushButton("Play", self)
        self.playAuido.move(100, 80)
```

```
        self.playAuido.pressed.connect(lambda: self.player.play())


app = QApplication([])
myapp = PracticalApp()
myapp.show()
sys.exit(app.exec())
```

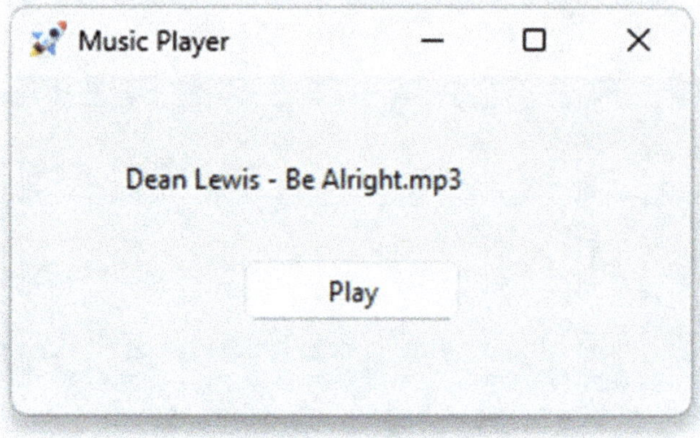

setVideoOutput(video)

Sets a widget or sink to display video (e.g. ***QVideoWidget***).

</> Python

```
import sys
from PyQt6.QtCore import *
from PyQt6.QtGui import *
from PyQt6.QtWidgets import *
from PyQt6.QtMultimedia import *
from PyQt6.QtMultimediaWidgets import *

class PracticalApp(QMainWindow):

    def __init__(self):
        super().__init__()

        self.setWindowTitle("Music Player")
        self.resize(300,150)
```

```
        self.setWindowIcon(QIcon("images/rocket.png"))
        self.setStyleSheet("background:#ebebeb")

        self.player = QMediaPlayer(self)

        self.video = QVideoWidget(self)
        self.video.setGeometry(5, 5, 400, 200)
        self.player.setVideoOutput(self.video)
        self.player.setSource(QUrl.fromLocalFile("D:/Video/movie.mkv"))

        self.playVideo = QPushButton(self)
        self.playVideo.move(150, 230)
        self.playVideo.setIcon(QIcon("images/play.png"))
        self.playVideo.setIconSize(QSize(30, 30))
        self.playVideo.setFlat(True)
        self.playVideo.pressed.connect(lambda: self.player.play())


app = QApplication([])
myapp = PracticalApp()
myapp.show()
sys.exit(app.exec())
```

videoOutput( ) and **audioOutput()**

videoOutput()	→	Returns the current video output object.
audioOutput()	→	Returns the current audio output object.

```python
player = QMediaPlayer(parent)
player.audioOutput()
```

play( ), **pause()** and **stop()**

play()	→	Plays audio or video or resumes playing audio or video if paused.
pause()	→	Pauses or breaks playing audio or video.
stop()	→	Stops audio or video from playing.

```python
player = QMediaPlayer(parent)
player.play()
player.pause()
player.stop()
```

isPlaying( )

Returns True if media is currently playing.

```python
player = QMediaPlayer(parent)

if player.isPlaying():
    player.pause()
else:
    player.play()
```

setPlaybackRate(rate) and **playbackRate()**

setPlaybackRate()	→	Speed up or slow down playback (e.g. 1.5x speed).
playbackRate()	→	Returns the speed of playback rate.

</> Python

```
player = QMediaPlayer(parent)

forward = QPushButton("forward", parent)
forward.pressed.connect(lambda : alterPlayback( 2 ) )

reverse = QPushButton("reverse", parent)
reverse.pressed.connect(lambda : alterPlayback( -2 ) )

def alterPlayback(value):
    currentPlayback = player.playbackRate()
    player.setPlaybackRate(currentPlayback + value)
```

playbackStateChanged and **playbackState()**

playbackSateChanged	→	Signals emitted when state is changed.(eg, play – pause)
playbackState()	→	Reflects state: **Playing**, **Paused** or **Stopped**.

</> Python

```
player = QMediaPlayer(parent)
player.playbackStateChanged.connect(lambda: getState())

def getState():
    state = player.playbackState()
```

hasAudio() and **hasVideo()**

hasAudio()	→	Booleans indicating presence of audio tracks.
hasVideo()	→	Booleans indicating presence of video tracks.

setLoops(int **)** and **loops()**

setLoops()	→	Sets number of times media should loop.
loops()	→	Returns the number of times media can loop.

</> **Python**

```
player = QMediaPlayer(parent)
player.setLoops( 10 )
```

setPosition(ms time **), position()** and **duration()**

setPosition()	→	Sets the current playback position in milliseconds.
position()	→	Gets the current playback position in milliseconds.
duration()	→	Total length of the media in milliseconds

</> **Python**

```
player = QMediaPlayer(parent)
player.setPosition( 900 )
```

Signals

durationChanged and **positionChanged**

durationChanged	→	Signals emitted when duration is updated.
positionChanged	→	Signals emitted when the position is updated.

</> **Python**

```
player = QMediaPlayer(parent)
player.positionChanged.connect(lambda: onPositionChanged())

def onPositionChanged():
    position = player.position()
```

Finalizing Project - Developing a Music Player

</> Python

```python
import sys
from PyQt6.QtCore import *
from PyQt6.QtWidgets import *
from PyQt6.QtGui import *
from PyQt6.QtGui import QIcon
from PyQt6.QtMultimedia import *

class PracticalApp(QMainWindow):

  def __init__(self):
      super().__init__()

      self.setWindowTitle("Music Player")
      self.setFixedSize(500,400)
      self.setWindowIcon(QIcon("images/rocket.png"))
      self.setStyleSheet("background:#ebebeb")

      appName = QLabel(self)
      appName.setGeometry(0, 200, self.width(), 50)
      appName.setAlignment(Qt.AlignmentFlag.AlignCenter)
      appName.setWordWrap(True)
      appName.setFont(QFont("Georgia", 25, 50 ))
      appName.setStyleSheet("color:#0C3B2E;font-family:Georgia;")
      appName.setText("My PyQt Player")

      self.fileName = QLabel(self)
      self.fileName.setGeometry(0, 250, self.width(), 30)
      self.fileName.setAlignment(Qt.AlignmentFlag.AlignCenter)
      self.fileName.setWordWrap(True)
      self.fileName.setFont(QFont("Comic Sans MS", 12 ))

      self.openFile = QPushButton(self)
      self.openFile.setGeometry(450, 205, 35, 35)
      self.openFile.setIcon(QIcon("images/upload.png"))
      self.openFile.setIconSize(QSize(35, 35))
      self.openFile.setFlat(True)
      self.openFile.clicked.connect(lambda:self.openFileDialog())

      self.progress = QProgressBar(self)
      self.progress.setGeometry(100,280, 300, 30)
      self.progress.setRange(0, 100)
      self.progress.setValue(0)

      self.player = QMediaPlayer(self)
      self.audio_player = QAudioOutput(self)
      self.player.setAudioOutput(self.audio_player)
```

```
        self.player.positionChanged.connect(self.getDuration)

        controllers = QWidget(self)
        controllers.setGeometry(100, 300, 300, 100)

        self.reverse = QPushButton()
        self.reverse.setIcon(QIcon("images/prev.png"))
        self.reverse.setIconSize(QSize(35, 35))
        self.reverse.setFlat(True)
        self.reverse.setSizePolicy(QSizePolicy.Policy.Expanding, QSizePolicy.Policy.Expanding,)
        self.reverse.clicked.connect(lambda:self.seek(-500))

        self.startPlay = QPushButton()
        self.startPlay.setIcon(QIcon("images/play-button.png"))
        self.startPlay.setIconSize(QSize(35, 35))
        self.startPlay.setFlat(True)
        self.startPlay.setSizePolicy(QSizePolicy.Policy.Expanding, QSizePolicy.Policy.Expanding,)
        self.startPlay.clicked.connect(lambda: self.playerFunction())

        self.forward = QPushButton()
        self.forward.setIcon(QIcon("images/nextt.png"))
        self.forward.setIconSize(QSize(35, 35))
        self.forward.setFlat(True)
        self.forward.setSizePolicy(QSizePolicy.Policy.Expanding, QSizePolicy.Policy.Expanding,)
        self.forward.clicked.connect(lambda:self.seek(100) )

        controllerLayout = QHBoxLayout(controllers)
        controllerLayout.addWidget(self.reverse)
        controllerLayout.addWidget(self.startPlay)
        controllerLayout.addWidget(self.forward)

        self.thumbnail = QLabel(self)
        self.thumbnail.resize(500,200)
        self.thumbnail.setPixmap(QPixmap("images/newbg.png").scaled(500,500))


    def openFileDialog(self):
        audioFile,_ = QFileDialog().getOpenFileName(self,"Choose Audio File", "", "Audio (*.mp3 *.wav *.ogg)")

        self.player.setSource(QUrl.fromLocalFile(audioFile))
        name = self.player.source().fileName()
        self.fileName.setText(name)

    def playerFunction(self):
        try:
            state = self.player.isPlaying()
            print(state)
            if state:
                self.player.pause()
                self.startPlay.setIcon(QIcon("images/play-button.png"))
            else:
                self.player.play()
                self.startPlay.setIcon(QIcon("images/pause.png"))
        except:
```

```
            print("error")

    def getDuration(self):
        try:
            pos = self.player.position()
            duration = self.player.duration()
            progValue = (pos/duration)*100
            self.progress.setValue(int(progValue))
        except:
            print("error")

    def seek(self, value):
        newPosition = self.player.position() + value
        self.player.setPosition(newPosition)


app = QApplication([])
myapp = PracticalApp()
myapp.show()
sys.exit(app.exec())
```

Chapter 9

Packaging Application (Creating Executables)

Chapter Objectives

- Learn about application packaging
- Understand why packaging is needed
- Explore packaging tools
- Review relevant Python modules
- Access PyQt documentation and community support

Packaging Applications

PyQt has many powerful widgets that can be used to build market-ready, industry-standard applications. If you've followed the guides above on using these widgets, you should now have a solid foundation in app development with PyQt.
After acquiring this knowledge and building your app, what comes next?

During development, we've been running our applications from the ***source code***—our Python and PyQt logic. This stage is known as **debugging**: testing and refining the app to ensure it runs without errors.
But once you're sure your code is stable and error-free, you'll want to distribute it to others who don't have (or need) your source code. That's where packaging comes in.

Packaging is the process of converting your project into a **standalone executable** that can run independently of your development environment. This is typically the final stage of development before release.

Why the Need to Package?

1. **Portability**
   After packaging, your app can be copied and run on different systems without installing Python or your source code.

2. **Platform Independence**
   Tools like PyInstaller and cx_Freeze let you generate packages for Windows, Linux, or macOS.

3. **Independence from Requirements**
   The packaged app contains all needed libraries. Users don't need to install Python or PyQt.

4. **Professional Presentation**
   An executable looks and feels like a real app to users. No command-line knowledge is needed.

5. **Ease of Distribution**
   You can share your app via email, websites, app stores, or USB sticks.

6. **Security of Source Code**
   Packaging hides your Python source code from casual users.

7. **Installer Creation**
   Packaging often includes the ability to make installers (EXE, DMG, etc.) for even easier user setup.

8. **Versioning and Updates**
   Packaged apps can be bundled with versioning info, making maintenance easier.

9. **Better User Experience**
   One-click launch instead of manually setting up environments or running

Packaging Tools

Application packaging is straightforward when you understand the tools needed for the job. Most packaging or installer tools use either command-line interfaces (CLI) or graphical user interfaces (GUI) to take input and produce platform-specific executables.

These inputs typically include:'

- Indicating the target platform (Windows, Linux, macOS)
- The icon to use for the application
- The output folder for the packaged files
- Whether it's a console-based or windowed application
- Application name and version
- Company or author information
- Included data files (images, configs, databases, etc.)
- Hidden or excluded modules
- Additional Python packages to bundle
- Compression options to reduce package size
- Digital signature or code-signing for security (optional)

After packaging, the tool produces application files with extensions specific to the target platform:

- 📌 **Windows** ➜ .exe
- 📌 **Linux** ➜ typically an **AppImage**, .bin, or just an executable binary without extension
- 📌 **macOS** ➜ .app bundle or .dmg disk image

When packaging Python applications, there are special tools you'll need to install. These tools are external Python libraries and can be easily installed via the pip command.

Some packaging tools are command-line only, requiring a bit of CLI knowledge, while others provide a graphical user interface (GUI) to make the process easier and more visual.

Below are recommended packaging tools, with installation instructions and usage guidance.

✏️ PyInstaller

PyInstaller is one of the most popular tools for turning Python scripts into standalone executables. It supports **Windows**, **macOS**, and **Linux**.

Installation

```
pip install pyinstaller
```

Usage (Command-Line)

```
pyinstaller yourapp.py
```

This will create a dist/ folder with your executable.

Common Arguments

➜ --onefile
Bundle everything into a single executable file.

```
pyinstaller --onefile  yourapp.py
```

➜ --noconsole

Suppress the terminal or console window (useful for GUI apps).

```
pyinstaller --onefile --noconsole yourapp.py
```

➜ --name Name

Set a custom name for the executable.

```
pyinstaller --onefile --name=MyApp yourapp.py
```

➜ --icon=icon.ico

Set a custom icon for the executable.

```
pyinstaller --onefile --icon=myicon.ico yourapp.py
```

➜ --add-data

Include extra data files.

```
pyinstaller --onefile --add-data "data_folder;data_folder" yourapp.py
```

(On Windows use ;, on Linux/macOS use : as separator)

➜ --clean

Clean old builds before building new one.

```
pyinstaller --clean yourapp.py
```

Auto-Py-to-Exe

Auto-Py-to-Exe is a **GUI front-end for PyInstaller**. It makes packaging easier by providing checkboxes and text fields for PyInstaller's options.

Installation

```
pip install auto-py-to-exe
```

Note

Note: Installing auto-py-to-exe automatically installs PyInstaller and its dependencies.

Usage (GUI)

1. Open the terminal or command prompt.
2. Type:

```
auto-py-to-exe
```

3. Press **Enter**.
4. A **graphical application** will open where you can:
   - Choose your script.
   - Select **onefile** or **onedir** mode.
   - Add **icons**.
   - Include **additional files**.
   - Set **advanced PyInstaller flags**.
   - Build the executable with one click.

It's **perfect for beginners** who don't want to memorize CLI commands.

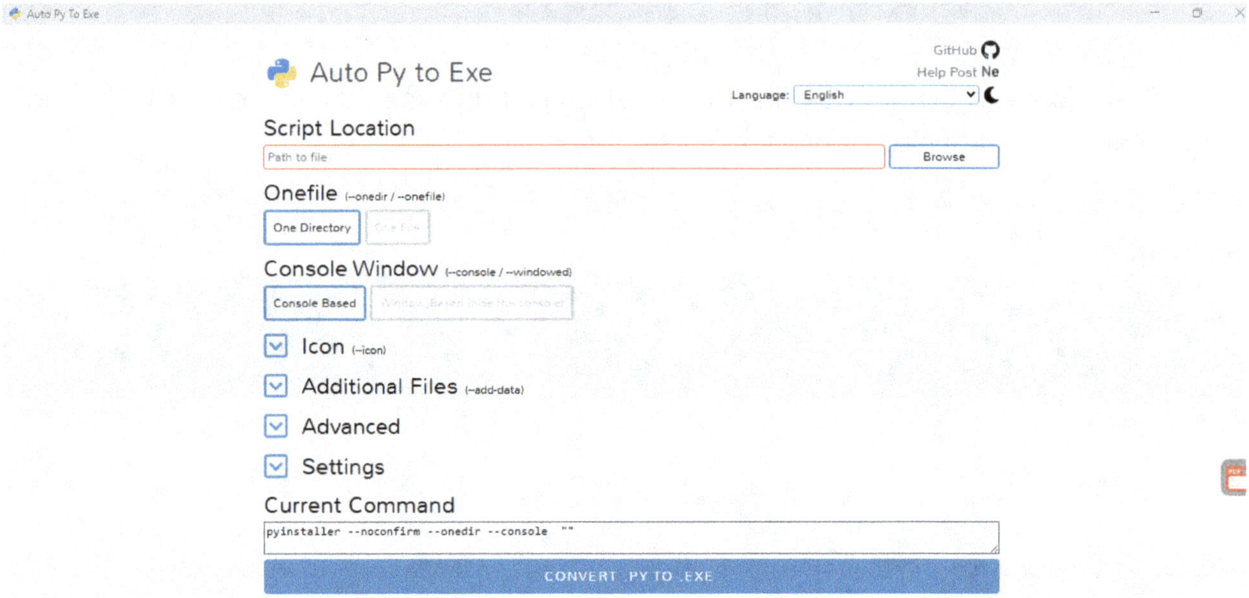

Figure 9.0 : Auto-py-to-exe interface

cx_Freeze

A flexible cross-platform packager. Good for distributing on **Windows**, **Linux**, and **macOS**.

Installation

```
pip install cx-Freeze
```

Usage (Command-Line)

```
cxfreeze your_script.py --target-dir dist/
```

Typically used with a **setup script** for fine-grained control:

```python
# setup.py
from cx_Freeze import setup, Executable

setup(
    name = "MyApp",
    version = "1.0",
    description = "My PyQt App",
    executables = [Executable("your_script.py")]
)
```

Then build with:

```
python setup.py build
```

Py2app

For **macOS** users to create .app bundles.

Installation

```
pip install py2app
```

Usage

Create a **setup.py**:

```python
# setup.py
from setuptools import setup
```

```
APP = ['your_script.py']
OPTIONS = {
    'argv_emulation': True,
    'packages': ['required_packages']
}

setup(
    app=APP,
    options={'py2app': OPTIONS},
    setup_requires=['py2app'],
)
```

Build with:

```
python setup.py py2app
```

Briefcase

From the BeeWare project—designed for **cross-platform** packaging including desktop and mobile apps.

Installation

```
pip install briefcase
```

Usage

```
briefcase new
briefcase build
briefcase package
```

Briefcase supports Windows, macOS, Linux, iOS, and Android. It's more advanced but very powerful.

Nuitka

Compiles Python to **C** for highly optimized executables.

Installation

```
pip install nuitka
```

Usage

```
nuitka --onefile your_script.py
```

Many advanced options are available for optimization and bundling.

Once your application is built, you have **two main options**:

Deploy it commercially

- Upload to marketplaces (Windows Store, macOS App Store, Linux repos).
- Sell or distribute via your website.
- Package installers or ZIPs for download.

Use it personally

- Install on your own devices.
- Share privately with friends or colleagues.

Final Thoughts

Throughout this tutorial, if you **couldn't get enough idea** about:

- A topic
- Syntax
- Application
- Class, methods, or properties of a widget

You can **explore more** using Python's built-in functions:

Use **dir()** to list all available properties and methods of an object and **help()** to get detailed documentation.

Python Module Docs

Python also has the **"Module Docs"** tool (pydoc), which gives you **manual-style help** for modules, classes, and functions—even for PyQt.

<u>How to open it:</u>

On Windows:

1. Go to **Start** or **Windows Search**.
2. Type **"Python Module Docs"** or **"pydoc"**.
3. Click to open it.

Alternatively, use Command Prompt:

```
python -m pydoc -b
```

This opens a **browser-based documentation server**.

On Linux:

Use terminal command:

```
python3 -m pydoc -b
```

This will launch the browser-based docs on localhost.

Alternatively, get text-based help:

```
python3 -m pydoc module_name
```

On macOS:

Use Terminal:

```
python3 -m pydoc -b
```

Opens a local browser server for easy navigation.

Or for quick CLI help:

```
python3 -m pydoc module_name
```

PyQt Documentation and Community Support

PyQt and Qt have **large, active communities**. You can get help, read examples, and ask questions on various forums and official docs.

Official Documentation

- PyQt6 Documentation
- PyQt5 Documentation
- Qt Official Documentation

Author's Remarks

Thank you sincerely for picking up and reading this resource. I am truly grateful for your time and dedication. It is my hope and prayer that you excel in your journey—whether as a developer, educator, or enthusiast. May your path be filled with growth, innovation, and fulfillment.

I trust that you've found this book valuable and insightful. At **Ouereila Publishing**, our mission is to make coding and software development accessible to everyone—at little or no cost. We are committed to producing high-quality, practical and affordable learning resources to empower future creators.

We deeply value your support and feedback. Your suggestions, reviews and critiques help us improve and grow. We believe in building a thriving learning community—and we're honored to grow with you.

If you'd like to share your thoughts, offer suggestions, or leave a review, please connect with us through the following:

- **Feedback Form**: forms
- **Email**: ouereila@gmail.com

Together, let's make learning better for everyone. Thank you again—and keep building!

Warm regards,
Williams Asiedu
Author & Educator
Ouereila Publishing

About the Author

Williams Asiedu is a seasoned software engineer, educator, and philanthropist with a PhD in Computer Science. With years of experience in software development, application design and instructional writing, Williams has played key roles in several innovative projects across the app development and book publishing industries.

His work is driven by a passion to make programming accessible, practical and enjoyable for learners of all levels. Beyond his technical expertise, Williams is committed to community empowerment through technology education, often contributing to initiatives that promote coding literacy in underrepresented areas.

As an author, he has written and published several impactful books focused on Python and modern application development, including:

1. **Mastering Python**
2. **App Development with Python and Flet**
3. **Python Graphics and More**

Williams continues to inspire the next generation of developers by sharing his knowledge through teaching, mentorship, and open educational content. His mission is to make learning software development simple, affordable and empowering for all.

www.ingramcontent.com/pod-product-compliance
Lightning Source LLC
LaVergne TN
LVHW080012210926
848481LV00011B/2996
* 9 7 9 8 3 4 9 4 7 4 0 8 8 *